Women and Microfinance

Women and Microfinance

Prospects and Challenges

AMIT KUMAR

RAWAT PUBLICATIONS

Jaipur • New Delhi • Bangalore • Hyderabad • Guwahati • Kolkata

ISBN 978-81-316-0719-0

The publication of this book was financially supported by the ICSSR. The responsibility for the facts stated, opinions expressed, or conclusions reached, is entirely that of the author and that the ICSSR accepts no responsibility for them.

ICSSR Consultant: Professor P.K. Jain, Director, Faculty of Management Studies, Mohan Lal Sukhadia University, Udaipur.

Published by
Prem Rawat for **Rawat Publications**
Satyam Apts, Sector 3, Jawahar Nagar, Jaipur 302 004 (India)
Phone: 0141 265 1748 / 7006 Fax: 0141 265 1748
E-mail: info@rawatbooks.com
Website: www.rawatbooks.com

New Delhi Office
4858/24, Ansari Road, Daryaganj, New Delhi 110 002
Phone: 011 2326 3290

Also at *Bangalore, Hyderabad, Guwahati* and *Kolkata*

Typeset by Rawat Computers, Jaipur
Printed at Nice Printing Press, New Delhi

Contents

Foreword

There is a paradigm shift in our thinking on poverty alleviation. It is now widely recognized that the poor can be brought into the mainstream of development if they are provided with marketable assets. The assets can comprise physical as well as social capital. In order to convert the assets into income stream, credit plays an important part. It lubricates the process. In a way credit is command over goods and services. In India, we were following this approach since long. Rationale provided for bank nationalization, and subsequent organizational and procedural innovation was to bring as many people as possible, particularly the poor, in the fold of formal banking, so that they may avail credit on reasonable terms. The main vehicle for implementing this policy was the public sector banks.

This objective was only partly fulfilled as banks found the transaction cost of dealing with the requirements of the poor high, and perceived that it would involve larger risks. Urban-oriented approach of the bank employees did not make things easy. It was in this context that the movement for micro-credit started. Once it was demonstrated that the poor are credit worthy, 'for profit' micro-credit institutions as well as 'not for profit institutions' sprung up in large number. The latter were further supported by the government policy of linking women self-help groups, the primary units for microfinance, with the banks.

To what extent this approach has succeeded is a matter of debate. Dr Amit Kumar dwells on this aspect in a competent manner. He has focused on one state, a relatively backward state in respect of micro-credit movement, and brought out different aspects of organizations and procedures that help or hinder the growth of the movement. His conclusions are based on fairly representative survey together with case studies and situational analysis.

He has emphasized the need for social cohesion, of capacity building, and importance of skill formation and marketing links, and illustrated his points by ground level examples. His emphasis on quality of the primary units, i.e. women self-help groups, rather than their number should be taken seriously. What adds value to this study is that Dr Kumar has studied both models of micro-credit, namely 'for profit' and 'not for profit' institutions, and has brought out their salient features.

At this point of time when micro-credit movement seems to have reached a plateau, this study is of particular value to all those who are involved in policy making, organization and operation of micro-credit institutions.

V.S. Vyas
Former Member, Economic Advisory Council to the Prime Minister of India
Former Deputy Chairman, Rajasthan State Planning Board

Acknowledgement

I sincerely express my gratitude to my guide Dr Raju Agarwal for continuously guiding me and providing necessary inputs throughout the research. Many organizations and practitioners helped me in gaining an understanding of the microfinance sector and the institutions. Many people whom I met over the last couple of years gladly spared their time, and the institutions that I visited willingly shared their resources to enable me to gather insights into the developments of this field. I owe a debt of gratitude to many. My special thanks to Shri Hanuman Sahay Sharma and Shri Ramavatar Jat from Laxmi Nidhi Primary Women Multipurpose Cooperative Society Limited, Niwai (Tonk), Shri Deepak Yogi from Shree Shyam Sanskriti Sewa Samiti, Chithwari, Chomu (Jaipur), Shri Kailash Khandelwal from Humana People to People India – Microfinance Division, Thanaghazi (Alwar), Shri Mohan Dangi from Prayatna Sansthan, Udaipur, Smt. Shashi Tyagi and Shrikant from GRAVIS, Jodhpur for supporting me to do the field survey in their respective project areas. I am deeply indebted to Chandrika Das, Tara Hill and Quentin Chaplet for their valuable inputs. The information base placed in public domain by RBI and NABARD has been of great use in this thesis. Shri Sourabh Roy has been very supportive throughout, with ideas and suggestions. I thank Prof.

V.S. Vyas and Institute of Development Studies for allowing me to have access to their rich library and issue books for study.

My sister Anupama, mother Karuna, father Dr Awadh Prasad, daughter Kriti and wife Seema kept me on my toes and were continuous source of inspiration and helped me navigate a couple of tight situations for which I am extremely thankful.

It is difficult to list all those who had directly and indirectly supported me. My sincere apologies to those whose names might have been inadvertently left out. Despite best efforts put in, the information presented might not be complete. I take full responsibility for any error or omission that may have occurred.

Amit Kumar

List of Abbreviations

ASSEFA	Association for Sarva Seva Farms
BAAC	Bank for Agriculture and Agricultural Cooperatives
BMI	Body Mass Index
BNDA	Banque Nationale de Développement Agricole
BoB	Bank of Baroda
BPL	Below Poverty Line
BRGB	Baroda Rajasthan Gramin Bank
CBI	Central Bank of India
CBMFIs	Community Based Microfinance Institutions
CBO	Community Based Organizations
CGAP	Consultative Group to Assist the Poor
CIG	Common Interest Groups
CmF	Centre for Microfinance
CMML	Camel Mahila Macs Ltd.
CRPs	Community Resource Persons
DLCC	District Level Coordination Committee
DPIP	District Poverty Initiative Project
DRDA	District Rural Development Agency

DWCD	Department of Women and Child Development
FGDs	Focused Group Discussions
GAPCL	Grameen Aloe Producers Company Limited
GDP	Gross Domestic Product
GoI	Government of India
GRAVIS	Gramin Vikas Vigyan Samiti
GSS	Gram Sahakari Seva Samities
HDFC	Housing Development Finance Corporation
HDI	Human Development Index
HH	Household
HPPI	Humana People to People India
ICDS	Integrated Child Development Scheme
IGNP	Indira Gandhi Nahar Pariyojna
IIBF	Indian Institute of Banking and Finance
IMR	Infant Mortality Rate
IPO	Initial Public Offering
IRDA	Insurance Regulatory and Development Authority
IRR	Internal Rate of Return
IRV	Individual Rural Volunteers
JLG	Joint Liability Groups
KCC	Kissan Credit Card
KIGS	Kumarappa Institute of Gram Swaraj
LIC	Life Insurance Corporation of India
MACS	Mutually Aided Co-operative Society
MDG	Millennium Development Goals
MFI	Microfinance Institution
MFT	Microfinance Transparency
MGB	Marwar Ganganagar Bikaner Grameen Bank
MGNREGS	Mahatma Gandhi National Rural Employment Guarantee Scheme

MIS	Management Information System
MIX	Microfinance Information Exchange
MLM	Multi-level Marketing
MMR	Maternal Mortality Rate
MPOWER	Mitigation of Poverty in Western Rajasthan
NABARD	National Bank for Agriculture and Rural Development
NBFC	Non-Banking Finance Company
NGO	Non-Government Organisation
NPA	Non-Performing Assets
NRLM	National Rural Livelihood Mission
NSSO	National Sample Survey Organisation
OBC	Oriental Bank of Commerce
OBC	Other Backward Class
PACS	Primary Agriculture Societies
PEDO	People's Education and Development Organization
PNB	Punjab National Bank
PS	Prayatna Samiti
PSB	Public Sector Bank
RBI	Reserve Bank of India
RNBC	Residuary Non-Banking Company
ROE	Return on Equity
ROI	Return on Investment
RRB	Regional Rural Banks
RRLP	Rajasthan Rural Livelihood Project
SBBJ	State Bank of Bikaner and Jaipur
SBI	State Bank of India
SBLP	Self-help Group-Bank Linkage Programme
SC	Scheduled Caste
SEBI	Securities and Exchange Board of India

SEWA	Self-help Women's Association
SGSY	Swarnjayanti Gram Swarozgar Yojana
SHG	Self-help Group
SHPI	Self-help Group Promoting Institution
SIDBI	Small Industries Development Bank of India
SKDRDP	Shri Kshetra Dhamrmasthala Rural Development Project
SLBC	State Level Bankers Committee
SSV	Sakh-Se-Vikas
ST	Scheduled Tribe
UNDP	United Nations Development Programme
WBIS	Weather-Based Insurance Scheme

1

Introduction

> Self-realization and self-initiative are the two most powerful weapons to wash poverty out from the world.
>
> —**Chanakya**
> *(World's Greatest Ancient Economic and Political Scholar)*

Microfinance has become widely recognized today as an effective tool in combating poverty and empowering the world's marginalized populations. Case studies have highlighted its potential role in creating social capital and advancing human development. As the sector continues to expand, the need for comprehensive analysis on the role and structure of microfinance as well as its problems and prospects, increases. Microfinance and specifically micro-credit have the power to transform people's lives, through providing the poor with credit to stabilize their income, while also enabling them to invest in income-generating activities. Microfinance promotes financial inclusion among those who have never been considered 'credit-worthy' or 'bankable' before, and provides the poor with the services of micro-credit, micro savings, micro insurance and remittances.[1] The economic role of microfinance in eradicating poverty is only one aspect of development that it targets. Microfinance also has the potential to promote social development through empowering women and promoting gender equality, providing the poor with sustainable livelihoods and creating social security and support for the poor, particularly women.

Despite the numerous benefits of microfinance, its limitations must also be considered. Does microfinance genuinely benefit those living under crushing poverty, or are its clients limited to the non-poor, or those on the very cusp of the poverty line? Under which circumstances do microfinance institutions flourish the most, and under which circumstances do they face significant obstacles? What are some of the predominant risks that microfinance institutions face when operating, with specific reference to India and Rajasthan? These are all questions that this documentation will address.

The extent of microfinance operations in India has seen a significant surge in recent years. This documentation, therefore, proposes a comprehensive survey of the current structure and role of microfinance in India and Rajasthan, taking into account its economical and social impact and potential, as well as its risks and setbacks.

Local Context of Microfinance Sector

Microfinance sector and its growth are dependent on the local context of the state, its geo-climatic conditions and livelihood systems of people. Microfinance needs of poor are guided by the larger development context and the opportunities emerging from economic growth. This chapter tries to detail out the local context of Rajasthan, the status of economy, livelihood systems, poverty and its reasons, and livelihood opportunities for poor so that the importance of microfinance services are understood in the context of Rajasthan.

About Rajasthan

Rajasthan has a very rich history and culture. It is one of the forefront tourist destination of India. The state has the western 'Thar Desert' with average annual rainfall of 250 mm and also has eastern parts where annual rainfall is about 700 mm. The geographical location of Rajasthan poses challenges for its inhabitants (low and erratic rainfall and droughts, extreme heat in summers, etc.) but it has certain advantages as well. To name a few, its rich culture and architecture attract domestic and foreign tourists which help a large number of people to gain livelihood. State has the largest average landholding in country. Rajasthan is also the leading producer of pulses and oilseeds. Its northern part is in close vicinity of our national capital and thus has the potential to develop as an industrial hub. Rajasthan also connects Gujarat and Mumbai with Delhi. Its rich mineral deposits, especially of marble and granite are very famous. Rajasthan is also famous for its colourful handicrafts.

Rajasthan is the largest state in the country in terms of total geographical area, with 3.42 lakh sq km, which is about 10 per cent of country's area. Out of this, only 40 per cent area (1.64 lakh sq km hectare) is under cultivation. There are vast areas, which are uncultivated due to non-availability of water. Western Rajasthan has the maximum uncultivated lands.

The population of Rajasthan (2011 census) is 6.85 crore of which 75 per cent is in rural areas. The density of population is 200 persons per sq km. The sex ratio is 928 females for every 1,000 males. Rajasthan has one of the highest proportion of Scheduled Caste (SC) population in India (17.8%) and a high proportion of Scheduled Tribes population (13.5%). The SC population is fairly distributed all over the state (though with higher concentration in western part). The tribal area is mostly in south-eastern parts.

The Aravali hill ranges divide the state into two parts from north to south. The western part is the Thar Desert. Nearly 60 per cent of state area is under Desert Districts and about 40 per cent population lives in this part of state. This is characterized by extreme temperature and scanty rainfall.

The eastern part of Arawali hills is mostly hilly with ravines. Large part of it drains out into the Bay of Bengal through

Chambal river and its tributaries. Most of the top soil in this part has already been washed away. Almost the entire tribal population of Rajasthan lives in this area.

There is no perennial river in Rajasthan. Though the average annual rainfall is 536 mm but there is large variation across districts. The western districts like Jaisalmer and Barmer get about 100 to 250 whereas Banswara and Jhalawar in the eastern part get about 900 mm. Both regions have acute shortage of water. Any decline in either rainfall pattern or in total rainfall results into drought.

Agriculture and animal rearing are two main sources of livelihood on which about 70 per cent of rural population is completely dependent. Rajasthan has 10 per cent of India's land but only one per cent of its water. Only 28 per cent of its cultivated land is irrigated. About 50 per cent of the farmers have access only to 10 per cent of cultivated land. Around 35 per cent of India's livestock population is in Rajasthan, whereas it produces only about 10 per cent of the country's milk and 30 per cent of its mutton. Livestock provides 15 per cent of the state agriculture domestic product.

Literacy rates in Rajasthan increased from 60 per cent to 66 per cent during the period 2001–2011. As per 2011 census, there is a wide gap in male and female literacy; Male 79 per cent and Female 48 per cent. There is also a wide gap in literacy between urban and rural areas; Urban–80 per cent and Rural–61 per cent. Literacy in SC/ST and tribal is extremely low and within that woman literacy rate is worse. Dropout rate in primary education is about 50 per cent and majority of dropouts are from SC/ST children.

Life expectancy in Rajasthan has improved over the past 5 decades. In western districts, it is higher than other parts of the state. Dungarpur, Banswara, Chittorgarh, Dholpur and Pali are at the lowest in terms of longevity. Health indicators in Rajasthan are amongst the poorest in the country. The Infant Mortality Rate (IMR) of the state (63 per 1,000 live births) far exceeds the national average (India, 53) and exhibits a wide rural-urban differential (Rural – 69; Urban – 38).[2] While the Maternal Mortality Ratio (MMR) of the state has reduced, it continues to be unacceptably high. Anaemia level amongst women of reproductive age, especially pregnant women continues to be a matter of grave concern. Though Rajasthan continues to have a lower sex ratio than that of India, the gap between the two has reduced over the years. State is plagued by high level of child and adult malnutrition. About one-third children under 3 years age are underweight and similar proportion of married adult men and women have Body Mass Index (BMI) below normal.[3]

Economy, Livelihood and Employment

During the Tenth Five-Year Plan (2002–07) the overall growth in the state was 5.95 per cent. The growth in primary sector was only 2.15 per cent in the plan period whereas, the secondary and the tertiary sector registered a growth of 8.58 per cent and 7.16 per cent respectively. The growth in non-agricultural employment has not been fast enough to compensate for the decline in employment in the agriculture sector. Underemployment is widespread especially in the agriculture sector and is very significant in the urban informal sector. The industrial-based labour force is quite thin, just 7.15 per cent, indicating its backwardness.

In Rajasthan, the main sector in terms of people employed continues to be in agriculture and allied sector. The main sector in terms of income is services sector. The livelihoods in Rajasthan are based on agriculture, animal husbandry, mineral and textiles. Considerable percentage of adult are employed on daily wages. The tertiary sector showed the greatest GDP contribution with 41 per cent, followed by the primary (32%) and secondary sectors (27%).

Agriculture and animal husbandry were two major sources of livelihoods for 66 per cent[4] of people in state in 1999–2000. The agriculture is mainly rainfed and the irrigation is only to about 30 per cent of the cropped area. Majority of small and marginal farmers do agriculture at subsistence level (they grow food and fodder for household consumption). Even if they have small surpluses, they sell it off to buy other subsistence needs of the household.

Main produces in Rajasthan include millets (coarse grains) in western Rajasthan, soyabean and spices in eastern region, wheat and cotton in north-western region while maize, millets, pulses and grains in the hilly region. The water for irrigation comes from wells and tanks. The Indira Gandhi Nahar Pariyojna (IGNP) irrigates north-western Rajasthan.

In western Rajasthan, livestock is the main livelihood for farmers and nomadic groups. Farmers who have better quality land and some irrigation source rear cattle, while small and marginal farmers and landless people rear goat and sheep. As per NSSO (59th round) survey, number of sheep and goats per 100 farmers was 280, which was highest in India. Animal husbandry contributes over 19 per cent to State's agriculture GDP. In Rajasthan, wool is a major livelihood in animal husbandry. Wool is mainly used for carpets and blankets. The state also accounts for 10 per cent of total production of milk in India.

Rajasthan is pre-eminent in quarrying and mining in India. The state is the second largest source of cement in India. It has rich deposits of salt, copper, zinc, sand stone, etc. However, large numbers of people working in quarries are in the informal sector and work without safety gears. Many of them suffer from tuberculosis, silicosis and other such diseases. Rajasthan is the second largest producer of polyester fibre in India.

In Rajasthan, a significant percentage of unskilled workers are employed on daily wages. Some 65 lakh households have been provided employment through MGNREGS (Mahatma Gandhi National Rural Employment Guarantee Scheme) till 2010. Under this scheme, 89.29 lakh households have been allocated MGNREGS job cards by 2009–10.[5]

Women Empowerment

Rajasthan has historically been a patriarchal and feudal society where gender discrimination has been a concern. This has drastically affected women's health, financial status, literacy level and political involvement.

The problems are further aggravated by high levels of seasonal migration. For many men in Rajasthan, migration is required since rural parts of Rajasthan often lack a sufficient economy to provide income for a family year-round. Women are commonly left behind to care and provide for the entire household. This has been increasingly difficult because it is estimated that an average woman's wage is 30 per cent lower than a man's wage working in a similar position. While these mothers work, they must also tend to domestic responsibilities. This leaves little resource for the growth and development of women's rights and education levels.

A strong 'son preference' exists in the region, as it does throughout the country, and high rates of female infanticide and female feticide plague the area. A strong need for women empowerment is evident considering the present status of Rajasthan's women.

Government's Strategy for Poverty Alleviation

The strategy of the government towards poverty alleviation is three pronged; targeting the poor and providing subsidy to give initial boost, helping poor to take up income generating activities by accessing credit from financial institutions, and creating infrastructure like roads, irrigation, marketing facilities, etc. The government subsidies to poor are critical for their survival needs but for sustainable economic development of poor, public investment in infrastructure and access to financial services are very crucial.

Role of Microfinance

Access to financial services plays a very crucial role in economic and social development of people. The impact assessment of microfinance programmes in Rajasthan and elsewhere clearly indicates the change in income level of beneficiaries; reduction of dependence on moneylenders; increase in expenditure/ investment on children education, health, agricultural inputs, increase in production and most important the increased awareness and self-confidence among poor.

Microfinance due to its inherent qualities of timely supply of financial services and flexibility of products can give impetus to potential sectors such as animal husbandry, wool and mutton processing, Information Technology, tourism, etc. In addition to harnessing potential sectors of development, microfinance helps in reaching out to the vulnerable segments of the society like women, SC and ST, which are outside the purview of formal financial institutions.

> Kele Devi is an illiterate rural woman who lives in Khidrath village; Tehsil Baph of Jodhpur district along with her husband and six children. She is the member of Kamdhenu SHG in village Khidrath which is about 22 km from Baph town. Earlier, all the villagers and especially members of the SHG had to go to Baph to get their wheat grinded into wheat floor in the wheat flour mill. They used to lose lot of time in this and couldn't make it a part of their day-to-day life. So to get it, either they made it on 'aata chakki' at home or had to go to the town. As a consequence children also participated in the labour and therefore, didn't go to school so as to help the family.
>
> Ever since then Kele Devi has received a loan of ₹ 10,000 from the SHG to which she belongs, life has become easier for the whole community. She has bought a small aata chakki and installed it at her house. Now, all the members of the SHGs are using it and are saving precious time that they can use it for other tasks as well. Moreover, not only the members but also all villagers from Khidrath are benefitting from this investment as they all use it. In addition to this, Kele Devi has found a sustainable source of livelihood that has also a positive collective impact on the villagers around.

Significance of the Study

Women self-help groups (SHGs) are at the centre of the microfinance revolution that India has been witnessing over the past two decades. The Self-help Group Bank Linkage Programme (SBLP) introduced in the beginning of the 1990s under the aegis of the National Bank for Agriculture and Rural Development (NABARD), mainstreamed the institution of SHG as an innovative system based on the principles of trust and mutual help that can effectively deliver affordable financial services to households with low net worth. The use of peer pressure within the group as collateral substitute helps in avoiding the usual risks associated with such lending. As on 31 March 2010, 69.53 lakh groups have been linked to banks across the country under the SBLP. Out of which 16.94 lakh SHGs have been promoted under the Swarnjayanti Gram Swarozgar Yojana (SGSY), the umbrella programme of centrally sponsored rural development schemes introduced in April 1999. The number of groups with loans outstanding stood at 48.51 lakh at the end of the financial 2009–10. The collective savings of the groups with the formal banking system amounted to ₹ 6,198.71 crore, while the cumulative loan outstanding stood at ₹ 28,038.28 crore (NABARD, Status of Microfinance in India, 2009–10). SGSY accounted for 24 per cent of the savings and 22 per cent of outstanding loans.

Purpose of the Study

This study aims to look into the functions of microfinance in women SHGs and organizations, to analyse the problems and prospects of microfinance, to study the impact of microfinance on various issues such as poverty eradication, supporting sustainable livelihoods, women empowerment, informal financial sector, social security in the State of Rajasthan with the help of systematic research. The main objective of the study is to understand the factors that lead to savings and loan procurement by women SHGs' members.

Objectives of the Study

The specific objectives of the study are as follows:

1. To study the status of microfinance and SHGs in India and Rajasthan.

2. To assess and analyse the status and functioning of women SHGs and its members – their socio-economic profile, reasons for joining SHG, reasons for group conflicts, satisfaction level with the working of SHG, democratic set up of SHGs, etc.
3. To study the mechanisms followed by women SHGs in their operations.
4. To study the role of formal financial institutions such as banks in their day-to-day operations.
5. To study loan disbursement to the SHG members – rules, penalties, purpose, etc.
6. To study the problems faced by members in the management of SHG operation, loan repayment, training, etc.
7. To study the impact of microfinance on various issues such as poverty eradication, supporting sustainable livelihoods, women empowerment, informal financial sector, social security.

Sampling Methodology

Secondary data such as Departmental Reports, periodicals, articles, books, reviews, etc. were made use of.

Being exploratory in nature, the study used a descriptive methodology. Both quantitative and qualitative methods were used for collection and analysis of data. The quantitative data collection instruments included structured and precoded schedules. These were mainly used to collect information relating to membership profile, savings and loans; and maintenance of records of the SHGs. Qualitative methods like focus group discussions and in-depth face-to-face interviews were used to elicit information from SHG members, banks and SHPIs on their experience and for getting feedback. Step-wise sampling process adopted for the study was as follows:

Selection of the Study Area (Districts)

A consultation meeting was convened with the microfinance experts to take the feedback on design, concept, methodology and outcomes. It was decided that the area selection should be in a manner which gives a glimpse of diversity of the state. Based on the brainstorming session; Jaipur, Udaipur, Alwar, Jodhpur and Tonk were selected to geographically represent the central, south, north, west and east region of the state.

Selection of Blocks

The next step after the district selection was the selection of block(s) in each of the five districts for data collection. Five blocks, one per district was selected for the study. The selection was based on the outcome of discussions and meetings with the experts, interaction with prominent SHPIs in the district and review of literature.

Selection of SHGs

The lists of SHGs were drawn from the selected NGOs/MFIs in each selected block and SHGs were selected in such a way that they represented different promoters and schemes in a proportionate manner.

Method of Data Collection

Being exploratory in nature, the study uses a descriptive methodology. Both quantitative and qualitative methods were used for collection and analysis of data. The quantitative data collection instruments included structured and precoded schedules. Schedules were developed separately for SHGs and members. These were mainly used to collect information relating to membership profile, savings and loans, and maintenance of records of the SHGs.

Qualitative methods like focus group discussions and in-depth face-to-face interviews were used to elicit information from SHG members, banks and SHPIs as regards their experience and feedback. A set of discussion guidelines were prepared before hand for this purpose.

Thus, the study set out to cover 5 districts, 5 blocks, 50 SHGs (i.e. 10 SHGs per district), 100 SHG members (i.e. 2 SHG members per SHG) and important people from the society who have witnessed changes from SHG movement and NGO/MFI/Cooperative Society. It was also proposed that case studies with best practices will be documented as part of the study.

Table 1.1

Distribution of SHGs by District and Blocks

District	*Block*	*Number of Groups Surveyed*	*Number of Members Interviewed Face-to-Face*
Tonk	Niwai	10	20
Jaipur	Chomu	10	20
Alwar	Thanagazi	10	20
Udaipur	Bhinder, Girwa	10	20
Jodhpur	Bhap	10	20
All		50	100

Five NGO promoters were captured by the study. These are:

1. Laxmi Nidhi Primary Women Multipurpose Cooperative Society Limited, Niwai (Tonk)
2. Shree Shyam Sanskriti Sewa Samiti, Chithwari, Chomu (Jaipur)
3. Humana People to People India – Micro Finance Division, Thanaghazi (Alwar)
4. Prayatna Sansthan, Udaipur
5. GRAVIS, Jodhpur

The field survey was carried out by me with the help of trained field staff of the respective NGOs during January–February 2011.

Notes

1. Hans, V. Basil, 'Innovations in Microfinance – Looking beyond income poverty', electronic copy available at: <http://ssrn.com/abstract=1292623>.
2. Sample Registration Survey Bulletin 2009.
3. National Family Health Survey–3, 2005–06.
4. NSSO data.
5. NREGA, Rajasthan www.nrega.nic.in

2

Microfinance in India

History of Informal Credit in India and the Emergence of Microfinance

For a long time in India, as in many other countries across the world, there was a distinct lack of formal financial institutions available to the poor. Instead, the only option available to the marginalized was to obtain credit from traders and money-lenders. However, this traditional system was often exploitative. in nature, with loans usually made at exorbitant rates of interest. Microfinance creates a new means of providing credit to the poor without creating the oppressive cycle of debt that existed under the traditional system. Instead, loans are made at lower, sustainable rates that the poor can realistically repay. As such, microfinance has proved to play a key role in increasing the extent of financial inclusion in India.[1]

Despite its obvious advantages over the traditional money-lender system, the new developments in microfinance were not immediately accepted or established in India. Initially, factors such as low grant levels to microfinance institutions and an unfavourable policy environment restricted the rapid spread of microfinance.[2] The first significant development in the field occurred when policy support was given to enable informal self-help groups (SHGs) of 15–20 members to transact with commercial banks.[3] To this day, the self-help group model of microfinance, which links these groups to banks, continues to be the predominant method of microfinance across India as a whole, and the national movement of microfinance now includes 1.4 million of such self-help groups, involving over 20 million members.

The National Bank of Agriculture and Rural Development (NABARD) was largely responsible for spearheading the microfinance movement within India, particularly in the form of self-help groups. Other mainstream institutions that have led the way in providing microfinance in India have been the cooperatives, followed by the Regional Rural Banks (RRBs), the Small Industries Bank for Agriculture and Development (SIDBI), and the Housing Development Finance Corporation (HDFC).[4] One other important institution on the scene in Indian microfinance is Sa-Dhan, a network body of the majority of Indian Microfinance Institutions, which was founded in 1999 as the Association of Community Development Finance Institutions. Its mission is to 'build the field of community development finance in India to help its members and associate institutions to better serve low-income households, particularly women, in both rural and urban India, in their quest for establishing stable livelihoods and improving quality of life'.[5] Membership of Sa-Dhan has increased drastically since its foundation, rendering it one of the most relevant and encompassing microfinance associations in India.

Beyond this, there are several other leading microfinancial institutions working in the sector, including the following: Association for Sarva Seva Farms (ASSEFA), Mitrabharati – The Indian Microfinance Information Hub, Mysore Resettlement and Development Agency (MYRADA), Self-help Women's Association (SEWA), Swayam Krishi Sangam (SKS India), Streedhan – Banking with Rural Women and the Working Women's Forum, Madras, India.[6]

Indian Microfinance Institutions in a Global Context

Today, microfinance has definitively earned its place as an important component to social development in India. Indian microfinance institutions (MFIs) are growing at a rapid pace, aiming to achieve what is known as the double bottom line of both financial sustainability and socially relevant engagement.[7] From a global perspective, a good number of Indian institutions are present in the two lists of top microfinance institutions in the world from Mixmarket and Forbes. In 2008, eight Indian MFIs made it to the top 50 in Microfinance Information Exchange (MIX) list with the highest at rank 4, seven MFIs made it to the top 50 Forbes list with the highest at rank 2. Except for the Kolkata-based Bandhan, which figures on both the lists within the top 10, no other MFIs figure in both the lists, within the top 50. The reasons are the different assessment parameters used by the evaluators. MIX market has used the criteria of outreach, efficiency and transparency. Forbes has applied the criteria of scale, efficiency, risk and return. While client coverage and efficiency are common to both the assessments, the differences are in MIXs, use of transparency and Forbes' use of risk (Table 2.1).

Table 2.1

Indian MFIs in the Top 50 Lists

MIX Top 50		*Forbes Top 50*	
Rank	*Name of MFI*	*Rank*	*Name of MFI*
4	Grama Vidiyal	2	Bandhan (society and NBFC)
6	Bandhan Konnagar	13	Microcredit Foundation of India
7	Sarvodaya Nano Finance	15	Saadhna Microfin
8	Evangelical Social Action Forum	19	Grameen Koota
12	Spandana Spoorthy	23	Sharda Womens Association
21	Share Microfin	29	Asmitha Microfin
35	Basix	44	SKS Microfin
50	CMML		

CMML: Camel Mahila Macs Ltd.

There is a lot of debate on the lists, the assessment methods, criteria and the number of better performing MFIs that are not in the lists. But a large number of Indian MFIs making their entry into both the lists even while the sector has the lowest interest rates (in global comparison) is a matter of satisfaction to all those who are in the sector. The lists have been drawn based on the year 2006 data, and might be dated for drawing conclusions with implications for the future. The market dynamics have changed a lot since then, and so would the leadership positions.

The top five MFIs as per the client coverage and loan outstanding (as on 31 March 2008) are listed in Table 2.2. No assessments have been made in this listing, which is based on data reported in Quick Data published by Sa-Dhan.

Table 2.2

Top Five MFIs by Outreach and Loan Portfolio

Top 5 MFIs – by Clients	*No. (million)*	*Top 5 MFIs – by Loan Outstanding*	₹ *(million)*
SKS Microfinance	1.88	SKS Microfinance	7,818
Share Microfin	1.29	Spandana	7,285
Spandana	1.19	Share Microfin	5,953
Bandhan	0.76	SKDRDP	3,370
Asmitha Microfin	0.70	Asmitha Microfin	3,360

SKDRDP: Shri Kshetra Dhamrmasthala Rural Development Project.

There is no centralized database on the number of microfinance institutions that operate in the country. Estimates have put it anywhere between 800 and 1,200. National Bank for Agriculture and Rural Development (NABARD) has put out a list of MFIs on its website, where 446 institutions have been named of which some may not be engaged in financial intermediation. New institutions are being set up at a rapid pace. These institutions look to exploit the market opportunities available for providing loans to small clients, and achieve the double bottom line of financial sustainability and socially relevant engagement. It is evident that even within the global context, Indian microfinance institutions have earned their place and recognition.

Distribution of Microfinance Across India

Sa-Dhan[8] brings out a comprehensive, annual document providing information on a number of microfinance institutions from which the data is collected. For the year-end, March 2008, Sa-Dhan brought out the report, which provided information on 223 MFIs.[9] As per the Sa-Dhan's report,[10] the outreach and portfolio size of MFIs have been accelerating fast. The clients, outreach increased[11] from 10.04 to 14.1 million over the year 2007–08, recording an impressive growth rate of 39 per cent; but this was lower than the growth rate of 53 per cent achieved last year, albeit on a smaller base. The loan portfolio outstanding was ₹ 59.54 billion as at the end of March 2008, representing an increase of 72 per cent on a large base, which is remarkable, but a shade lower than the 77 per cent growth recorded in the previous year. The growth rate of loans outstanding was 1.8 times that of increase in clientele, indicative of the deepening troubles taking place in the sector. The average loan outstanding per client increased from ₹ 3,442 to 4,222 by 22 per cent across all clients. While 80 per cent of the clients were women, more than 75 per cent of the clients had received loans of less than ₹ 10,000.

Quality of Growth

An analysis made from the data throws up some interesting features. The first is the skewed nature of the spread of microfinance[12] spearheaded by the MFIs, reflecting the trends noticed in the last few years in case of SHG–Bank Linkage Programme (SBLP). The southern region had a much larger share of the outreach and volumes than the other three regions put together. As in the case of SBLP, the MFIs also have strong presence in the southern states of Andhra Pradesh (AP); Karnataka and Tamil Nadu, which accounts for almost 52 per cent of clients and 59 per cent of the portfolio outstanding. If we add the next three best states as of Odisha, West Bengal (WB) and Maharashtra, to the clients of the top three states, we find 82 per cent of clients and also the loan outstanding were accounted for, by these six states. The traditionally low intensity states such as Madhya Pradesh, Bihar, Uttar Pradesh, Uttaranchal, Chhattisgarh and Jharkhand have not really seen a surge in microfinance activities, either under SBLP or under the MFI programmes. Northern and western regions have a share of 4 and 9 per cent, respectively, in terms of clients accounted for 6 and 4 per cent share in terms of loan portfolio. The south has a lion's share of 66 per cent of clients and 75 per cent of the portfolio (Table 2.3).

Table 2.3

MFI Client and Loan Outreach

State-wise Client Outreach			*State-wise Loan Portfolio*	
Name of the State	*Number*	*%*	*Amount (₹)*	*%*
Andhra Pradesh	36,53,115	25.97	19,44,50,23,878	31.75
Karnataka	19,63,373	13.96	11,03,84,81,244	18.02
Tamil Nadu	16,92,560	12.03	5,75,41,00,628	9.40
Odisha	15,77,600	11.21	5,32,35,29,239	8.69
West Bengal	15,40,927	10.95	5,29,85,97,926	8.65
Maharashtra	11,69,306	8.31	3,84,05,48,354	6.27
Uttar Pradesh	5,33,041	3.79	3,46,94,41,228	5.67
Gujarat	4,16,375	2.96	64,03,02,867	1.05
Kerala	3,82,001	2.72	1,27,73,05,126	2.09
Bihar	2,41,651	1.72	9,08,23,380	1.48
Chhattisgarh	2,35,063	1.67	1,15,64,23,043	1.89
Madhya Pradesh	2,29,300	1.63	1,04,53,50,073	1.71
Assam	1,37,239	0.98	45,87,01,844	0.75
Jharkhand	1,15,444	0.82	51,93,08,567	0.85
Rajasthan	83,873	0.60	38,03,84,265	0.62

Cont'd...

Cont'd...

Tripura	37,687	0.27	12,79,42,065	0.21
Delhi	27,761	0.20	43,93,41,552	0.72
Uttaranchal	16,798	0.12	7,17,10,412	0.12
Puducherry	13,161	0.09	2,87,85,907	0.05
Haryana	1,468	0.01	1,12,50,000	0.02
Manipur	651	0.00	45,60,000	0.01
Andaman Nicobar	239	0.00	17,86,389	0.00
Nagaland	12	0.00	48,000	0.00
Arunachal Pradesh	0	0.00	0	0.00
Himachal Pradesh	0	0.00	0	0.00
Meghalaya	0	0.00	0	0.00
Punjab	0	0.00	0	0.00
Grand Total	1,40,68,645	100.00	61,24,11,56,410	100.00

The loan size significantly differed from region to region. North recorded the largest average loan size of ₹ 6,300 with the west having the lowest average loan size of ₹ 1,900 (Table 2.4). The average loan size in the north was more than three times of the loan size in the western region. Surprisingly, the most mature southern region had a lower average loan size compared to the nascent north. The small loan size indicates that client acquisition is pursued more intensively than deepening the engagement with the acquired clients. The portfolio growth is a function of not only the number of clients but also the average loan per client. A healthy loan average per client is likely to improve profitability and bring down the operational cost per unit of loan.

Table 2.4

Region-wise Average Loan Size 2008

Region	*Average Individual Loan Size (₹)*
East	3,126
North	6,323
South	4,735
West	1,924

Microfinance Institutions in a Period of Crisis

Andhra Pradesh is considered to be the epicentre of the microfinance sector in India.[13] This section may help to explain how the microfinance sector was quacked by the downfall of Andhra Pradesh, one state of the most predominant one (in terms of geographic strength situated in the south and concentrating five of the largest NBFC-MFIs institutions in India).

As it was referred before, the microfinance institutions have paved the way for success and stability; however, their role during the last two decades has been marked by several developments in terms of outreach and penetration in unbanked areas.[14] But several setbacks were also felt. This was even more significant with the outbreak of Andhra Pradesh crisis (2012).

Therefore, the sector immediately reacted through strong regulatory initiatives; greater emphasis was put on client protection and on improving governance with the purpose of improvement social focus, as is stated in the report.[15]

This response was an attempt in the sector to move away from this pessimistic scenario characterized as the 'worst and dark times' of microfinance in India. The data gathered by The Bharat Microfinance Quick Report–2012 published by Sa-Dhan has exactly measured the consequences of 2012 with respect to the previous year. There was a manifested reluctance by several MFIs to share information. Only 167 of 264 have contributed with their figures to the report.

Secondly, as Table 2.5 shows the client outreach and loan portfolio registered a negative downfall in 2012, even when there was a small decline in the gross loan of 3 per cent. The customer outreach achieved 26.8 million with a gross loan portfolio of ₹ 209.13 billion. However, there is a negative growth in client outreach and loan portfolio in 2012 that is indicated by the decrease in the number of customers by 15.7 per cent.

This scenario has ensured a structural defeat in terms of retaining the client account liquidity that is mainly caused due to the huge losses of clients in AP. On the other hand this can be perceived as a good indicator of lesser number of loans available per person.

Table 2.5

Progress of MFIs

	2010	*2011*	*Growth Rate (%)*	*2012*	*Growth Rate (%)*
No. of MFIs reporting	264	170	—	167	—
Customer Outreach (million)	26.7	31.8	19.1	26.8	–15.7
Outstanding Loans (₹ Billion)	183.44	215.56	17.5	209.13	-3.0

Source: Data from Sa-Dhan's 'The Bharat Microfinance Quick Report–2012'.

This entire micro-economic scenario had also some implications in the 10 ranking of the MFIs. The current data indicates a complete change in the positions of the best MFI's performance in comparison with the previous data of 2008.

CASHPOR assisted a new entrant in the list of the 10 institutions, SKS retained the 1st place in terms of client outreach, and Bandhan moved up to the second place. However, this last MFI has been considered as the largest MFI in India in terms of gross loans.

Table 2.6

Top 10 MFIs by Outreach

Year	*Outreach (million)*		*Outreach Growth %*	*Loans o/s (₹ billion)*		*Loans Growth %*
	2011	*2012*		*2011*	*2012*	
SKS	6.24	4.26	–32	41.11	16.69	–59
Bandhan	3.25	3.62	11	25.07	37.30	49
Spandana	4.19	3.44	–18	34.58	27.15	–21
SHARE	2.84	2.16	–24	20.65	21.10	2
Equitas	1.53	1.19	–22	7.94	7.24	–9

Cont'd...

Cont'd...

SKDRDP	1.38	1.02	–26	9.58	6.01	–37
Ujjivan	0.84	0.82	–2	6.25	7.03	13
Grama Vidiyal	0.93	0.82	–12	5.2	5.20	0
BASIX	1.53	0.57	–63	12.49	2.92	–77
CASHPOR	0.43	0.46	7	2.38	3.23	36

Source: Data from MIX.org

Among the top 10, only Bandhan and CASHPOR could achieve a positive growth in outreach. All the others have shown a negative growth, with an insignificant decrease towards BASIX. As the Table 2.6 shows BASIX and SKS showed a real negative decline of 63 per cent and 32 per cent each in terms of client outreach. This data is even more overwhelming when it is referred to the gross loan portfolio with an expressive decline of 77 per cent towards BASIX and 59 per cent of SKS. In conclusion, all the MFIs with a large portfolio exposure in Andhra Pradesh were negatively affected. As the graph indicates only CASHPOR and Bandhan could achieve a larger loan portfolio of 49 per cent and 36 per cent respectively and have shown that they are quite independent of the Andhra Pradesh economy.

The loan capital in comparison with the previous year has increased slightly by 15 per cent to ₹ 7,803 as the Table 2.7 indicates.

Table 2.7

Per Capita Loan Size

Year	*2008*	*2009*	*2010*	*2011*	*2012*
Per capita loan nominal terms (₹)	4,223	5,192	4,223	6,870	7,803
Per capita loan real terms (₹) 2004–05 Prices	3,521	4,120	3,521	4,963	4,984

Source: MIX market.

However, as the report mentions[16] the loan size nominal is still behind the demand for livelihood development, as the inflation rate is very high.

Simultaneously, the regional distribution in terms of outreach and loan portfolio has shown an unchangeable trend towards the dominance of the southern region, counting almost 50 per cent in outreach and portfolio followed by the eastern region (25%) (Table 2.8).

Table 2.8

Comparison of Market Share of Different Regions

Region	*Share of Clients 2010–11%*	*Share of Clients 2011–12%*	*Share of Loans 2010–11%*	*Share of Loans 2011–12%*
North	4.8	4.2	3.7	4.2
North-East	3.2	4.2	3.6	6.1
East	17.9	25.1	18.1	23.3
Central	16.7	9.6	14.3	9.7
West	12.1	7.2	11.4	7.6
South	45.3	49.7	48.9	49.1

Source: MIX market.

Therefore, as has been documented through all the tables the MFIs were obliged to do some internal restructurization due to the negative consequences of the Andhra Pradesh Law (2012), as it caused several aftershocks in the microfinance sector, causing almost an abrupt stagnation.

In this context MFIs were obliged to adopt several austerity measures to reduce the operational costs, which has caused a reduction in the workforce and also either closed down and/or merged branches to reduce cost of operation. Some MFIs have cut down upon their staff, as it was the case in PWMACS and CRESA. In conclusion, the institutions have suffered a reduction in their branches' infrastructures and client portfolio (Table 2.9).

Table 2.9

AP-MFIs Operational and Financial Performance

AP based MFIs	*2001*	*2012*	*Decline (%)*
No. of Branch	6,426	5,227	19
No. of Staff	55,512	39,067	30
Active Clients (million)	16	12	25
Loan Portfolio (₹ million)	1,39,430	79,120	43
Disbursement (₹ million)	1,91,800	62,900	67
PAR 60 (%)	30	31	
Total Asset (₹ million)	1,35,210	91,730	32
Net Owned Fund (NoF) ₹ million	31,490	25,380	19
Yield (%)	22	10	
Operating Expense (%)	10	6	
Operational Sufficiency – OSS (%)	111	55	
Return on Asset (RoA) (%)	2	–8	
Return on Equity (RoE) (%)	2	–35	

Source: Sa-Dhan Bharat Microfinance Quick Report 2012.

A short overview of the crisis shows a devastating impact also on the clients. Several have abandoned the MFI and started to do wage labour for their livelihoods, and to solve their liquidity problem they started selling their valuable goods such as gold, cattle, etc. which was also done to accomplish the severe high interest rates, as is stated in study conducted by Sa-Dhan. At the same time they started to deny accessing the credit once it started getting very difficult. Around 90 per cent of the respondents of the study have affirmed that they want to repay the loan if MFIs started disbursing them fresh loan as it was referred in the same study conducted by MicroSave.

A Critical Overview of the System Performance: In the Aftermath of AP Crisis

The Centre for Microfinance (CmF), at IFMR, Chennai[17] felt the need to conduct a study in order to perceive whether the RBI guidelines were in accordance with the clients' profiles. The findings are overwhelming. There is a lack of understanding of the client's needs on this sector for many reasons. First they are not accomplishing with the RBI guidelines that requires that 75 per cent of the loan should go to income generating activities. Only 49 per cent of the respondents affirmed that the income was invested in the current business, and 17 per cent have utilized it for consumption purposes. Secondly, more than 62 per cent of client households have at least one bank account but it is not the primary source of credit.

In addition to this, around 11 per cent of the respondents have never used the banking system to take loans. There are several reasons highlighted that are in accordance with this pessimistic approach such as: 'the customers feel that their demand for a specific credit is not provided by the banks (30%); documentation and application procedures are too complicated (25%), there is a lack of knowledge about the products and services provided by the banks (11%)'.[18]

Among the others who do not have a bank account, the inability to cooperate with the banks is permanent: 20 per cent feel that their low savings are not relevant in the banking system, as well as 19 per cent confessed that they have a lack of knowledge about the financial products and finally, 13 per cent reported that their demands for loan have been neglected or rejected.

In comparison with self-help groups model that was also analysed by this study, the picture is also blurred. Taking this kind of model into analysis it was stated that more than 76 per cent of the clients do not have any SHG account, as 47 per cent said that they are totally ignorant about the function of this kind of model. These findings were even more predominant in the semi-urban areas.

In the eyes of the clients the loan recovery has been awkward (just assuring high profits to MFIs and coercive money collection practices). Among these practices there were several complaints such as: the obligation to someone else's instalments, high interest rates and selling practices that resulted in indebtedness.

To solve all these incoherences it was required that MFIs ensure proper compliance through a code of conduct (that was established in the India Summit 2011 in New Delhi) and other regulations. The main purpose was to strengthen and enforcing a way that is ethical and transparent and benefits clients in a holistic manner. This should include the following principles:

- Integrity and ethical behaviour
- Transparency
- Client protection
- Governance
- Recruitment
- Client education
- Data sharing, and
- Feedback/grievance redressed mechanisms

The two companies Sa-Dhan and MFIN are making all the efforts to gather their staff according to these rules. Along with this a code of conduct was enforced to assess whether the MFIs have participated to assure protection, governance, transparency and social involvement towards their clients in a more systematic manner on a daily basis.

Simultaneously, this entire context has paved way to create a new product design as a basis for reducing operational costs, and tackling the local needs of their clients. Therefore, it has resulted in a mixture of services and products.

The new era of products is characterized not only to generate income but also to provide consumption needs of the clients. This period, remarkably established what is called 'beyond credit innovation' as is stated in the report.[19] New products have emerged in terms of savings, micro-insurance, micro-pension and credit support. There is a general awareness that contributes to more responsible and wise clients who now know how to plan their wealth and tackle all their external and internal threats (health problems, emergencies outbreaks from social obligations, etc.) thus giving more profits to the banking system. Therefore, all this amalgamation of products has recently developed.

The first one related to the savings especially conceived towards the poor who often face distressing problems because of social and religious obligations or even because of a downfall of their incomes from agriculture. They are also the most vulnerable group as they are not keen on planning their savings to face these emergencies. Moreover, they are also used to taking credits from informal sources that is more costly and it creates hard losses without using any structural life cycle planning to tackle the emergencies and needs that often result in financial stress. In the eyes of the MFIs, this possibility also increases the diversity of products that can get more profit, by not putting all the products in the same basket, as well as assuring, for instance, the client loyalty through retention. This can be an asset in periods of downfall.

There are several saving options provided by the MFIs sector such as: Bank-led savings options (concerning commercial banks to provide savings in terms of deposits through electronic and mobile banking solutions), Proprietary options (centre on the Gold Acquisition Loan), Mutual Fund products (whose main purpose is to invest in the government debt), and Pension products (directed to the most vulnerable groups of the society that can be planning for periodical withdrawals from a voluntary base or even under the Government of India's New Pension Scheme (NPS) and finally the Insurance products in partnership with life insurance companies. However, all these innovative achievements have also been a subject of criticism with respect to their real profits and security to the customers. In the Microfinance Report of India 2012, eight sensitive points were found. These savings options may not be beneficial to the customer integrally. There are nevertheless some constraints that should be taken in account in terms of: cost for the client (some expenses for the transactional cost); the returns to the client (are dependent to the market ranges); the period of withdrawal as it can be focused only on a long-term perception; the security aspects of the institutions should be developed by receipts to avoid risk markets for the clients and finally, the regulatory aspects should be an asset as well as the return to the organization should be done in a more transparent manner, as sometimes they are dependent on the partnership organization.

Secondly, the micro-insurance in terms of health insurance is very important especially in an era where poverty alleviation and universal health care are the landmarks of development policy worldwide. In India this is even more important as the government is already planning to spend 1.4 to 2.5 per cent of the GDP on health care by the end of the 12th Five-Year Plan (2017).[20] Besides, there is a situation that it is reported in the same report of poorness facilities and capabilities of the public health service in comparison to private ones. This increase in the daily household expenses is detrimental to the poor people who cannot afford any kind of service.

Women in Indian society are considered as the 'Care Givers' of the family. However, most of them suffer from lack of information and awareness about health treatments. Despite this, they are seen as the most important persons in the family as they are responsible for the nutrition and health status of their families. Therefore, several MFIs are developing this kind of insurances that tackles maternal care and childhood illnesses as well as malnutrition, HIV/AIDS, hygiene and sanitation. Along with these programmes it is also known that there is a lack of information in the remote locations and among poor people about these issues. Therefore, the microfinance should perform these activities with the Self-Help Groups assuring low cost solutions towards the bottom layers of the social pyramid. This is also perceived as an opportunity to develop better labour supply, as all the members of the family with a healthy status can contribute to the family income.

Along with these new initiatives, we can also highlight the water and sanitation (WATSAN) loan. A larger number of international non-governmental organizations are cooperating with banks, government institutions and agencies to provide proper water and sanitation through microfinance to the poor.

These kinds of products were also seen as a form of duty from the financial institutions to provide social protection for their customers as they can be healthier and assure more revenues in long term for the institutions, developing in that way their financial security. As is described in the same report, these are considered as products that are not 'income generating' but 'income saving'.

The micro-insurance is also considered under the umbrella of social security schemes. In that sense, community-based micro-insurance infrastructures have been created in India to tackle some 'women specific risks' as is the case of Vimo SEWA, Yeshasvini and Karuna Trust. Another product that is starting to be developed is the pension, as India is predicted to reach 200 million ageing people by 2030.

Similarly, to the other products this innovation brought some challenges on it design to establish a real development in the income of the poor people. There are several constraints that should be rethought: the awareness should be generated among the society that is clearly fragile, the time life of the products and consequently the revenues generated, etc.

The housing microfinance was also initiated to tackle the low-income households of the society that want to make a 'progressive build' houses that could include repair, renovation or rehabilitation. The biggest concern in this product is that often the poor do not have the owner's rights nor the proper awareness to make use of these kinds of products. Therefore, MFI's sector should invest more in financial literacy in order to empower the poorest of the poor in the society, before putting all these products in the market on a large scale, so as to not threaten their financial inclusion.

In conclusion, the utmost concern of MFI's innovations is to tackle the real needs of their customers instead of having a 'panacea for all ills'. In doing this, they should also recognize how to work out the regulation provisions, information systems and outweigh the risks or costs of every product created.

MFI's sector should be tuned for this purpose to help poor people improve their livelihood, income and avoid any kind of commercial grievance.

Therefore, all these innovations recently developed have at the same time created a need to improve regulations, transparency and good governance among the sector.

The Credit Bureau was expressively designed to audit directly the transparency of MFIs by imposing a register service about the credit information of the companies as well as all the liabilities of its borrowers. Since June 2012, MFI's sector has made mandatory for all members to use the credit bureau in order to report all the loan process.

To sum up, this bureau can monitor and also create more confidence in the borrowers once the borrowers create credit histories. The main objective is to empower the clients about their rights, responsibilities and duties to manage the loans and debts in a better way.

The governance and transparency as such were also not forgotten by the MFIs. The first one has been the result of many attempts to assure that the board members of the companies are well qualified and are willing to conduct and combine their work in terms of social and financial goals. It is a need referred in the report for the CEOs to have a code of conduct through social goals in outreaching and setting targets for the clients who can move out of poverty levels.[21] However, it is also mentioned in the report that there is a need to create a culture of outreach in terms of social goals, as well as set a working plan with precise targets to make financial inclusion a reality.

Finally, the transparency requirements were also not forgotten. The absence of a single market rate and the disparity of the prices has damaged the sector. Therefore, there is an emergency to regulate the pricing norms through several clauses: educating low-income clients on all products, enabling them to understand policies and ensuring that the product and policies are not distorted, especially in terms of interest rates. This kind of methodology should be applied in the sector, as done in India, where MIX platform information set up by SIDBI has already started. The transparency should be done on a daily basis, to update the information in all markets.

The RBI guidelines were created in that way to have more specificity about the pricing that can be charged on microfinance loans and also recommended the MFIs to inform their clients about the effective interest rates.

Conclusion

The performance of MFIs was characterized by some setbacks and improvements. Therefore, some points should be highlighted to re-conceptualize their functions and place in the market. The first one is related to the main purpose of the MFI's creation, in order to empower rural women through Self-Help Groups that slowly started to shift for commercial purposes with a severe negative impact on the sector, especially because of the grievance of some players.

Second, microfinance could not target the right segment as it has no definition about how to characterize the poor clients and differentiation of products in terms of income. There was only a uniform type of products which are hard to root and address the clients' preferences.

Third, the spillover of the MFIs had a negative impact in the sector. The boom of several institutions has exhausted the market, offering multiple loans to the same households in the same operational areas, causing an interest of conflicts in the sector.

Fourth, there has been a high interest rate that nowadays was reconsidered to be fixed under a cap. The final issue was concerning the grievance from some borrowers who wished to have more loans than their capacities to repay them, and it has been largely damaging the sector and the market.

Microfinance has to battle for a more customer-oriented approach in which it can create awareness and preparedness among the people to use financial credits. Furthermore, it should design proper products to improve the livelihood conditions of the poor. Providing them a better capacity building could be an asset. There is an urgency to improve the infrastructure support and marketing arrangement along with good monitoring of the practices. However, it is also recognized the good work that MFI have performed in 'reaching the unreached areas', as well as its working for a better social inclusion. One example of this success is, for instance, the great effort that Bandhan has done especially in the north and eastern regions of India, as well as other stakeholders. Along with this, there is general recognition that the microfinance sector has been consolidated in India. There are several models that have come forward such as SHGs, NGOs cooperative models, as well as some sponsored by different institutions such as NABFINS[22] that can emerge to tackle the specificity of every region, local or place.

The Microfinance Bill should be passed in the Parliament and should bring to the sector a greater emphasis on social performance towards good governance and transparency in the institutions for better protection of their customers.

The future steps on the Microfinance sector in India should pave the way for more financial inclusion. The World Bank survey concluded that India is only a step behind other countries worldwide in terms of bank account penetration but is in the same line with respect to borrowings from formal institutions.[23] Therefore, the next generation of the SHG called SHG–2 should improve a diversity of factors such as: strengthen the possibility for voluntary savings; prioritizing cash credit in the scope of lending, and providing multiple borrowers on the basis of financial capacities of the costumers and finally, diversify the profits in order to improve the livelihood of the people.

The AP crisis has proof that the sector requires tremendous ability to re-adapt in severe times as well as in emergencies to fulfil the needs of the poor in a more costumer-friendly approach. The establishment of a Credit Bureau, a unified code of conduct and at the same time more awareness towards good governance and transparency can, in the near future, help in the consolidation and the growth of this sector in India.

Notes

1. Hans, V. Basil, 'Innovations in Microfinance – Looking beyond income poverty', electronic copy available at: <http://ssrn.com/abstract=1292623>.
2. Arora, Sukhwinder Singh. 'Microfinance Matters – The Future of Microfinance in India.' *UNCDF/FENU*. Web. 15 June 2010. <http://www.uncdf.org/english/microfinance/newsletter/pages/2005_06/news_india.php>.
3. Ibid.
4. Hans, V. Basil, op. cit.
5. *Microfinance-India-Home*. Web. 17 June 2010. <http://www.sadhan.net/>.
6. 'Microfinance and NGOs', article available through Kumarappa Institute of Gram Swaraj.
7. Srinivasan, N. 'Microfinance India, State of the sector report 2008'.
8. Sa-Dhan is a national network of microfinance institutions.
9. The Bharat Microfinance Report – Quick Report 2008, Sa-Dhan. The report contains data about operational and financial details of 223 MFIs of which, 196 are members of Sa-Dhan and 97 non-members. There are some MFIs that have not reported to the Sa-Dhan database. Their data is not a part of the analysis and to that extent, allowances have to be made for the conclusions drawn in this chapter. But the volumes involved are not expected to be significant in the overall context of the sector, but the significance of what the institutions do, remains outside the report.
10. Some of the institutions reporting data do not seem to have their own clients, but have clients working in promotion, development and umbrella support. Significant numbers have been reported,

for example, by Maharashtra Mahila Athik Vikas Mahamandal (MAVIM).

11. In the previous year's report, the number of clients was reported as 10.4 million, but revised to 10.04 million in the current year's report.
12. The Bharat Microfinance Report – Quick Report 2008, Sa-Dhan. At the end of chapter 2, contains the state-wise client outreach and loan portfolio details.
13. http://www.microsave.net/files/pdf/What_are_Clients_doing_Post_the_Andhra_Pradesh_MFI_Crisis.pdf
14. Microfinance India: State of the Sector Report 2012, Chapter 3, Microfinance Institutions – sign of recovery, page 47.
15. http://www.microsave.net/files/pdf/What_are_Clients_doing_Post_the_Andhra_Pradesh_MFI_Crisis.pdf
16. Microfinance India: State of the Sector Report 2012, Chapter 3, Microfinance Institutions – sign of recovery, page 50.
17. Microfinance India: State of the Sector Report 2012, Chapter 3, Microfinance Institutions – sign of recovery, page 56.
18. Ibid.
19. Microfinance India: State of the Sector Report 2012, Chapter 5, Microfinance – Beyond Credit, page 106.
20. Ibid.
21. Microfinance India: State of the Sector Report 2012, Chapter 3, Microfinance Institutions – sign of recovery, page 67.
22. Is a subsidiary of National Bank for Agriculture and Rural Development (NABARD) with equity participation from NABARD, Government of Karnataka, Canara Bank, Union Bank of India, Bank of Baroda, Dhanalakshmi Bank and Federal Bank.
23. Microfinance India: State of the Sector Report 2012, Chapter 1, Overview.

3

Status of Microfinance in Rajasthan

Rajasthan is located in the north-west of the country, in an area which Sa-Dhan's survey specifically highlighted as remaining less targeted by microfinance institutions. The rate of growth in microfinance may not be as high as in other states, yet Rajasthan has still seen a rapid increase in the microfinance sector. According to the 'Status of Microfinance Sector in Rajasthan' published by the Centre for Microfinance in 2010, the number of self-help groups and credit disbursal had increased three times in the previous three years.[1] As with the general trend across the country, the primary model used to deliver microfinance services in Rajasthan is the SHG-Bank linkage model. However, there still remains a much greater need for microfinance outreach in the region than what is currently being provided.

Government programmes on poverty alleviation and its policies impact the microfinance sector to a great deal. The microfinance needs also get impacted by various developments at district, state and centre level. This chapter captures some of the major developments from the government, banks and voluntary organizations in terms of new interventions and policies that would impact the microfinance sector in Rajasthan. Only the schemes and trends which bear direct relation to microfinance services of the poor have been captured in the chapter.

Developmental Scheme Updates

Mahatma Gandhi National Rural Employment Guarantee Scheme (MGNREGS)

The scheme provides a legal guarantee for one hundred days of employment in every financial year to adult members of rural households willing to do unskilled manual work at the statutory minimum wage. The objective of the scheme is to provide employment to rural poor on one hand and to build assets for rural development on the other.

Money Spent on Wages – MNREGS in Rajasthan[2] *(in ₹ Crore)*

Year	*Amount*
2008–09	4,365.31
2009–10	3,930.48
2010–11	2,272.02
Total	10,567.81

MGNREGS started in 2006 in selected 100 districts and from 2008 it was upscaled to all districts. In Rajasthan its implementation is considered successful. Till March 2011, 58 lakh households have got employment and over ₹ 10,567 crore have come in the rural economy of Rajasthan in the form of payments to labourers. A cash inflow of this quantum has helped the poor to meet expenses on child education, food and fodder, agriculture inputs, etc. It can be said that had MGNREGS not been there, the poor would have taken loan from moneylenders at 25–60 per cent interest rates to meet such expenses or would have migrated. Over 50 per cent of households in Rajasthan are estimated to have benefitted from the scheme.[3]

Financial progress as per data provided by MGNREGS indicates that the scheme has been successful in providing employment to rural poor. However, it is not known as to what extent the assets for poverty alleviation have been built. Though there has been no impact study to prove or disprove asset creation, preliminary findings indicate that in Rajasthan, majority of projects have been on making rural roads and desilting old waterbodies and digging new waterbodies on common lands.

MGNREGS is often criticized for raising the agricultural wage and thereby increasing the agricultural costs. However, in Rajasthan, agriculture is primarily sustenance agriculture. Therefore, the chance of wage rate increasing is unlikely, even though no evidence is present for or against the argument. The payments under MGNREGS are routed through banks, post offices and cooperative societies. Thus, people have started getting exposed to these formal institutions. This is a positive development and would help in financial inclusion as well.

National Rural Livelihood Mission (NRLM)

NRLM has been conceptualized by Ministry of Rural Development, Government of India. It is to replace the (SGSY), a scheme which was primarily designed to promote self-employment oriented income generating activities for the Below Poverty Line (BPL) families in the rural areas.

NRLM aims at taking a different approach to issues faced in SGSY. Main thrust areas in NRLM comprise (a) Targeting all poor and not just BPL; (b) The subsidy to be used as seed capital for long-term credit linkage; (c) Focus on building institutions of the poor, e.g. community based organizations (CBOs, SHG federations, etc.); (d) Dedicated support structure for SHGs and SHG federations; (e) skill development trainings specially off-farm trainings; (f) Resource mapping at various levels and matching it with market demand before selecting activities for community livelihood promotion; and (g) tracking financial conditions of households over a period of time.

District Poverty Initiative Project (DPIP) II

The Government of Rajasthan completed DPIP Phase I in December 2007 and is preparing to follow it up with a second phase called Rajasthan Rural Livelihood Project (RRLP). The RRLP is expected to build on the experience from DPIP, and other ongoing livelihood projects in India. The RRLP aims to increase and sustain income of the poor, especially women, in 17 districts covering 111 blocks.

Loan Waiver and One-Time Settlement of Debts Scheme

Following the farmers distress and farmers suicides in various parts of country, Government of India launched loan waiver and one-time settlements of bank debts scheme in 2008. The scheme was to waive off ₹ 60,000 crore bank loan of marginal and small farmers so that they can get fresh credit from banks and do not have to fall in debt trap by usurious informal loans.

Small and marginal farmers holding land up to two hectares were entitled for complete waiver of loans, while farmers holding more land than that were eligible for a one-time settlement relief of 25 per cent. It was envisaged that loan waiver will bring out the distressed poor from clutches of debt trap and strengthen them to build their livelihood.

The scheme got implemented but there are different opinions on whether it really benefitted the poor. Data is not available on the number of poor (whose loans were waived off) who could get fresh loans from banks. There are anecdotal evidences from the field that people faced enormous difficulties in getting fresh loans from banks. Many bank managers still consider them defaulters (as they have not repaid the loan) and strongly believe that such schemes would have negative impact on financial discipline of the poor.

According to the National Sample Survey (59th Round, 2004–05), 51.4 per cent or just over half of farmer households in the country did not access credit, either from institutional or non-institutional sources. Further, despite the vast network of bank branches, only 27 per cent of total farm households had any loans from formal sources (of which one-third also borrow from informal sources). Among the marginal farmer category, as many as 80 per cent did not have any borrowing from formal sources. Therefore, it can be deduced that the target group of loan waiver scheme was not exactly for which the scheme was launched.

In loan waiver scheme, only agricultural loans were waived off. Since SHG's microfinance loans did not fall in this category, SHG loans were not waived off. This resulted in resentment in some SHGs who perceived them to be sufferers at end of the day, rather than beneficiaries. Repercussion of the scheme included adverse effect on repayment rate of SHGs, who thought that their loans too will be waived off.

The massive scale of loan waiver scheme squeezed the human resource capacity of banks to an extreme. During 2008–09 and 2009–10, significant proportion of bank staff was engaged in loan waiver claim processing. This had negative impact on SHG-Bank linkage.

Financial Inclusion

Dedicated Fund to Promote Financial Inclusion

Government of India set up Financial Inclusion Fund and Financial Inclusion Technology Fund in NABARD in 2007–2008. With an aim to support developmental activities through promotion and technology, these funds will see infusion of aggregate ₹ 1,000 crore in both the funds. The funding will be contributed by the GoI, Reserve Bank of India (RBI) and NABARD in a ratio of 40:40:20.

Financial Inclusion in Villages with Population in Excess of 2000

Finance Ministry, in consultation with RBI, has decided to provide banking facilities, along with insurance and other financial services, to habitations having population in excess of 2000 by March 2012. (This will be followed by targeting habitations having population in excess of 1,000). This will be achieved through business correspondents and business facilitators.

Mushrooming of Multilevel Marketing to Collect Savings from the Poor

In the last few years, there has been an influx of 'doorstep financial services providers' which provide savings linked schemes to the poor in Rajasthan. Their activities have ballooned in last few years. Their structure mirrors that of a Ponzi scheme in which returns are paid to investors from their own money or money paid by subsequent investors, rather than from any actual profit earned. A Ponzi scheme is meant to default later, if not earlier in its day of operations, when the bubble gets burst.

There has also been an influx of (multilevel marketing) schemes in which members are incentivised to add more members under each member to do business. With every new addition, existing members get benefitted.

A quick learning from successful operations of such schemes, many of which are not regulated by RBI, SEBI or IRDA, indicates that a fertile ground exists for banks to meet demands of the poor. It is ironic that Doorstep Financial Services Providers which are regulated by none, hold a free hand in whatever they do and are able to run scot free in case of frauds. The State government and RBI need to take stern action to bring such unregulated entities under their purview, which usually come to public notice only in case of fraud alarm.

Interest Subsidy of 50 per cent on Loans Taken by Women SHGs[4]

The state government has decided to give 50 per cent subsidy on interest to Self-Help Groups (from July 2010) if the SHGs repay to banks on time. This is a positive trend and incentivises SHGs to be regular in payment. This development should also encourage banks to give more credit to SHGs.

Standard Micro-insurance Product for Rural and Social Sector

IRDA's proposed standard product is aimed to provide a comprehensive package of insurance covers to relevant persons belonging to economically weaker sections in rural and urban areas. The product is proposed to link with KCC, farmer clubs, SHGs which would enable the insurers to reach out to the policy holders easily for premium payment and other servicing.

Policy Trends Having Impact on Microfinance Sector

In the last few years, there has been a paradigm shift observed in the policy and programmes of poverty alleviation. Now the policy makers and development practitioners are looking at financial inclusion and microfinance from a different perspective. Some noticeable trends are discussed below:

Addressing all Poor Rather than Targeting Only Below Poverty Line (BPL)

In the past, approach of poverty eradication was limited to targeting 'Below Poverty Line' families only. The idea was to provide relief and propel growth of the BPL poor by providing them with one-time subsidy. For example, under SGSY (Swarnjayanti Gram Swarozgar Yojana) scheme, subsidy was given to SHGs of BPL members. However, this approach of targeting BPL has not fetched desired results. A negative implication of this policy has been increase in demand of 'BPL card' from relatively richer segment of poor and, therefore, lot of BPL benefits not reaching intended beneficiaries.

New poverty alleviation programmes like MGNREGS, NRLM, RRLP, MPOWER, etc. are approaching poverty eradication through 'financial inclusion', in which focus is not just on BPL but a set of poor people, including BPL. The new approach aims at impacting more and more poor irrespective of whether they fall in BPL, thereby increasing outreach and building strong institutions of the poor.

Focus on Institutions of Poor (e.g. SHG Federations and CBOs)

Mobilization of all the rural poor households into functionally effective, self-managed and self-governed institutions of the poor has now become top priority of policy makers and local development practitioners. It is perceived that 'institutions of poor' are more sustainable and effective as compared to individuals dependent upon outside support. Federating self-help groups in higher-level institutions increases their 'voice' and bargaining power with the private sector, market and other state actors. NRLM, which has replaced SGSY, and DPIP II (RRLP), which has replaced DPIP I, have 'focus on institutions of poor' as one of their key thrust areas.

NGOs involved in the sector have found 'federations' to be the next step for SHGs' growth. There is growing acceptance of the whole idea of federating SHGs. This is pronounced by increasing number of federations over the years.

Use of One-time Subsidy and Grants as Seed Capital

In the past, focus has been on providing one-time subsidy/grant to BPL households and SHGs. Government schemes like SGSY and DPIP Phase I have focused more on subsidy component to individuals rather than building their credit linkages with banks. Such schemes have resulted in leakages, delay in payments, false delivery and bureaucratic interventions. Adding to that, amount of subsidy has been limited and is not replenishable.

Compared to schemes mentioned above, new schemes like MPOWER, NRLM and DPIP Phase II (RRLP) focus more on building credit linkages of the poor with banks rather than providing one-time individual subsidies. The idea is to invest in building institutions of the poor by providing seed capital and then grooming them to save. Remaining amount for growth is fetched from banks as credit. This approach is more sustainable. Moreover, since bank credit is unlimited (of course, if repaid regularly), it serves as a reliable, long-term solution as compared to short-term focused subsidy/grant.

From Group Enterprise to Micro-Entrepreneurs' Group

SGSY scheme supported and promoted group enterprises. However, group enterprise approach has been proved wrong beyond doubt over time. It has been well established that individual enterprises (or at max, partnerships) are natural, more sustainable and more effective from the business point of view. Individual enterprises have got wider acceptance over the years.

Rollback of Private Banks from Microfinance

In microfinance sector, many private sector banks came forward, 3–4 years back, to provide credit to the poor through SHGs and MFIs. The models involved, to name a few, partnering with microfinance institutions, using business facilitators for microfinance services, etc. However, either due to operational losses or due to implementation issues, these banks faced expansion issues. Rather than finding solutions to the problems, these banks started rolling back. The implication was that the channels for provision of financial services to the poor were narrowed.

Shrinking Donor Funds for Promotion and Nurturing SHGs and SHG Federations

Due to influx of large number of microfinance institutions, which are raising commercial capital and which are returning commercial Return on Investment (ROI) to investors, donor agencies have started taking a relook at the microfinance sector. Over the last 2–4 years, microfinance has become somewhat of a new 'asset class'. A number of private equity investors and commercial venture capitalists have made significant investments into the sector. Same microfinance institutions, who were hand-held and groomed by donor agencies during initial days, have now become favourites of large commercial investors, who are willing to deploy huge amounts of cash for minority stake of equity.

These developments have led to change in perception of many donor agencies which are now looking at this sector as 'profit-making' and 'commercial'. Donor agencies have, therefore, started distancing themselves from the microfinance sector. This has negative implications for community based microfinance programmes (read SHGs), which are meant for empowerment of the poor. Community based microfinance is being deprived of financial support that is required at the initial stage.

Impressive Growth by MFIs

Credit outstanding by MFIs is estimated at ₹ 527 crore as of March 2010 while credit outstanding through SHG-bank linkage is estimated at ₹ 501.3 crore as of March 2010. This indicates that out of ₹ 1,028.3 crore total credit outstanding in microfinance sector as of March 2010, almost 51.25 per cent has been captured by MFIs. What is more interesting is that this 51.25 per cent has been captured in a period of little over 3 years, while SHG-bank linkage has been there for more than 10 years.

Innovations in Microfinance Sector

Over the last few years, microfinance sector in Rajasthan has seen innovative approaches being tested to counter the challenges of poverty alleviation. A few of them have been captured below:

Producer Companies

Last few years have seen producer companies becoming a reliable and successful model of empowerment for the poor. This reinforces the belief that future lies in promoting 'people's institutions'. A producer company is owned by its members who are required to be 'primary producers', that is, persons engaged in an activity connected with, or related to, primary produce.

Members' ownership or equity in a producer company is not publicly traded. Some examples of successful producer companies that have emerged in Rajasthan include Grameen Aloe Producers Company Limited (GAPCL), Ginger Producer Company, Jhadol, Maitree, Tonk, Jhambu Khand Kisan Producer Company Limited.

Mobile Phone Based MIS

MITRA (Mobile Information Technology for Rural Development) is an initiative of People's Education and Development Organization (PEDO), a Dungarpur based NGO. MITRA is a mobile-based management information system (MIS), which generates full-fledged reports. MIS captures real time information through mobiles and generates reports with following information: Capital, cash book, deposits, ledger, investment, member history, saving report, etc.

Financial Inclusion of Tribal Through Community Based Microfinance (Dungarpur Project)

Bank of Baroda, in collaboration with PEDO and CmF, took up Dungarpur as a pilot district for SHG-Bank Linkage and for strengthening livelihoods of poor by providing timely and sufficient credit through Self-Help Groups. Initiatives involved credit of ₹ 55 crore through SHGs, support for promotion of 300 new SHGs, training of all branch managers of Bank of Baroda and its sponsored RRB, skill training of SHG members, issuance of Kisan credit cards, banking products counselling and microfinance training to tribal youth.

Over the last three years since launch of the project, about 12,000 tribal families have accessed credit of ₹ 320 million and used it for their income enhancement.

The major learning from this pilot project has been that commercial banks can reach out to the poor effectively through Self-Help Groups. The project has also demonstrated that SHG-bank linkage is done in focused manner and on scale, can contribute towards financial viability of rural bank branches.

Secondly, banks should invest in creation of new SHGs and link it with credit targets. A unit of 300 SHGs in two years will cost the bank ₹ 15 lakh and generate a credit portfolio of minimum ₹ 150 lakh per year, earning gross annual revenue of ₹ 15 lakh.

Weather-based Insurance Scheme (WBIS)

Weather-based insurance scheme is running in the pilot stage in Rajasthan. This scheme provides payouts only if the key weather indicators, such as rainfall, temperature exceed or fall short of the specified range. WBIS will prevail for farmers who have availed loans. Private players like ICICI Lombard charge insurance premium in the range of ₹ 138 to ₹ 2,647 to provide compensation for various crops in range of ₹ 5,000 an acre to ₹ 40,000. In another instance, the compensation for every acre of paddy, maize and ground nut is ₹ 10,000 while the premium is ₹ 276 for paddy, maize and ₹ 386 for groundnut.

Demand for Microfinance

In Rajasthan, cash inflow for a household broadly includes daily wages from agriculture and non farm (including MGNREGS); sale proceeds from agriculture and animal products, 'animal sale', remittances by family members who have migrated, etc. The cash outflow is primarily on expenditure incurred on food, clothes, education of children, household expenses, cattle feed, local conveyance, health, alcohol, etc. In addition, there is substantial expenditure on life events like marriage, birth, death; on health related events and construction of house; and investments like deepening of wells/new wells, pump sets, tractors, etc.

Given this context, savings and credit have been found to be the two prime financial services that the poor needs. However, as most of their livelihoods are uncertain in nature (for example, uncertainty due to illness, death of livestock, crop failure, etc.), insurance is of utmost importance. Further, due to increased migration of workforce from villages to cities within and outside Rajasthan, remittance has become a key service that migratory workforce needs these days.

Profile of Poor in Rajasthan

Rural Poor

Most of the rural poor depend on agriculture for their livelihood while others, rear animals to supplement their income. The average annual income of rural household is estimated to be ₹ 54,159.[5] A large number of poor in rural Rajasthan migrate to earn their livelihoods. Over 64 per cent of rural households in southern Rajasthan report migration, which contributes to 46 per cent of household incomes (UNDP, 2004). Key reasons reported for migration are stagnant agriculture and lack of diversified sources of livelihood. People from tribal areas in the southern part go to adjoining Gujarat. In rest of the places, there is substantial migration from villages to nearby towns and cities like Jaipur, Kota and Jodhpur.

Urban Poor[6]

In urban areas, a significant proportion of the poor are daily wage labourers working on construction sites and other works, followed by those employed in shops, factories on salary basis, followed by those who are self-employed (but comprise less than 20 per cent of the urban poor). Urban poor are a heterogeneous group consisting of recent migrants/fresh settlers at one hand and permanent settlers at another end. Urban poor live in slums which typically lack even meagre infrastructure. Around 16.9 per cent of the urban population consists of slum dwellers in Rajasthan. Most of urban poor have irregular cash flows. Majority of their income is spent on procuring basic necessities like medical expenses, food, child education, debt servicing, etc. The average annual income of urban household is estimated to be ₹ 77,000.[7]

Demand of Savings

More than 72 per cent of rural families and over 90 per cent of urban families have been found to save.[8] Apart from few families, mostly destitute, who live from hand to mouth, others (even beggars) have been found to be saving some amounts for future needs. Most poor families save for repair of house, construction of new house, marriage of children, celebration of festivals; buying agriculture inputs, pay old debts, etc.

Rural Poor

For rural poor, the income from agriculture and allied activities is seasonal in nature, primarily around the harvest season. Thus, most rural households have surplus for some time after the harvest of crops. Even the landless agriculture labourers, generally considered at the bottom of the poverty index, have regular employment in this season and tend to save. Rural poor save money as cash in pocket/house, saving in recurring deposits in post office, buying insurance (mainly life insurance of LIC), saving in SHGs, chit funds/committees, and in companies.

During the last 5–10 years, companies like Tulip Global Pvt Ltd.[9], Mitashi Tradelink Ltd.[10] among many have started a successful 'MLM' (Multi-level marketing) scheme to mobilize deposits. Other companies like Peerless,[11] Sahara Financial Services[12] mobilize savings from rural areas by providing 'service at doorstep'.

Households earn from remittances and non-agriculture wage labour, therefore, saving products that offer 'recurring' deposits and 'daily' collection at 'doorstep' are in demand, e.g. ₹ 50 collected every day 25 days a month. The market size of saving products in rural Rajasthan is estimated to be over ₹ 11,000 crore.[13]

Urban Poor[14]

Fresh settlers/recent migrants save cash at home. Families that have lived in the city for more than five to ten years (called permanent settlers) have a bank account and most of the family surplus is deposited in the bank. Saving is also done through loaning to friends and purchase of property in one's native village. Agents of RNBCs like Sahara, Pearless, etc. and Chit Fund managers are active in the slums and play a key role in financing of life cycle events.

Fresh settlers express their insecurity about saving at home. However, due to the lack of saving products and services, they use informal ways of saving. This lack of saving options further increases their dependence on credit for meeting their expenditure. Permanent settlers have relatively more saving avenues but still crave for better saving options, viz. doorstep financial service. The market size of saving products in urban Rajasthan is estimated to be over ₹ 4,500 crore.[15]

Demand of Credit

The credit need of the poor can be classified into three categories: (a) Credit needed for investments such as capital investment (to buy assets) or as working capital; (b) Credit needed to meet household consumption; (c) Credit needed to finance life events like marriages, house construction, serious health emergencies, etc. The poor are not a homogeneous group and their livelihoods vary a great deal in wage labour, agriculture, animal rearing, petty businesses, etc. Therefore, their credit need varies too.

Rural Poor

It has been found that about 24 per cent outstanding credit to rural families is from banks and cooperatives, whereas rest 76 per cent is from various informal sources like moneylenders, friends and relatives, etc.[16] The credit from informal sources comes at very high cost, i.e. at 24 per cent to 60 per cent annual interest. The immediate propensity of the poor is to pay off costly loan from moneylenders[17] and then to use it for meeting their consumption needs, health expenditures and after some time, to make small investments to augment their livelihood sources, e.g. seeds and other inputs, fodder for animals, etc. Once these needs are fulfilled, they start making investments on assets (capital investments) like deepening of wells, pipes for irrigation, purchase of animals and so on.

On an average a poor family needs about ₹ 15,000 credit (in multiple doses) every year to meet their consumption and small working capital needs. This translates into total annual credit demand of ₹ 8,700 crore.[18] If sustainable livelihood is to be ensured and people have to be brought out of poverty, then a family would need at least ₹ 50,000 credit (cumulative) over a period of 2–3 years.[19] If the demand is to be seen within the overall framework of 'livelihood finance' then the micro-credit market can be estimated to be around ₹ 29,000 crore in next 2–3 years.[20] Out of this, total credit need in agriculture and allied sector is estimated at ₹ 19,200 crore[21] (Agriculture crop loan 15,100 crore, Term Loans 3,800 crore and agro processing 300 crore).

Urban Poor

It has been estimated that more than three-fourths of the poor households in urban areas are indebted, with moneylenders emerging as the main source of credit.[22] Less than 10 per cent have been found to avail credit from banks. Most of the credit is available at the rate of 24 per cent to 36 per cent per annum. Most loans are taken for life cycle events and housing. In case of fresh settlers/recent migrants, credit is primarily for consumption, for sending remittance, for marriages and for unpredictable expenditures due to illness, accident, loss of spouse's job, etc. In case of permanent settlers, availing credit is relatively easier. It is normal for tea vendors and fruit stall owners, etc. to get 2–10 days credit. Such settlers take credit at interest rates of typically 2 per cent per month to meet large expenditures like marriages, property acquisition, etc.

As per study conducted by Aajeevika Bureau, credit needs of migrants are: Food loan – for ensuring food and nutrition to families left behind as migrants move to new places in search of jobs; Transportation loan – for travel expenses from the village to the destination point; Tools loan – for newly trained plumbers, electricians and carpenters; Uniform loan – for those in catering and hotel services and Enterprise loan – for those confident enough to set up seasonal businesses outside villages, for example ice cream and sugarcane juice vending.

Total annual credit demand in urban areas is estimated to be ₹ 2,700 crore.[23] If the demand is to be seen within the overall framework of 'livelihood finance' then the urban micro-credit market can be estimated to be around ₹ 9,000 crore in next 2–3 years.

Demand of Insurance

Rural Poor

The major risks that the rural household faces are of four types[24]: life, health, animal illness and death of earning member of the family.

Risks faced by rural households in last three years:

1. Death in family – about 17 per cent households faced this risk
2. Death of livestock – about 57 per cent of households faced this risk
3. Health and illness – about 43 per cent of households faced this risk
4. Crop failure – about 69 per cent of households faced this risk

Current Practices of Rural Poor[25]

Poor households in rural areas spend 19 per cent of their income on health and illness, 14 per cent of income on livestock death and 20 per cent of income on crop failure. Therefore, more than 50 per cent of their household expenses in rural areas are lost on items that should ideally fall under non-life insurance coverage. In contrast, only 7.5 per cent of the households have insurance policy, that too of life insurance. Non-life insurance is something unheard of.

Need and Potential for Insurance Products

Estimating demand for insurance assuming (a) 'life' insurance coverage equal to two years' household income and 'non-life' insurance coverage equal to 50 per cent of household income, it can be deduced that there is demand of ₹ 1.35 lakh[26] of insurance coverage per household in the rural area, provided household is ready to pay[27] around ₹ 50 as premium per month.[28] This translates to market demand of over ₹ 1,30,000 crore[29] market of insurance coverage in rural areas in Rajasthan. In other words, this translates to potential premium turnover of over ₹ 600 crore for insurance companies per annum in rural areas.

Urban Poor

The major risks that urban households face are health and life.[30]

Risks faced by urban households in the last three years:

1. Death in family – about 18 per cent households faced this risk
2. Health and illness – about 42 per cent of households faced this risk

Current Practices of Urban Poor[31]

Poor households in urban areas spend over 26 per cent of their income on health and illness. Therefore, more than 26 per cent of urban poor's household expenses are lost on items that should ideally fall under non-life insurance coverage. In contrast, only 10 per cent of the households have insurance policy, that too of life insurance. At times of crisis, they resort to taking credit at very high rate of interests from informal sources and sometimes, end up losing all their savings and assets during the course.

Need and Potential for Insurance Products

Estimating demand for insurance assuming a 'life' insurance coverage equal to two years' household income and 'non-life' insurance coverage equal to 26 per cent of household income, it can be deduced that there is a demand of ₹ 1.74 lakh[32] of insurance coverage per household in urban area, provided the household is ready to pay[33] approximately ₹ 70 as premium per month.[34] This translates to market demand of over ₹ 50,000 crore[35] market insurance coverage in urban areas in Rajasthan. In other words, this translates to potential premium turnover of over ₹ 250 crore for insurance companies per annum in urban areas.

Demand of Remittance

It is estimated that there are around 1.39 crore[36] migrants in Rajasthan accounting for approximately 5.68 per cent of the total migrants in the country. Migrants use informal sources like self carry, transfer through friends/relatives, or in kind remittances in the form of consumer goods, etc. Formal financial institutions offer the remittance services such as bank transfers and money orders. But recent settlers/migrants do not approach formal institutions and services. Moreover, the service fee charged by banks (7%) and post offices (5.3%) makes remitting small amounts at frequent intervals unviable. Primary research indicates that there is unmet demand as far as remittances are concerned, though there is no authentic data for estimation.

Institutional Set-up for Delivering the Microfinancial Services

The microfinance providers can be broadly grouped into three categories, viz. informal, semi-formal and formal. In Rajasthan, the Bank-led SHG-Bank Linkage Programme (SBLP) and MFI-led microfinance programme are reaching out to the poor in a most significant way.

Sector	*Microfinance Delivery Institutions*	*Products*
Informal Sector	Moneylenders who typically charge interest rate of 24–60% per annum	Credit (with collateral and without collateral)
	Friends and relatives	Credit (largely on interest and sometimes without interest)
	Commission agents	Credit for all purposes – Deposits
	Petty shopkeepers, Kirana shops	Groceries on credit

Cont'd...

...Cont'd

Semi Formal Sector	Self-Help Groups which are members based institutions, the SHGs are unregistered	Thrift, Credit (Also link members to other (microfinance services like insurance, etc.)
	SHG's higher-level organization like 'clusters' and 'federations' come under Semi-Formal category. They are registered.	Intermediate between banks and SHGs (Mainly capacity building of SHGs, facilities linkages with banks, etc.) and insurance services
	Beesi , Chit fund	Saving
Formal Sector	Commercial Bank	Savings, credit, money transfer, payments of MNREGA, insurance linked with loan
	Primary Agriculture Cooperative Societies	Credit (agriculture) and Agri. Inputs – Savings from members in form of equity, payments
Formal Sector	Cooperative banks	Credit, Savings
	Regional Rural Banks	Credit, Savings (Crop insurance along with crop loans)
	Insurance Companies	Insurance term and endowment
	Post Offices	Savings, money transfer, payments of NREGA
	Not for Profit Microfinance Institutions	Credit, mainly through SHGs but to individuals also
	For-profit Microfinance Institutions	Credit and insurance – Savings in the form of term deposits only after permission from RBI
	Residuary Non-banking Companies (RNBCs), e.g. Sahara India Financial Services	Savings in form of recurring deposits
	Pawn shops and Gold loan NBFCs, e.g. Muthoot Finance and Manappuram Finance	Gold Loan – Provide credit against collateral of jewellery. They typically charge interest rates of 12–27% per annum on declining basis.

Informal Systems of Microfinance

With the formal financial institutions reaching only about 30–35 per cent households, there is an obvious dependence on informal sources. Through 15 short studies carried out collaboratively with other agencies/individuals across the state, CmF tried to capture some insights into the savings, credit and risk mitigation mechanisms prevalent in the twilight zone between needs of the poor and access.

From the cash flow study,[37] it came out that the most important source of credit is friend/relative and about 40 per cent of total credit is from them (37 per cent on interest and 3 per cent without interest). The second most important source of rural credit is moneylenders, who provide about 37 per cent of credit. It is found that the moneylenders have their own assessment about credit worthiness of the borrower and they ask for a guarantor. But from very poor people, they also ask for collateral.

The studies have confirmed that savings are an important source towards asset creation. Savings often get channelled into purchase of land, livestock and jewellery. These do not generate any regular income for families but there is a sense of appreciation of value of the same.

Temporary surpluses also get channelled to short-term loans to friends and relatives. This enables liquidity as well as safety and ensures a source of finance in times of need. Sharing of resources through systems such as '*notra*' – prevalent in South Rajasthan – where families raise funds for a specific purpose from the community. The norm of reciprocity is strong with the amount being received as an interest-free advance that must be returned when the contributor organizes a *notra*. Similar systems for providing gifts for marriages were evidenced elsewhere in the state.

Following are some of the ways that are commonly adopted by the poor to save money:

Cash Saved at Home

This is the most prevalent way of savings. Rural households save large amounts at home due to limited outreach of banks. Both men and women save cash at home, though the latter at times saves even without the knowledge of other members in the household. In most households women also save from the amount meant for household expenditure. Money is stashed away in spice pots, red chilli pots, under mattresses, *gulaks,* in the granary and many other places. Majority of the small deposits are stored as cash parked at home, also because liquidity and accessibility is the determining factor and not returns from savings while selecting a saving avenue. In rural areas, about 75 per cent of the savings (number and not amount) is in the form of cash at home.

Besides saving to meet household expenses, people also save for festivals like Diwali to exchange gifts, buy new clothes and for emergency situations. In urban areas, the situation varies, as it is generally the recent migrants/fresh settlers who save at home, other poor households find it unsafe to keep cash at home.

Saving in the Form of Loans Given to Friends/Relatives

This is the most common means of saving in both rural and urban areas. Loans are given to known people with or without interests. In fact, in rural areas loans from friends/relatives have the largest share in fulfilling the credit need of the population. It is an attractive form of saving for households with surplus, as it ensures high returns and security. The average returns on such savings is around 24 per cent per annum, much higher than offered by any formal institutions. Cash saved at home and money loaned to friends/relatives accounts for about 34 per cent of total savings in rural areas.

Gifts to Relatives and Other Community Members: The Notra System

The *Notra* system is generally practiced within the members of a caste residing in one village, a practice of mutual exchange of gifts and money during functions especially marriage. A family receives gifts and money from relatives and other members of the community during a marriage in the house. The gift received is formally noted down and a list maintained of all the gifts received. The practice is to give higher value gifts when the guests have a function in their house. Households have been reported to take loans for giving gifts in particular when a close relation is involved. Likewise the cost of the gift also varies on the closeness of the relation with the family. This traditional way of saving is the *notra,* an important source of financing expensive functions amongst many communities in the state.

Savings through Chit Funds

Chit Funds though not common in rural Rajasthan are quite prevalent amongst urban poor. It is generally the men who are members of a chit fund. Households with regular source of income are members of more than one chit fund. In a chit fund a particular number of individuals come together to pool a specific amount of money periodically. The total amount of money collected in one meeting is given to a member through lottery or via bidding. In case of bidding, the highest bidder gets the amount and has to pay an interest on it. The advantage of chit fund is that people are able to get a large sum of money at one time, which can be used for purchase of high price products or to meet social expenses like on daughter's marriage.

Saving with Moneylender

People in rural areas save with moneylenders as and when they have surplus, and in turn get an interest on it. The moneylender in turn lends the money out for a higher interest rate. The benefit of this avenue is easy accessibility and liquidity as the person can withdraw his saving from the moneylender when he needs the money. However, this is limited to economically better off families.

Investment in Land

With rapid urbanization and rising land prices, purchase of land in pan-urban areas has become an important avenue of saving. This is done by people residing in urban areas and also rural people in villages adjacent to the city/town. The land is sold to a real estate developer at a much higher price after 4–5 years or even lesser time. People have also taken loans in villages adjacent to Jaipur to buy additional land, as they are sure that the value of land would almost double in the next couple of years.

Remittances are an important source of purchasing more agriculture land in rural areas. Temporary migrants save and invest in land in their native village.

Investment in the Form of Ornaments

Investing in silver ornaments is an important way of saving. Most women receive jewellery at times of marriage and other social functions like childbirth. In most households ornaments are either inherited or received as gifts. It is rarely that women buy ornaments for their own use. Most households have silver ornaments; gold is limited to a few economically better off households. Though rarely sold, the ornaments are commonly used as collateral for loans from informal sources.

Credit

Moneylenders and friends/relatives provide loan for all events. Overall, 92 per cent of loan for meeting the expenses on events like marriages, death feast, etc. comes from informal sources like moneylenders, friends/relatives, etc. and only 8 per cent loan (for events) comes from banks and cooperatives. With the increasing policy thrust towards inclusion of the poor in the mainstream financial institutions, it is important to also learn of informal systems and draw lessons from that to reach out.

Money lending is no more a monopoly of traditional moneylenders (Mahajans, traders, etc.). These days, people who have surplus income provide a large part of credit. Lack of saving avenues in rural areas has also given impetus to money lending by non-traditional moneylenders. They provide credit to people whom they know well or to their kith and kin. They also charge interest almost equal to the rates charged by traditional moneylenders.

Informal Credit Systems Prevalent in Rajasthan

Khandi System

The Khandi system of credit is the most popular. Under this system the loan has to be repaid in fixed monthly instalments. The loan is convenient to both lenders and borrowers, as instalments are paid regularly. However, the effective rate of interest is very high in this system. The cash transactions are well-documented in this system – the moneylender maintains his books and also a diary is maintained by the borrower in which he takes the signature of the lender after every repayment. The effective rate of interest is around 3.6 per cent per month under this system. Increasingly, in villages the repayment period is being fixed as equal instalments in 10 months. This makes the lenders money secure as the repayment period has reduced. However, the effective rate of interest is further increased up to 4. 27 per cent per month.

Balloon Loan System

The credit for agriculture purpose is available at 2 per cent monthly rate of interest. For amount below ₹ 20,000 no written formalities like stamp agreement is required. The amount is just written in the diary for keeping a record. The repayment is done when agriculture harvest comes. This includes principle plus interest for the agriculture season. If harvest fails then it is rescheduled for the next season. If the repayment is not done on time even after rescheduling of the loan, then the moneylender starts cultivating the land of the borrower till he/she repays the amount with interest.

The rate of interest varies with the type of client. If the client's credibility with the moneylender is good and terms are good then the loan is provided at 2 per cent monthly rate of interest. In other cases the rate of interest becomes 3 per cent. This is especially when the need is urgent and amount is more. Loan for agriculture purpose involves seed purchase and for land levelling purpose.

There is no instalment system but to repay the principal and interest rate at the end of the loan term. Like Mr Ramesh has taken a loan of ₹ 20,000 and committed to repay ₹ 25,000 after a year. After one year he repaid the committed amount at 25 per cent annual interest rate.

Cash Security

In some cases the cash security of 10 per cent is taken at the time of providing loan. Although presently this is rarely practised but such practice involved providing credit at 2 per cent rate of interest and upfront deduction of 10 per cent cash security at the time of providing credit and interest is charged for entire amount. There is no provision of providing interest on the security amount. e.g. if a person needs ₹ 10,000, he gets ₹ 9,000 in hand and repays at the end of year ₹ 12,400. Interest on ₹ 1,000 for one year becomes ₹ 240. Thus the cost of credit for ₹ 10,000 is ₹ 2,640. Thus, effective rate of interest becomes 26.4 per cent annually and 2.2 per cent monthly.

Satki system: This system for taking credit is now rare. It was prevalent few years back. Under this system, lenders deduct 10 per cent of what is demanded by borrower at the time of disbursal of loan. But the borrower has to return the full amount with interest.

Beej Babna: This system is very unique in nature as it does not involve transactions of money but seeds. During session farmers borrowed seeds from Sahukars, relatives, etc. and at the time of harvesting they return double the quantity. This system is called Beej Babna and is still in practice.

Grains and Fodder Lending

This system is happening within the village where people lend grains and fodder. People could borrow grain/fodder from a farmer at the time of harvest and returned in a one and half times of the gram/fodder at the time of the next harvest. In case fodder or grain is not available to recover then the loan has to be repaid in cash.

Notra System

Notra system is a very common system of mutual help in the form of monetary help or in kind at the time of a person's need. In this system the needy family invites close relatives and friends on a particular day for a special cause like help for marriages, health care, house repairing or building, repayment of loan amount. People help in a monetary form, which ranges from ₹ 50 to ₹ 2,000 as per their financial capacity and closeness to the needy person. In this system, people anticipate the return of their helping amount back, at the time of their own *Notras*. In this *Notra* system one cannot calculate the return on investment, because it is a system of mutual help in the society.

Example: Binod Meena has organized a *Notra* for repairing of his house. He invited around 30 families with an expectation amount of ₹ 20,000/and had got help of ₹ 18,000/. Two of his close friends named Suna Meena and Kishan Lal contributed ₹ 1,000 and ₹ 2,000 respectively in that *Notra*. Mr Suna also organized *Notra* next year for his daughter's marriage and receives back from Binod Meena ₹ 1,200. And after two years Mr Kishan Lal organized *Notra* for purchasing of a agricultural land where Mr Binod contributed only ₹ 1,000.

Security Deposit (Girva System)

This method is very popular in the village. In this case people are depending upon traditional moneylenders by depositing securities like ornaments (silver or gold) with fixed rate of interest per month. The borrower has to deposit some ornament and will get half of the actual market rate of the ornament cost from the moneylenders. For example: Mr Goutam has need of ₹ 3,000 loan from the moneylender, so he went with 300 gms of silver ornament which cost around ₹ 6,000 and got the required amount at the rate of 2 per cent per month. He returned the loan amount with interest after six months, which is ₹ 3,360. So here, the effective rate of interest is 24 per cent per month.

Delinquency Management

There is no such hard and fast rule in between lender and borrower. In case of not repayment of loan, the borrower has to lose his or her security deposit/mortgage. No doubt the moneylender always keeps continuous watch on borrowers for repayment, if a borrower is being shown as defaulter then the lender uses help of local people and abusive language. In *Notra* system if anybody is not involving or escaping from this mutual help concept then that family may be debarred from the social inclusion system.

Moneylender/Sahukar

This system of taking credit is prevalent in the state. Person who needs money approaches the moneylender and after an informal discussion on interest rate and time of repayment, money is given to the concerned person. This process of taking credit is of two types:

1. *With security deposit:* Although this method is not very popular in the village, but in some cases the moneylender asked for some security deposit. It can be land, jewellery, house utensils, livestock, etc. – the demand of security deposit from moneylender's side becomes quite demanding when the borrower is new to the lender. This mechanism of security also affects the rate of interest, i.e. lower than the market rate of informal system. For example, if a Sahukar lend at 6–7 per cent to a new borrower then with security deposit the rate may come to a lower value of 5 per cent per month.

2. *Without security deposit:* Very few people in the state go for security deposit due to constraint of resources. Majority of people take credit without security deposit with variable interest rate which depends on some factors like:
   (i) *Credibility of person in the eye of lender:* If the person has good record of repayment in the past, then he can easily take credit, otherwise he has to convince the moneylender and sometimes it becomes very frustrating for the borrower.
   (ii) *Introducer of the borrower:* This is one of the crucial factors in deciding the interest rate. If introducer (a person known to lender and borrower) is well known to the lender and his (introducer) record in terms of the cases he brought earlier are good then the interest rate generally goes down.

Grain Commission Agent (Arhatia)

Grain Commission Agent or locally known as *Arhatia* is a common source of credit among farmers. The money is loaned usually for agricultural use such as fertilizers, pesticide, and cultivation but it is not only confined for such purposes. Often, as wedding ceremonies are expensive events, especially female wedding, the loan for paying wedding bills is also taken from *Arhatia.*

Based on interviews with the villagers, from *Arhatia,* the duration of loans vary between six months to a year, or until the time of harvest. Generally, outstanding credit with interest is paid back by selling the crop to *Arhatia.* Often, time of harvest is seen as the time for repayment of credit and beginning of new credit for the preparation of sowing of next crop.

Depending on trading relations with *Arhatia,* the amount of loan and interest rates varied between 2.5–4 per cent, calculated every six months. If unpaid, the outstanding interest is added to the principal and on this new principal, interest is charged.

The amount of credit could also vary. Generally, for most villagers, it varied between ₹ 10,000 to ₹ 50,000. This credit amount could be much higher (between 1–2 lakh) in certain cases but is available to few, whom the *Arhatia* trust and have surety about its return. Higher amount of credit is given at much lower rates of interest than in comparison to smaller amounts.

However, the landless or daily wage labourers have no access to such credit from *Arhatia.* This does not strictly translate that *Arhatia* does not give credit to non-farmers. Often, Arhatia does extend small credit to landless or daily wage labourers but requires collateral to ensure repayment and a financially well-to-do witness from the village, often not exceeding ₹ 10,000 (generally ₹ 5,000) and at higher interest rates. The interest can vary from 4–5 per cent.

Local Shopkeeper

There are four grocery shops in the village. All shopkeepers are Meo by caste. The oldest grocery shop, which is 20 years old, is the busiest shop in the village. Goods are available to shopkeepers from their wholesalers on credit. Usually, this credit is limited to a one month period without interest. After one month, the wholesaler charges interest to the village shopkeepers.

The information given below is based on an interview with the most prosperous shopkeeper in the village.

This shopkeeper also owned agricultural land and hence it was easier to make repayment in crop to *Arhatia.* According to him, *Arhatia* was their preferred source of seeking credit. Usually, the credit was given at the rate of 2–3 per cent.

In the village, often, goods and groceries were sold on credit. The shopkeeper kept an account of the sale and charged Re 1 extra on the goods price, if sold on credit. For example, if a customer bought goods on credit worth ₹ 20, at the time of payment, the customer was charged ₹ 21. Almost all villagers were able to seek such credit from the shopkeeper. According to the shopkeeper, there were no cases of defaulters in the village and most villagers were able to pay their dues sooner or later.

Additionally, the shopkeeper did not charge any interest, even if the creditor failed to pay in time or on request.

Barter system is another common form of transaction between the villagers and shopkeepers especially during harvest season. Villagers could trade their harvest such as mustard, and pay their outstanding credit. Furthermore, the shopkeeper also procured mustard or wheat from the villagers, usually in small quantities, at market price and exchanged it for goods available in the shop. While we were there, two kids from the village brought few kilos of mustard (by collecting mustard left over, after harvest in the mustard field) to sell to the shopkeeper in exchange for some goods from the shop.

Milk Trader or Doodwalla

Milk trader or commonly known as *Doodwalla* in the village, is a popular source of credit among villagers who raise animals for milk. Especially, buffaloes are a common source of milk for the family and raising income by selling milk to *Doodwalla.* Milk traders buy milk from animal owners and sell it for profit in the nearby cities.

The *Doodwalla* gives credit to potential families for purchasing milk animals such as buffaloes, varying from ₹ 10,000–20,000. Such credit is paid off by selling milk back to respective *Doodwalla.* In return, *Doodwalla* buys milk from creditors for ₹ 2 less per litre than the existing rate of the milk in the village. For example, in *Nandanheri,* the current rate of milk per litre was ₹ 12 and if a person took a credit for ₹ 10,000 the *Doodwalla* will pay for milk, ₹ 10 per litre (₹ 2 less than existing rate), until the credit is paid. However, interest on credit is not customary among *Doodwalla* in this village.

Doodwalla also gives credit in small amounts such as less than ₹ 2,000. Such credit is also paid back in milk. Such credit is given without any reduction in milk price or interest. By giving small loans without any incentive, *Doodwalla* creates permanent clients to buy milk.

From non-credit suppliers of milk, *Doodwalla* purchases milk on credit. Milk payments usually vary between weekly, fortnightly or monthly. On request, *Doodwalla* also supplies animal feed for some houses in the village.

Small Loans from Friends/Relatives without Interest

This type of loan from villagers/friends/relatives without interest is common among villagers, especially, among the daily wage labourers or the landless. This loan is given in small amounts usually less than ₹ 3,000 dependent on borrower's relation with the lender. Often, there is no fixed time of return for such credit. Since, the credit is given in small amounts, it is assumed by the lender, that it will be returned within a short period, for example, within a month or few days. Further, in some cases, such loan can be as much as ₹ 10,000 taken from close relatives for marriages.

From the Informal Societies in the Village

As has been discussed earlier the village level informal society acts as the most important source of credit for its members. Members can avail credit facilities in one of the following two ways:

- *Credit auction:* Here in the monthly meeting, after the money is collected, members who need credit declare the amount of money they would pay back extra (interest) if they are allowed to take the money collected during that meeting (this means that the pay back money includes principal amount plus interest). Whoever bids the highest money can avail all the money collected during that meeting as loan.
- *Chit system:* Here names of all the members who have not taken loan from the society are put in a bowl in the form of chits. A lucky draw is taken out and that person is given all the money collected during that meeting. In this system the member does not have to pay any interest. So even if the lucky member does not need the full money he takes that (as the money is interest free).

The informal societies have strict rules. They are as follows:

- If somebody defaults then two guarantors have to come forward to promise that they would make sure the money gets repaid.
- Penalty for default varies from ₹ 10 to ₹ 50 per day as decided by the members of the society.

Loan from Big Vegetable Wholesalers

The rickshaw pullers work in the Lal Kothi vegetable market of Jaipur. Here, big vegetable wholesalers generally employ them. During the times of need these wholesalers act as the main source of providing credit to these people. This method is very good for the creditors too. They can comfortably deduct instalments from their daily wages and so do not have to worry about defaults to a great extent. Interest rate varies between ₹ 4 to ₹ 5 per month per ₹ 100 of loan taken.

Why are these Informal Sources so Prevalent?

The informal system caters to the needs of a large chunk of population. The major reasons for their success, over the years, are:

- *Easy access:* Moneylenders are easily accessible to the poor. They can be contacted at odd hours, at the time of emergency to take credit.
- *Timely disbursement:* Borrower gets the credit on time from moneylenders. Generally the borrower and lender are known to each other, so the credit is disbursed at the time of need. This helps in proper and full use of the loan, which is almost impossible with the formal financial system.
- *Minimum or no formality:* There is no paperwork except that some lenders maintain a personal diary in which the amount and time of loan disbursement and repayment is written. Only in the case of a new borrower, the moneylender asks for collateral.
- *Flexibility in repayment:* There are no fixed schedules of repayment. It depends upon the borrower. At the time of disbursement, the borrower mentions the time frame in which he will repay the whole amount with interest.

What are the Interest Rates in Informal Credit?

The interest rate in the rural informal system varies from 2 per cent to 10 per cent per month. The rate of interest depends on various factors:

- *Relation of introducer with lender:* Generally there is a person who accompanies the borrower at the time of taking credit. This person (introducer) is known to both the borrower and the lender. If the moneylender thinks that this person (introducer) has substantial impact on the borrower, then the rate of interest may be low as compared to a situation where the borrower directly approaches the moneylender.
- *Credibility of borrower:* If the past record of the borrower is good in terms of repayment, there is a chance of a slightly lower interest rate.
- *Urgency of loan:* If a person needs credit instantly, then interest rate increase (during emergencies like health-related issues, it could go up to 10 per cent).
- *Collateral:* If a security deposit or collateral is provided, the rate of interest goes down.

Mode of Repayment

In most cases, there is *one-time settlement*. At the time of taking the credit, the borrower promises that he/she will repay the amount with interest after a certain period. There is no hard and fast rule between the lender and the borrower. In case of default, the borrower has to lose his or her security deposit/mortgage. Moneylender keeps continuous watch on the borrower for repayment and takes the help of guarantor, community pressure and even muscle power to recover his dues on case-to-case basis. Informal systems have very good repayment rates.

Who are the Clients of the Informal System?

During the study, focus was to identify those who have the access, or those who are the major clients of this system. It was found that persons who are not connected to any formal or semi-formal system (SHG) are availing this service. These people were not aware about the services of formal financial institutions. When asked why they do not have a bank account, the reply was that opening an account was a cumbersome task; bank officials asked for too many documents; and, also that the bank account does not serve their purpose as they need credit in small amounts.

Ramkanya Rana is a common rural women who lives in Nala village; Tehsil Niwai of Tonk district along with her husband and three children. The only source of income for this family was what her husband could get by being the member of the band who played at the wedding processions. As a result, the money would come in the family only during the wedding season. Worried about the fluctuating income of the family she joined the SHG of her area upon the insistence of the neighbouring women. Soon enough, she started attending the meetings and was inspired to save money.

One day, Ramkanya's son got seriously ill. Both husband and wife got frightened, since they did not have any health centre in their village. The only way left was to take their son to the nearby city hospital. Alarmed at this prospect, Ramkanya's husband tried his best to borrow some money – but to no avail. When he shared his predicament with his wife she assured him saying that she had taken the money from the SHG and the repayment of the money could be done in instalments. Relieved, Ramkanya and her husband took their son to the hospital and got his treatment done.

Ramkanya thanks the SHG and the help they gave her at such a crucial time and says that if it had not been for the SHG, her son's treatment could have been indefinitely delayed.

Notes

1. Centre for Microfinance, 'Status of microfinance report in Rajasthan 2007'.

2. www.nrega.nic.in
3. Assuming number of members per household in Rajasthan remains same as 5.6 which were found in Population Census 2001, number of households by March 2010 can be estimated to be 1.27 crore. Out of which, over 65 per cent households have benefitted from MGNREGS.
4. finance.rajasthan.gov.in/doc/1011/pressbriefe1011.pdf
5. Risk profiling study of 493 households conducted in 5 districts of Rajasthan.
6. Cash flow study in five cities conducted by CmF, Jaipur.
7. Risk profiling study of 493 households conducted in 5 districts of Rajasthan.
8. Cash flow studies conducted by CmF in 2006.
9. http://tulipbusiness.com/mlm_in_india/
10. http://mitashitradelink.com/
11. http://www.peerless.co.in/
12. http://www.sifo.in/
13. Average household income in rural Rajasthan is ₹ 54,159 (As per risk profiling study of 493 households in Rajasthan over 5 districts conducted by CmF, Jaipur). As per NCAER, 2007, saving rate in rural India is 22 per cent. Number of households in Rajasthan as of March 2010 can be estimated at 97.2 lakh as follows – As per Population Census 2001, rural population is 75.45 per cent of total population and average strength of household in Rajasthan is 5.6. Extrapolating these figures to 2010 level assuming 2.6 per cent p.a. growth rate in population and assuming strength of households to remain same over last 10 years.
14. Cash flow study in 5 cities conducted by CmF, Jaipur.
15. Average household income in urban Rajasthan is ₹ 77,000 (As per risk profiling study of 493 households in Rajasthan over 5 districts conducted by CmF, Jaipur). As per NCAER, 2007, saving rate in urban India is 28 per cent. Number of households in Rajasthan as of March 2010 can be estimated at 29.7 lakh as follows – As per Population Census 2001, Urban population is 24.55 per cent of total population and average strength of household in Rajasthan is 5.6. Extrapolating these figures to 2010 level assuming 2.6 per cent p.a. growth rate in population and assuming strength of households to remain same over last 10 years.
16. Cash flow studies conducted by CmF in 15 locations in Rajasthan.

17. Assuming 'loan use pattern' of SHG members is taken as an indicator.
18. Extrapolating number of rural families in Rajasthan as of March 2010 to be 97.2 lakh and assuming about 60 per cent of them as clients of microfinance, total annual credit demand works out to be ₹ 8,700 crore.
19. However, it is important to mention here that 'credit alone' will not bring people out of poverty and a number of services like technical skills, market linkages, etc. will be needed along with credit. But credit as capital investment (long-term capital and working capital) is critical.
20. This is assuming only 60 per cent of clients avail micro-credit as discussed in last footnote.
21. State focus paper of NABARD 2010–11.
22. Cash flow studies conducted by CmF in 15 locations in Rajasthan.
23. Extrapolating number of urban families in Rajasthan as of March 2010 to be 29.7 lakh and assuming about 60 per cent of them as clients of microfinance, total annual credit demand works out to be ₹ 2,700 crore.
24. Risk profiling study of 493 households conducted in 5 districts of Rajasthan.
25. Risk profiling study of 493 households conducted in 5 districts of Rajasthan.
26. Assuming average annual household income of ₹ 54,159 which was found in cash flow studies conducted by CmF, Jaipur in rural areas.
27. Most Indians are willing to pay 1.35 per cent of income or more for health insurance As per survey conducted in 7 locations by David M Dror – 'Health Insurance for the Poor: Myths and Realities'.
28. Assuming premium to be around 0.5 per cent p.a. of insurance coverage amount.
29. Assuming number of rural households in Rajasthan by March 2010 to be 97.2 lakh (through extrapolation as discussed in notes above).
30. Risk profiling study of 493 households conducted in 5 districts of Rajasthan.
31. Risk profiling study of 493 households conducted in 5 districts of Rajasthan.

32. Assuming average annual household income of ₹ 54,159 as discussed in footnote above
33. Most Indians are willing to pay 1.35 per cent of income or more for health insurance As per survey conducted in 7 locations by David M Dror – 'Health Insurance for the Poor: Myths and Realities'.
34. Assuming premium to be around 0.5 per cent p.a. of insurance coverage amount.
35. Assuming number of urban households in Rajasthan by March 2010 to be 29.7 lakh (through extrapolation as discussed in notes above).
36. NSSO, Report 470, migration in India, Sept 2001, this also includes within the state migration: rural to urban migration, urban to urban migration and inter state migration.
37. Cash flow study, CmF 2006b.

4

Organizational Structure of MFIs and Women SHGs

As mentioned before, the growth of microfinance in India has been in response to a lack of institutional initiative to provide rural or informal credit, the result being that there are now over 1,000 NGOs implementing microfinance projects across India.[1] There are various models of microfinance institutions, some of the predominant models being Grameen banking, regulated financial institutions, and credit cooperatives.[2] The self-help group model is likewise a growing and important approach to microfinance, particularly through the Self-help Bank Linkage Programme (SBLP), the largest microfinance model in India. This chapter will focus on the range on the organizational and institutional structures of MFIs and SHGs, and how these are able to provide financial services whilst satisfying the needs of their customers.

Importance of MFIs Becoming Self-Sufficient

When microfinance was initially developed and put into practice, its primary focus was on delivering micro-credit. As such, most MFIs were created as non-governmental organizations, and continue to be created as such to this day. However, with time the focus of microfinance has shifted to incorporate a wider range of financial services to provide to the working poor, such as savings services.[3] As the number of microfinance institutions continues to increase rapidly, resources from donor funds inevitably begin to shrink.[4] It is, therefore, becoming imperative that MFIs work towards becoming financially self-sustainable, and as such the organizational and institutional structures of MFIs are beginning to diversify in attempts to best reach this goal. MFIs can take the form of formal, semi-formal and informal organizational structures, and all must be, 'able and determined to make visible progress towards financial self-sufficiency', in which the revenues from the institution's operations are enough to cover all of its costs.[5] The organizational and ownership structure of the MFI must, therefore, create long-term stability both financially, and with regards to its target group of clients to ensure that the MFI remains socially relevant. Thus, structurally, there must be a division of roles between the management and the board of directors or supervisory board.[6]

The Role of Partnerships

One important organizational feature of most MFIs is that they work alongside one or more development agencies or partners. These development agencies may consist of international NGOs, governments or donors that provide technical assistance, funding and training to the MFI itself.[7] These partnerships are important in strengthening local institutions and in providing the best services possible to the local, low-income clients. The relationship is one which is mutually beneficial for both the local MFI and the international NGO or agency. For the latter, the benefits of partnering with local institutions are numerous, as these have the advantage of knowing much more about local circumstances, such as the target group or clients, their situation and demand for financial services, the local financial market, and the local laws and habits.[8] For the local institutions, the benefit of partnering with an international NGO or agency comes from the funding, technical assistance and training that these can provide. Both partners must share a common goal, and a willingness to contribute to the achievement of this goal, through a relationship of openness and mutual respect.[9] Thus, what makes a good partnership is very much a case-by-case basis, but forming partnerships is something which microfinance institutions and development agencies should both consider.

Institutional Types: Formal, Semi-Formal and Informal

Each of these three categories of institutions can act as deliverers of microfinance products. Formal institutions are defined as those that are subject not only to general laws and regulations, but also to specific banking regulation and supervision. Semi-formal institutions are those that are formal in the sense of being registered entities subject to all relevant general laws, but informal in that they are not under bank regulation and supervision. Finally, informal institutions or providers are those to which special bank law nor general commercial law do not apply, and whose operations are usually so informal that disputes arising from interactions with them often cannot be resolved by seeking settlement through the legal system.[10] Within each of these broad categories, are many different institutional types, each of which has its own particular way of providing microfinance services.

The following are examples of formal institutions:

Public Development Banks

These are usually a special type of large, centralized, government-owned banks, most of which were founded with a significant amount of financial support from international organizations. Their aim is to provide financial services to specific and strategic sectors such as agriculture or industry. Large businesses constitute the traditional clients of these banks, although in the 1970s there was a trend towards several development banks providing their services to small farmers and businesses. However, the success of this initiative was limited as the banks failed to alter their credit technology and organizational structure to suit the needs of their new clients. Within this branch of public development banks are also the rural development banks and specialized small business development banks, which have several positive attributes. Most have a broad network of branches and are active collectors of deposits. In many rural areas they are the only form of large institutions to offer basic financial services to the poor.[11]

Private Development Banks

These work to broaden economic development by filling in the capital gaps in the productive sector which are considered too risky to be handled by commercial institutions. These exist in some developing countries, and usually have lower capital requirements than commercial banks.[12]

Development banks are able to lend both directly or indirectly through intermediaries. Cecile Fruman, collaborator from the World Bank on the Sustainable Banking for the Poor Project provides two examples of each type of lending. In the case of direct lending, an example is the Bank for Agriculture and Agricultural Cooperatives (BAAC) in Thailand. It was created in 1966 as a state-owned bank to financially assist farmers and agricultural activities. This bank lends directly to the farmers.[13]

The Banque Nationale de Développement Agricole (BNDA) in Mali is an example of a bank that began lending directly to borrowers, but due to low rates of repayment, switched their approach to lending through intermediaries in the early 1990s. It began to lend to village cooperatives and groups of farmers, and now has begun lending to microfinance institutions such as self-managed village banks, which in turn lend to their clients. This method has proved much more successful in terms of the repayment rates of the loans.[14]

Savings Banks and Postal Savings Banks

Savings banks are generally owned by a combination of private and public owners, and are usually not owned by the central government, as one of their primary attributes is their decentralized nature. They are often grounded in their local community and aim to serve the local small businesses there.[15] As their name suggests, savings banks focus on savings mobilization much more so than other banks that perhaps focus more on delivering micro-credit.

Postal Savings Banks operate through the counters of post offices, and as such are able to cover a wide area through a large network of outlets. These banks do not offer credit, but they do accept deposits and provide money transfer services. However, many of these banks suffer from organizational weaknesses, due to the fact that they are managed by the postal service, which lacks a genuine invested interest in their success.[16] Thus, most postal savings banks are in poor condition, a regrettable situation due to the potential of these banks to provide basic financial services within easy reach of the poor.

Commercial Banks

These are formal financial institutions which concentrate on providing long-term and short-term loans to established businesses. The majority of commercial banks have limited experience in providing financial services such as credit to micro-entrepreneurs or small farmers, but many are increasingly considering it beneficial to do so. Branch banking is the most common way in which this is done, with bank tellers providing financial services to low income clients from bank facilities.[17]

Non-bank Financial Institutions

These exist in some countries, where special regulation has been created in order to allow for the establishment of non-bank financial institutions. These sorts of institutions are created in order to resolve the problem that some MFIs have with meeting the standards and requirements of commercial banks due to the nature of their lending.[18]

The following fall under the category of semi-formal institutions, which usually consist of financial cooperatives and NGOs.

Credit Unions, Savings and Loans Cooperatives, and other Financial Cooperatives

There exists a wide variety of forms of financial cooperatives, many of which play an important role in providing financial services to the poor. These provide savings and credit services to their clients. The organizational structure of these cooperatives is as follows: there are no external shareholders, the members themselves are the owners of the institution, and each member has the right to one vote in the organization. The members are able to hold shares and redeem these, and are able to deposit money with the organization or borrow from it.[19] Membership usually arises due to a shared bond between members, often times through employment or through membership in the same community. Moreover, the leadership responsible for policy making is drawn directly from the cooperative members themselves, usually through a volunteer or on election basis.[20] Financial cooperatives are rarely under any form of banking regulation, and in general, cooperatives share the following characteristics: they serve low-income to lower-middle-income families, they provide virtually exclusively financial services, and they self-generate their capital to cover their operating costs without dependence on outside sources of funding.[21]

Financial NGOs

NGOs are the most common institutional type for microfinance institutions. It is important to distinguish between NGOs and other forms of non-profit and non-governmental institutions: self-help groups and cooperatives. Unlike these two latter forms of institutions, NGOs are owned and run by outsiders, not by the target group members themselves, and these owners are usually from the middle classes of society who aim to financially support and assist the poor. These NGOs, however, are close to the target group in terms of location and understanding, and are usually able to provide better services than government officials or traditional bankers.[22] Thus, financial NGOs have many advantages that place them in a favourable position to offer effective microfinance services. However, NGOs have several weaknesses that when combined, can inhibit the effectiveness of the institution, as clearly laid out in Ledgerwood's *Microfinance Handbook: An Institutional and Financial Perspective:*

- 'The lack of business acumen with which some NGOs are set up and operated.'
- 'Overly ambitious aspirations with regards to their social relevance.'
- 'The limited scale of their operations, which does not permit them to benefit from elementary economies of scale.'
- 'The frequent use of donated funds or soft loans from foreign development organizations.'
- 'The influence of people who do not belong to the target group and thus are not subject to peer pressure and are not directly hurt if the institution's money is eventually lost.'[23]

When these factors work together, a situation can be created in which the financial and business side of the NGO is not taken care of diligently enough. Many NGOs often suffer from a lack of long-term vision or strategy.

Informal Financial Providers

Within this category, it is more difficult to distinguish between different types of institutions, as many times, informal financial providers lack any form of formal institutional structure or organization. Often, informal financial providers are the largest source of credit and financial services amongst the poor. The informal sector ranges from moneylenders and money collectors, to a network of family and friends who provide informal loans.[24]

Self-help Groups

These prove difficult to classify, as while they follow what seems an informal structure of self-employed women who 'informally support the economic activities of their members by providing mutual guarantees that facilitate their members' access to bank loans, by borrowing and lending among themselves, or by encouraging each other to save regularly,'[25] these self-help groups are also formal enough to establish relationships with development agencies and banks, as shown by the Self-help Group Bank Linkage Programme. Self-help groups often exhibit strong common interests between its members and are particularly effective as they function on the principle of mutual peer pressure. They have a democratic structure and strong leadership, and are effective at empowering women in particular.[26]

One approach to microfinance is the SHG promotion approach, in which an NGO promotes SHGs and acts as a financial adviser for them. In this role as an adviser, the NGO is able to build the capacity of SHGs to mobilize savings, to link with banks and to start sustainable micro-enterprises by the SHG members.[27] The role of the NGO in this approach is to act as a mediator between the SHGs and the banks, examining the creditworthiness of the SHGs, thus enabling the banks to lend to them.[28]

SHG-based microfinance in India encourages members to manage the group's financial affairs such as savings and loan recovery, and the funds are deposited in a local commercial bank in the name of the SHG.[29] These savings are initially used to provide small loans to the most needy members; however, after the SHG has gained experience in handling credit, it is issued a larger loan by a commercial bank, and are free to determine the end use of this loan, including its purpose and repayment instalments, etc. without any external influence from the promoting NGO or the bank, as it is the SHG's sole responsibility to repay the loan.[30]

SHGs managed solely by women have seen a huge increase in India in recent years, and many state governments have provided strong support for the development and growth of this microfinance model. This model provides poor women with an opportunity to make their own decisions regarding themselves and their groups, and dramatically increases the capacity building of the rural poor.[31]

SHG-Bank Linkage Programme (SBLP)

This model, which has become the primary method of providing microfinance services in India, involves the SHGs being financed directly by banking institutions such as Commercial Banks, Regional Rural Banks and Cooperative Banks.[32] Many SHGs have loans outstanding with banks, and all SHGs save regularly. The project was launched by NABARD in February 1992, and constituted the first time that informal savings and credit groups were recognized as bankable clients.[33]

This proved to be a mutually beneficial relationship for both sides, as through this programme, banks were able to tap into a large market of predominantly low-income households, with low transaction costs and high repayment rates.[34] For the SHGs, this relationship was advantageous as it enabled them to scale up their operations with the increased financing, and provided them access to a wider range of credit products.[35]

However, as the programme has grown, problems have arisen. SHGs do face problems in dealing with banks. Often, initial loan volumes are low and banks require groups to place all their savings with the bank, which leaves little room for the internal lending of members' savings.[36] Many times branch staff also lacks the time to visit groups in their villages, and the lack of direct contact can also cause problems for the SHGs.[37]

Socially, the growth of SHG-Bank Linkage Programme has both benefited local communities, and encountered setbacks. The link between women's involvement in SHG programmes and their overall empowerment within their community is clear. Women's involvement in public affairs for example has grown significantly.[38] Although the number of women involved in politics still remains low, data shows that these numbers are on the increase.[39] Through SHG participation, women gain greater language and financial skills, which work to build their confidence in further engaging their community and societies.[40] SHGs have also shown to promote social justice within communities. Several cases have shown SHGs resolving disputes, such as arbitration and divorce, and whilst the role of dispute resolution used to belong solely to men, women SHG members have begun to assert themselves in this role too.[41]

However, recent data has also indicated that the impact of SHGs on the community at large have been limited, and that significant contributions to education, family planning, eradication of child labour and hygiene for example have remained low.[42] The reason for this is usually the financial limitations of the SHG, as undertaking such reforms and projects require significant economic commitments.[43]

One area in which SHGs have so far not made significant progress is in promoting social harmony and in managing social tensions.[44] Sometimes the composition of SHGs is exclusively of one social mix, and although there have been groups composed of members from a mixed social background, in almost all cases the group leaders have consisted of women from the dominant social group's category.[45] Thus, SHGs have a long way to go in becoming completely socially inclusive and equal.

SHG Federations

SHGs have also come together to form larger federations. Within these federations, about 15 to 50 SHGs constitute a Cluster or Village Organization, with one or two representatives from each group.[46] Several clusters or village organizations then come together to form a larger apex organization or SHG federation. This particular organizational structure allows for inter-group borrowing, exchange of ideas, sharing of costs and discussion of common interests at the cluster and federation level.[47] Usually, there are various subcommittees responsible for a variety of issues such as loan collections and accounting and social issues.[48] The larger scale of SHG federations is, therefore, an advantage, as well as the fact that they are formally registered entities under the Mutually Aided Co-operative Society (MACS) Act, 1995, and are thus recognized by bankers. However, there are also several limitations of SHG federations. The federation itself is comprised of groups that share informal common interests. Its members can, therefore, be somewhat informal and as a result its capacity for self-governance may be limited.[49] The systems and processes of an SHG federation may also be poorly defined. Finally, the financial cost of establishing SHG federations must not be underestimated, as registration is estimated to cost about ₹ 7,000 per SHG member.[50] In order to overcome these internal limitations, SHG federations require experienced external assistance and, unfortunately, there are too few high quality NGOs that are able to meet the needs of the growing number of SHG federations.

Ownership and Governance

Whilst many microfinance institutions are created with a social visionary mission, that to improve the lives of low income clients through providing them with financial services, it rapidly becomes evident to these institutions that a social vision alone is not sufficient. The institution must likewise have an efficient governance and management structure both to ensure the sustainability of the programme, and to attract skilled people who usually come from the private sector.[51] The governance of a microfinance institution refers to a system of checks and balances in which a board of directors is established to supervise the management of the MFI.[52] Members of the board should have a range of skills, to include legal, financial and managerial; and representation from the private sector is also particularly important.[53] The board members must have a set of common objectives, and must be independent from the MFI itself; selected for their own expertise as opposed to their own interests or political agendas.[54]

With regards to ownership, it is the owners of the MFI that select the members who comprise the board of directors. The owners are responsible for overseeing the management of the MFI.[55] However, ownership of MFIs can often be unclear, particularly as many receive funding from donors. NGOs and informal MFIs do not have formal ownership; however, formal institutions have shareholders who own shares.[56] This provides a way of holding the board of directors accountable, as shareholders have the ability to vote their shares to elect board members.[57] NGOs do not generally have shareholders, and instead it is the management who elects the board of directors. This, however, can create a conflict of interest, if the management selects board members who will conform to their interests.[58]

Microfinance Institutions (MFIs) in Rajasthan

Technically, any institution working in the field of microfinance can be called a Microfinance Institution. However, usually the organizations which do micro-lending as their prime work are included in 'Microfinance Institutions'. For clarity, it is worth mentioning that in this chapter, institutions that are delivering micro-credit as a 'business' are discussed as MFIs.

The emergence of MFIs can be rooted to Grameen Model of Bangladesh. Under this model of microfinance, the poor are called clients and about 5–6 clients are grouped in to 'Joint Liability Group (JLG)' and credit is provided to 2–3 members of JLG and all of the members take joint liability of repayment. Once repayment is received from first set of clients, loans are given to remaining members of the group. Experiences indicate that JLGs become unsustainable once loan sizes go beyond ₹ 15,000. Therefore, after 2–3 initial cycles of loaning through JLG mechanism, many MFIs start providing micro-credit to clients on 'individual' basis.

In early days, microfinance was being discussed as the next big innovation to address the poverty issues in India. In recent times, microfinance is discussed in terms of the next big investment opportunity, thanks to the phenomenon called MFIs. Owing to MFIs, the language of microfinance has undergone a fundamental change in the two decades of its evolution. With recent IPO (initial public offering) of SKS Microfinance Ltd., MFIs have become a buzzword in capital markets not just in India, but across the world. MFIs in India borrow from banks at 13 per cent, lend to the poor at 26 per cent to 27 per cent, and spend around 8 per cent to deliver the loans and have an interest margin of 5–6 per cent, almost double the margin that banks make. Adding to that, NBFC MFIs in India have 5–10 times leverage (debt to equity ratio). This results in healthy Return on Equity (ROE) for MFIs.

Over time, MFIs have become favourites of private equity funds and venture capitalists. Private equity/venture capital investors typically expect a return (ROI or IRR) of over 30 per cent per annum (p.a.) from investments in their fund's portfolio. MFIs, therefore, in their pursuit of generating over 30 per cent p.a. return are required to follow profit-maximizing strategies which are expected to generate over 30 per cent returns. This is done by hiring of professionals, by following industry's best practices and by making optimum use of technology. Further, PE/VC Funds set milestones for MFIs, at the time of investment, for scaling up at exponential pace. MFIs are expected to achieve these milestones over time.

In Rajasthan, MFIs started their operations in around 2007. And within a short span of three years, combined clients of MFIs have touched 8.06 lakh and the outstanding credit of MFIs has touched ₹ 527 crore. MFI outstanding credit in Rajasthan has surpassed SBLP outstanding credit.[59]

Products – Credit and Insurance

Products and services offered by MFIs are primarily credit led and insurance led. Since most of the NBFCs are non-deposit taking NBFCs, therefore, by regulation, they are not allowed to mobilize saving deposits. Credit-led products typically have loan sizes of ₹ 6,000 to ₹ 10,000 and increase with every loan cycle. MFIs also tie up with insurance companies to provide life insurance.

For repeat loans, credit records and attendance at the weekly meetings of the members is studied and based on this criterion the repeat loan is given out. The repayment rate for most of the MFIs is reported to be more than 98 per cent. However, information received from field officers and other informal sources reveals that repayment rates are actually not so high. Loan defaults do happen but are not reported by MFIs to the outside world.

Interest rates reported by MFIs vary from 15–30 per cent[60] on reducing balance basis. However, this reporting does not include flat loan processing fee charged to clients at the time of initiation of loan. Moreover, this also does not include certain amount of deposit that is kept as collateral with some MFIs. So the effective rate of interest charged comes out to be higher than that reported by MFIs.

Effective interest rate of a hypothetical MFI which charges 15 per cent flat interest rate

A 15 per cent flat interest rate charged on a 12-month micro-credit loan translates to over 27 per cent interest rate p.a. on a reducing basis. Now assuming that this MFI also keeps 10 per cent of credit given to a client as 'deposit' (or collateral), then the effective rate of interest becomes 33 per cent p.a. on a reducing basis. A flat processing fee of 3.5 per cent makes the effective rate of interest to be 36.5 per cent.

MFIs also act as insurance service providers (as an intermediary between insurance companies and clients). They collect an insurance premium on regular basis for insurance cover provided to MFI clients. It has been learnt that typically the insurance cover is only large enough to safeguard credit repayment to MFIs in case of a casualty. The insurance covers are usually not as per needs of the microfinance clients.

Microfinance Institutions in Rajasthan

There are currently 22 MFIs operating in the state. Eight of these MFIs are local with headquarters in the state while the rest are multistate players. SKS Microfinance is the largest player with 87 branches and a portfolio of ₹ 159 crore.

Till 2006–07, BASIX and SKS Microfinance were the only major players in the state, but in last three years, MFIs have seen an exponential growth in the state. The overall number of branches, areas of operations, client base and their portfolio has seen a steep rise. This is summarized in Table 4.1.

Table 4.1

Particulars of MFIs in Rajasthan as on March 2010

Name of MFI	*Loan Outstanding (₹)*	*No. of Branches*	*Area of Operation*	*Outreach (No. of clients)*	*Interest Rate*
Arth	8.12	9	Jhalawar, Kota, Baran and Jaipur	11,073	15% Flat
Basix (BSFL)	38.99	15 districts	Jaipur, Jodhpur, Kota, Udaipur, Bhilwara, Bharatpur, Ajmer, Bikaner, Dausa, Ganganagar, Chittorgarh, Hanumangarh, etc.	38,646	18–24% reducing
Bazaari Global	7.55	15	Abu Road, Balotra, Bhinmal, Bhopalgarh, Gudamalani, Jalore, Jodhpur, Pali, Phalodi, Rohit, Samadari, Sayla, Sanchore, Shiv, Sindhari, Siwana, Sumerpur	8,127	18% Flat
Mimo Finance	2.92	6	Ajmer, Beawar, Bhilwara, Jaipur, Nagaur	3,500	15% Flat
Pustikar	75.22	8	Three in Jodhpur, one each in Bikaner, Pali, Phalodi, Jaisalmer, Nagaur	Not Available	15%–17% reducing
Sahayata	60.98	70	Udaipur, Jaipur, Kota, Jodhpur, Ajmer, Beawar, Bhilwara, Chittorgarh, Pali, Rajnagar, Jhalawar, Kotputli, Bikaner, Fatehnagar, Merta, Neem Ka Thana, Kishangarh, Sikar, Chomu, Gulabpura, Kuchaman, Jobner, Shahpura	1,39,179 (64% in urban while 36% in semi-urban)	28.13% reducing
Equitas	0.35	2	Not Available	347	26.5%–28.5% reducing
Janalakshmi	2.89	1	Jaipur	3,460	28–30% reducing

Cont'd...

Cont'd...

Mitr	1.53	2	Alwar	2,700	15% Flat
SKS Microfinance	159	87	Jaipur, Bhilwara, Alwar, Ajmer, Tonk, Pali, Nagaur, Churu, Sikar	2,66,093	15% Flat
Share Microfin and Asmitha	100	50	Not Available	2,00,000	NA
Ujjivan	19.57	13	Jaipur, Jodhpur, Kota, Alwar, Ajmer, Bharatpur, Bundi, Kishangarh, Tonk, Pali, Dausa, Sawai Madhopur, Sri Ganganagar and Hanumangarh	32,499	22–25% reducing
Others (incl. NGO MFIs)	50	NA	NA	30,000	NA
Total	527			8,05,624	

Major Issues Related to Microfinance Institutions in Rajasthan

Microfinance institutions are providing credit to people who otherwise are not able to get it from commercial banks. The excellent growth registered by MFIs in Rajasthan in terms of number of clients and amount of credit is a good indicator of the 'demand of credit' and acceptability of MFIs. However, it is worth mentioning here that the clients of MFIs are those who have some economic activities which enable them to make weekly repayments. Therefore, the MFI clients are largely in semi-urban areas and somewhat in better off rural areas.

Rate of interest charged by MFIs has been a much debated issue. While it is largely accepted that the cost of credit to poor (small size of transactions and large distances) will always be more than what it is for economically better off middle class; there is no agreement on what should be 'just and appropriate' interest rate. It is also argued that market forces (competition) will force the MFIs to rationalize their interest rates but considering the number of people who do not have access to formal financial institutions, possibility of this happening is remote.

Initially, clients come to MFIs for loans because their effective rate of interest (30–35%) is lower than that of money-lenders who normally charge 36–60 per cent. But as the loan size grows, the interest rate of 30 per cent becomes a burden and defaults start happening. However, the local staffs of MFI give a top-up loan to get repayment instalment on time. Or the client starts approaching another MFI to repay the loan of another MFI.

Most MFIs are found to focus their operations in the same area. One can find lots of MFIs in few areas while none in other areas. However, this does not result in lowering of interest rates. The major reason attributable is that it takes around 15–20 days for a MFI to train and orient a new set of microfinance clients. The late MFI entrant finds it easier to deal with tried and tested set of microfinance clients rather than to start operations in a virgin territory.

The negative implication of this practice is occurrence of multiple lending. One set of clients are provided credit by more than one MFI. This leads to payment to one MFI by availing credit from the other and vice-versa, until the client falls into a debt trap and defaults.

Apart from a few big MFIs, majority do not reveal their cost structure and therefore, the justification of high interest rates. The salary structure of top executives working in some of the MFIs is same or even more than the commercial bank staff.[61] This adds to the total cost/expenses of MFIs, thereby impacting the interest rates charged to microfinance clients. MFI promoters need to understand that all these costs are ultimately borne by the poor.

If MFIs, like other for-profit NBFCs (read vehicle finance, gold loan finance, home finance, car finance NBFCs, etc.) can easily access capital markets to raise cheap finance, and if they have mastered the art of recovering loans from villagers and can reach where the banks can't, it may be argued whether or not they still require 'priority sector lending' support. Same reasoning is applicable to 'micro-credit' portfolios of 'gold loan' companies, which, too, fall under priority sector lending.

Emerging Action Points

MFIs currently operate in urban, semi-urban and relatively well-off rural areas. MFIs can target relatively poorer segments by collaborating with SHGs. SHGs provide a ready platform for MFIs to scale up and impact weaker sections of the poor. SHGs need more credit while MFIs look for disciplined clients with good credit record. MFIs can save on cost, given that SHGs are capable to take care of back-end operations (e.g. collection, distribution, book-keeping, etc.) by themselves. However, for this to happen, MFIs may have to give a relook at their cost structure and see where costs can be reduced so that they charge economical interest rates to clients.

Microfinancial Products and Services

With regards to the products and services that microfinance can offer to low-income families, these can be characterized as either direct or indirect, as either the tangible products and services that are on offer such as credit, savings and insurance, or the intangible services that microfinance offers, such as social security in old age, the ability to support a sustainable livelihood and eradicate poverty, and women's empowerment.

Direct Products and Services of Microfinance

Savings Mobilization

Described as the 'forgotten half of microfinance',[62] savings mobilization is one of the most important services that microfinance institutions can offer to low-income clients. Many poor people lack access to good quality, formal deposit services, and as a result rely on informal mechanisms to save. This could include tucking money away under mattresses, buying animals or jewellery that could be sold off at a later stage, or stockpiling inventory or building materials.[63] However, there is significant risk associated with these informal methods of saving, as cash can be easily stolen, animals can fall sick or die, etc. These methods of saving often render the money illiquid also, if money is saved in the form of animals or expensive jewellery, it is impossible to sell simply a part of these if there is a need for a small amount of cash. Thus, there is a great demand for secure and convenient deposit services that allow for small balances and an easy access to savings and funds.[64] Many low-income clients are unable to find access to savings services from traditional banks however, due to a limited branch network, and because banks are reluctant to deal with small amounts of money.[65]

Despite the unwillingness of traditional banks to offer savings services to low-income clients, it has become generally accepted that microfinance institutions which mobilize savings enhance their own sustainability.[66] Micro-credit and savings should be viewed as two complementary components of microfinance; too often, microfinance over focuses on providing credit instead of savings services. The advantages to doing so are numerous. By offering savings' mobilization services, the MFI is able to enhance its fund base, and work with an accountable client base that has a stake in the success of the MFI.[67] Furthermore, saving mobilization strengthens the asset base of the MFI, reduces risks faced by the institution and enhances financial viability.[68]

In order to mobilize savings, MFIs must fulfil two legal requirements, one regarding licensing and the other regarding reserve requirements. In general, an MFI must have a license in order to collect savings, which means that it is usually subject to some form of regulation.[69] Some MFIs who collect savings solely from borrowers or members and who proceed to lend these funds or deposit them in a formal financial institution do not necessarily have to be licensed and are not regulated or supervised closely in their deposit activities.[70] However, to accept deposits from the general public, and MFI must have a license and is subject to regulatory supervision.[71] Reserve requirements mean that a percentage of deposits accepted by the MFI must be placed in safe and liquid form in a central bank or other institution, to ensure that the depositors' funds are both safe and accessible.[72]

Credit

Providing credit to low-income clients remains the predominant idea behind microfinance. The multiple structures through which micro-credit can be delivered have already been discussed at length, and can range from formal microfinance institutions to self-sufficient self-help groups or cooperatives and to fully fledged commercial banks in some cases. Lending can be done either directly or indirectly. Borrowers are able to improve their livelihoods and increase their incomes through microfinance loans.[73] Micro-credit works towards reducing the economic vulnerability of its clients, by providing them with enough income to smooth over gaps or unforeseen shortages on their own.[74] It also aims to provide jobs through enterprise development, by providing clients with loans with the hopes that these loans will be invested into income-generating activities.[75] Research, however, shows that less than half of micro-credit loans are actually used for the purpose of enterprise, and that instead, most loans are put towards household management needs, medical expenses, or events such as weddings and funerals.[76]

However, because micro-credit loans consist of unsecured loans, or loans without collateral, there is inevitably a risk associated, known to MFIs as credit risk.[77] MFIs receive funding for their portfolios through external borrowings, through their own capital, or through mobilizing their clients' savings.[78] Thus, by providing a loan, the MFI is also inherently attracting risk to these funds. If clients default on their loans, an MFI may lose money to the point where it is no longer able to meet its financial obligations to its own depositors and lenders, and becomes a defaulter itself.[79] This, in turn, can result in the donors losing confidence or interest in the MFI, which only adds to the MFIs current and future financial losses.[80] Some causes related to higher risk MFIs are: a poor screening of borrowers, weak appraisal, unclear communication about the product and methodology, lack of immediate follow-up, natural disasters, corruption or demotivated employees.[81] All of these factors contribute to a higher risk associated with providing loans for the MFI. If an MFI does suffer from a delinquency problem in which its clients fail to repay their loans on time, this can have many negative repercussions on the MFI itself, ranging from a loss in its portfolio, to hampered growth, a loss of credibility, and a loss due to competition from other MFIs.[82] It is, therefore, very important that MFIs strictly manage their loan disbursements and monitor their repayment rates diligently, in order to avoid the problem of one delayed or defaulted loan to escalate and cause much more serious consequences.

Insurance

Micro-insurance is one aspect of microfinance that has enormous potential but that unfortunately has not yet become mainstream amongst the financial services provided to the poor. The poor face more risks than those from wealthier backgrounds and the poor are more vulnerable to the same risks.[83] The poor usually face risks that fall into two categories: idiosyncratic risks (those specific to the home), and covariate risks (common to all, such as drought, and epidemic, etc.).[84] The poor are in desperate need of social protection, and providing them with services such as micro-insurance reduces their exposure to many risks and lessens the impact of a disaster.[85]

According to a draft paper written by the Consultative Group to Assist the Poor (CGAP), micro-insurance was defined as, 'the protection of low income households against specific perils in exchange for premium payments proportionate to the likelihood and cost of the risk involved'.[86] Research has shown that micro-insurance has faced difficulties in penetrating the rural markets in India, and that micro-insurance remains relatively rare among the rural poor.[87] According to a study commissioned by the United Nations Development Programme (UNDP) titled, 'Building Security for the Poor-Potential and Prospects for Micro-insurance in India', found that 90 per cent of the Indian population, approximately 950 million people, are not covered by insurance.[88] The study also pointed to the important issues regarding the growth of micro-insurance in India. One issue is that there are often challenges in product design, which can result in a mismatch between the needs of the clients and the actual products on offer.[89] According to the report, difficulty in distribution is one of the most cited reasons for the lack of micro-insurance in rural areas.[90] Thus, the UNDP report suggests that micro-insurance should attempt at 'addressing key issues that will improve customer satisfaction (demand-supply gaps, appropriate products and pricing), provide distribution efficiencies for better outreach and remove procedural hassles facilitating easier renewals and claim settlements'.[91]

With regards to the delivery mechanisms for micro-insurance, there are four main models that were studied by the NABARD Committee in their Report on Financial Inclusion. The first is the *Partner-Agent Model,* in which insurers use MFIs' delivery mechanism to provide sales and basic services to clients. In this model there is no risk and a limited administrative burden for MFIs.[92] The second model is the *Full Service Model,* in which the provider is responsible for all aspects of product design, sales, servicing, and claims assessment. There is a certain amount of risk involved, as the insurers are responsible for all insurance-related costs and losses, but they retain all profits.[93] The third is the *Community Based Model* in which the policy holders own and manage the insurance programme, and negotiate with external health care providers. Finally, there is the *Provider Model,* in which the service provider and the insurer are the same, meaning that for example, hospitals or doctors offer policies to individuals or groups themselves.[94]

Types of insurance that would be most pertinent to low-income clients according to the NABARD Committee are life insurance, health insurance, crop insurance, livestock insurance and asset insurance.[95] Although there is a huge potential for growth in this sector, micro-insurance still remains a new concept, and insurers face significant setbacks, in that there is a lack of base line data on potential claims that can help them design and price the products. The main challenge however remains, and that is spreading awareness among the low-income segment of the population about micro-insurance.[96]

Indirect Products and Services of Microfinance

Many of the indirect products and services of microfinance have already been discussed, and it is evident that microfinance has a large capacity to empower women, to provide social security, to reduce poverty and to provide the poor with the ability to sustain a profitable livelihood. As mentioned before, the SHG model in particular has great potential for empowering women, as it provides women with direct responsibility and a sense of entitlement and financial independence. Microfinance, through providing micro-credit, enables low-income clients who already generate income through trading or through the fabrication of goods to invest in their small-scale enterprises. This stabilizes their income and makes them personally less vulnerable to fluctuations in demand, or other circumstances that may adversely affect their business. Vocational training, when coupled with microfinance can also provide positive results. It can 'help to improve efficiency and the quality of goods and service provision as a means of raising enterprise and workers' income'.[97]

One often cited criticism of microfinance, however, is that it does not truly benefit the really poor, and is only suited to those living on or slightly above the poverty line. However, 'the extreme poor are either less likely to participate in microfinance programmes, or such increases were too small and short-lived to enable sustainable poverty exit'.[98] Indeed, one reason is that microfinance institutions wish to provide loans to clients whom they will see using these towards income generating activities and enterprise as quickly as possible, and with the poorest of the poor this is often not the case. According to Marguerite Robinson, author of *The Microfinance Revolution,* her aim was not to reach the poorest of the poor, but to reach the 'poorest of the economically active'.[99] The truly destitute, are believed by many in the microfinance field to be the responsibility of the government, the Ministry of Social Welfare, private charities, etc. These are people who would benefit more from outright grants than from loans. Many have argued that by providing the truly poor with loans and consequently them not being able to repay the loan, simply further lowers their self-esteem.[100]

Self-Help Groups in Rajasthan

A self-help group (SHG) is a primary community institution usually composed of 10–15 women from similar socio-economic backgrounds, organized as internal group and managed through simple self-imposed norms. SHGs have established themselves as effective and self-managed financial intermediary at local level, aggregating financial needs of the poor in a more bankable proposition.

The Self-Help Movement started more as 'social mobilization' of women for their better place in family and society rather than 'microfinance movement' in Rajasthan. However, most development practitioners and policy makers gradually realized that mere women participation is not adequate and some direct action in terms of improving economic status of women is needed. That is how many voluntary organizations and government (together and/or separately) started organizing women into groups to take up small business (income generation activities) collectively.

Over the years, considerable progress has been made in organizing women into groups. The groups of women have to be promoted since new SHGs do not self-evolve. That is where Self-Help Group Promoting Institution (SHPI) plays a key role (see Table 4.2). Though the concept of SHGs was initiated by voluntary agencies, state government (especially its Department of Women and Child Development) has taken a lead in SHG promotion.

Table 4.2

Major SHG Promoting Institutions (SHPI)

S. No.	SHPI	Scheme/Project	Remarks
1.	Department of Women and Child Development	No Specific Scheme	Groups are organized by Anganwadi workers and Sathins
2.	Department of Rural Development	SGSY, Watershed Development Programmes, DPIP, MPOWER	BPL groups – mostly promoted in collaboration with NGOs
3.	NABARD and Banks	SHG-Bank Linkage, Individual Rural Volunteers (IRV)	Through NGOs, RRBs, Cooperatives
4.	Cooperatives		The cooperatives have very recently started forming SHGs
5.	Voluntary Organizations	With support from donor agencies and government programmes	Groups promoted by NGOs and government are often reported by both
6.	Others	Forest Dept., Elementary Education, Dept. of Industries	

Number of Self-Help Groups (SHGs) in Rajasthan

In Rajasthan, all of SHG promoters have different format for SHG information. Also there is double reporting, i.e. same group

Table 4.3

Numbers of SHGs Promoted by SHPIs as of March 2010

	DWCD	NGOs	Cooperatives	Others	Total
ICDS	1,96,273[101]	1,245[102]			1,97,518
SGSY		35,518[103]		11,839	47,357
NABARD-SBLP		11,069[104]			11,069
DPIP		18,000[105]			18,000
Others		11,417[106]	47,638[107]	27,690[108]	86,745
Total	1,96,273	77,249	47,638	39,529	3,60,689

is reported by different agencies (see Table 4.3). Therefore, reporting of SHG numbers becomes a difficult task.

Estimate of Actual Number of SHGs

As stated above, there is no comprehensive database of self-help groups in state. It is very difficult to compile the data on all SHGs in the state because of various reasons like: there is double reporting (more than one agency reporting the same group); the groups that have become defunct are not deleted from the list and there is no uniform reporting/MIS and many SHPIs are hesitant to share the information on their groups.

The only reference point for counting of SHGs is the data on bank accounts of SHGs. As on March 2010, a total of 2.17 lakh SHGs are reported as having bank accounts. But there is problem in taking this as reference as well. There are good numbers of groups that do not have bank accounts.

Many SHGs become defunct after some time due to various reasons like: the promoting organization is unable to regularly visit the group, there is conflict among group members, SHG fails to link with bank and members distribute their savings among themselves and stop meeting, and so on. But such groups are seldom removed from the list of SHGs reported by the SHPIs.

Considering the above factors, it will be highly useful if a comprehensive database of SHGs is prepared and managed at district and state level. Till such database is prepared, it is difficult to arrive at the exact number of SHGs existing. However, it might be safe to assume that about 2.6 lakh SHGs (about 70% of the SHGs reported) exist.

Outreach of Self-Help Groups

Taking the actual functioning 2.6 lakh SHGs and the average membership of SHG,[109] the total outreach of SHGs in Rajasthan would be near about 31.2 lakh members (while 44 lakh as per reported figures). Assuming that the members are from different families (though there is more than one member from a family in some groups), SHGs are reaching out to about 32 per cent of rural families.[110] As per the study conducted by CmF, about 40 per cent members in SHGs are from BPL.[111] Assuming this sample statistic as representative of the whole set, about 12.48 lakh rural BPL families can be assumed to be covered through SHGs, which is about 59 per cent of total rural BPL families in state.[112]

SHG movement is not uniformly spread out in Rajasthan. After taking into account data provided by SHPIs till 2009–10 on districtwise number of SHGs in a district and comparing it with population of the district, a 'Saturation Index' has been constructed. The index gives clear status of percentage of rural households covered under SHG movement in a particular district (Table 4.4).

Table 4.4

Saturation Index of SHG Movement in Rajasthan as of March 2010

District	*Saturation Index 2010*
Kota	91%
Jhalawar	80%
Dungarpur	57%
Bhilwara	55%
Baran	54%
Bundi	53%
Chittorgarh	50%
Banswara	49%
Bikaner	48%
Sirohi	46%
Udaipur	44%
Jaisalmer	42%
Bharatpur	42%
Ganganagar	42%
Hanumangarh	40%
Sawai Madhopur	37%
Tonk	36%
Sikar	36%

Cont'd...

Cont'd...

Jhunjhunu	36%
Churu	36%
Ajmer	34%
Jaipur	34%
Rajsamand	32%
Alwar	29%
Jalaur	28%
Pali	28%
Jodhpur	28%
Barmer	26%
Karauli	24%
Dausa	23%
Dholpur	20%
Nagaur	19%

On basis of analysis, SHG movement has been found to be weak (in terms of households covered) in districts like Nagaur, Dholpur, Dausa, Karouli, Barmer, Jodhpur, Pali, Jalaur, Alwar and Rajsamand. Nagaur, Dholpur, Dausa, Karouli, Barmer and Jalaur have been found to be under-banked too.

Further, SHG movement has been found to be strong in districts like Kota, Jhalawar, Dungarpur, Bhilwara, Baran, Bundi, Chittorgarh, Banswara, Bikaner and Sirohi. Jhalawar, Dungarpur, Bhilwara, Bundi and Chittorgarh have been found to have strong bank presence.

Self-Help Group Promoting Institutions

Various SHPIs are promoting SHGs in Rajasthan as a strategy for women empowerment and poverty alleviation. DWCD has been a leading SHG promoter in Rajasthan. The Department of Rural Development has adopted the Self-Help Group approach for poverty alleviation through social mobilization and micro-enterprise development under its programmes like SGSY, Watershed Development, and District Poverty Initiative Project and so on. Banks and Cooperatives have mostly focused on providing credit to SHGs. SHPIs are discussed in detail below:

Department of Women and Child Development (DWCD)

The Department of Women and Child Development (DWCD) has promoted the largest number of the groups in Rajasthan (1,96,273 till March 2010). The department has a cadre of women workers (Aanganwadi Workers and *Sathins* at village level) who organize Women Self-Help Groups. Total savings of the groups is ₹ 107.37 crore. Compared to savings, only ₹ 61.88 crore has been disbursed by banks as credit during 2009–10. This credit too is estimated to be distributed only among 10 per cent of SHGs. Further analysis of data provided by DWCD indicates that only 54 per cent SHGs are using their savings to give loans to members.

Department of Rural Development

Department of Rural Development, Government of Rajasthan is promoting Self-Help Groups through its three main programmes – Swarnjayanti Gram Swarojgar Yojana (SGSY), Watershed Development and District Poverty Initiative Project (DPIP).

SGSY (2009–10)[113]

The triangulation of data provided by government on SGSY is a tough task for any researcher. For example, under SGSY in 2008–09, 1,65,941 groups have been reported to be formed while in 2009–10 only 2,846 groups have been reported to be formed and in 2007–08, 7,952 SHGs are reported as formed during the year (Table 4.5).

Table 4.5

SHGs Promoted Under SGSY in Last Three Years

	2007–2008	*2008–2009*	*2009–2010*
SHGs promoted under SGSY in last 3 years	7,952	1,65,941	2,846

Figure 4.1

Money Spent on Wages (in ₹ Crore)

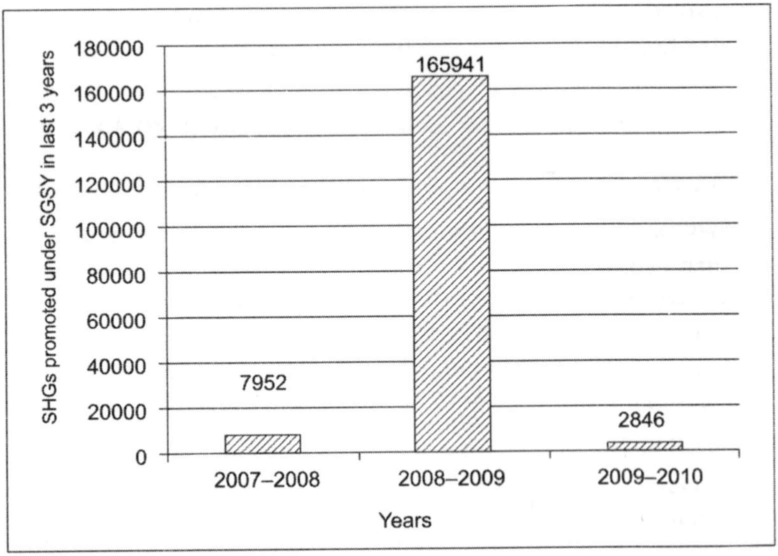

Further, as per data reported by NABARD banks provided credit of ₹ 20.26 crore and ₹ 44.58 crore respectively to SHGs under SGSY in 2007–08 and 2008–09. However, as per data reported by SGSY, banks have provided credit of ₹ 43.43 crore and ₹ 86.4 crore to SHGs under SGSY in 2007–08 and 2008–09, respectively.

Going by figures reported by SGSY, total 2,09,412 SHGs have been formed under SGSY in Rajasthan till March 2010. The SHG groups formed under SGSY are as per the guidelines by GoI and the revolving fund and bank credit is provided to the group if it passes the grading test. Out of total 2,09,412 groups, 39,464 groups (18.9%) have passed first grading and 16,927 SHGs (8%) have passed second grading as of March 2010. Total 13,488 SHGs have taken up some economic activity.

In last three years (2007–08 to 2009–10), total ₹ 1,327.5 lakh have been spent to form and nurture 1,76,739 SHGs under

SGSY in Rajasthan. Thus, the money spent for promoting one SHG in 3 years under SGSY comes to ₹ 751. The average cost of promoting a good quality SHG and also the norm in SGSY itself is ₹ 8,000 per SHG. This is one of the reasons for poor quality of SHGs under the scheme.

A total credit of ₹ 192.22 crore has been reported as mobilized from banks under SGSY during 2009–10. Most of it (approx. 80%) has gone through SHGs while only 20 per cent has gone to individual *swarozgaris*. Over the years, credit reported as mobilized from banks to SHGs under SGSY has increased by almost 100 per cent every year. However, the data from banks is yet to be published by NABARD. Considering the differences of almost 100 per cent in the data of Bank credit under SGSY (reported by SGSY and NABARD), credit mobilized to SHGs from banks is estimated to be about ₹ 90–100 crore.

CIGs under District Poverty Initiative Project (DPIP)[114]

DPIP was implemented in the seven poorest districts: Baran, Churu, Dausa, Dholpur, Jhalawar, Rajsamand and Tonk of the 32 Rajasthan's districts wherein 1,00,000 poor rural households were covered and 1,70,000 members were benefited. The project was initiated in July 2000 and ended in December 2007. These poor households were organized into Common Interest Groups (CIGs), provided with financial and technical support so as to improve their organizational capacity and maximize the utility of their productive assets, federating them and then linking them to markets. Some 18,000 CIGs were formed, of which nearly half were livestock and dairy groups. Of these, about 4,347 CIGs were linked to the Rajasthan State Dairy Federation for marketing and technical services support.

The impact evaluation of the project revealed that the project achieved significant results, viz. (i) assets were intact with CIGs, (ii) 82.14 per cent CIGs had shown full utilization, (iii) around 20 per cent CIGs acquired additional assets through bank linkage and (iv) the average income increased by 78 per cent over the base year 2001. The other positive lessons from implementation of DPIP include income from animal husbandry which increased by 267 per cent, around 95 per cent members of CIGs getting sufficient food daily around the year and increase in irrigated area from 1 bigha to 4 bighas for land-based groups.

Watershed Development Programme

As per the guidelines of the watershed development programmes, promotion of SHGs in watershed area is one of the strategies. There is a provision of ₹ 1 lakh as revolving fund in a micro-watershed. Though about 16,783 SHGs have been reported under Watershed Development Programme, the focus of the programme is more on water harvesting and land development.

NABARD, Banks and Cooperatives

In 1992, SHG movement was started with initial support from NABARD. By March 2009, NABARD had sanctioned ₹ 4.21 crore to SHPIs for group promotion in Rajasthan (see Table 4.6, Figures 4.2–4.6).

Table 4.6

Support to SHPIs by NABARD

SHPI	*No. of SHGs Aimed to be Promoted and Credit Linked*	*Amount Sanctioned (₹ Lakh)*	*Total Amount Released (₹ Lakh)*	*No. of SHGs Promoted*	*No. of SHGs Credit Linked*
NGOs	12,122	249.43	98.35	7,272	4,794
RRB	300	1.55	1.11	611	411
Cooperative Banks	5,315	79.17	1.74	316	158
IRVs	5,030	90.54	4.2	365	30
Total	22,767	420.69	105.4	8,564	5,393

Figure 4.2

Number of SHGs Aimed to be Promoted and Credit Linked

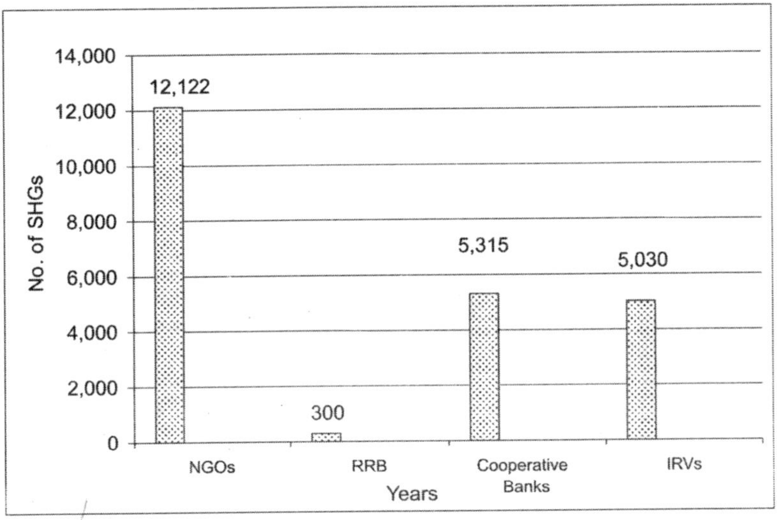

Figure 4.3

Amount Sanctioned (₹ Lakh)

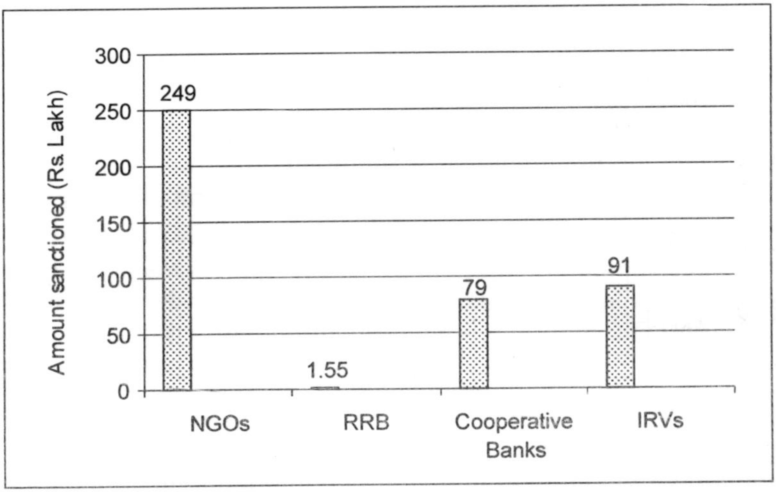

Figure 4.4

Total Amount Released (₹ Lakh)

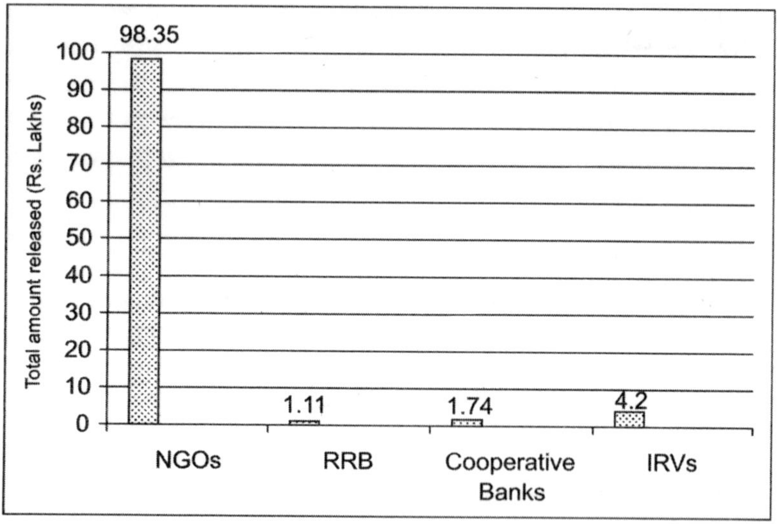

Figure 4.5

Number of SHGs Promoted

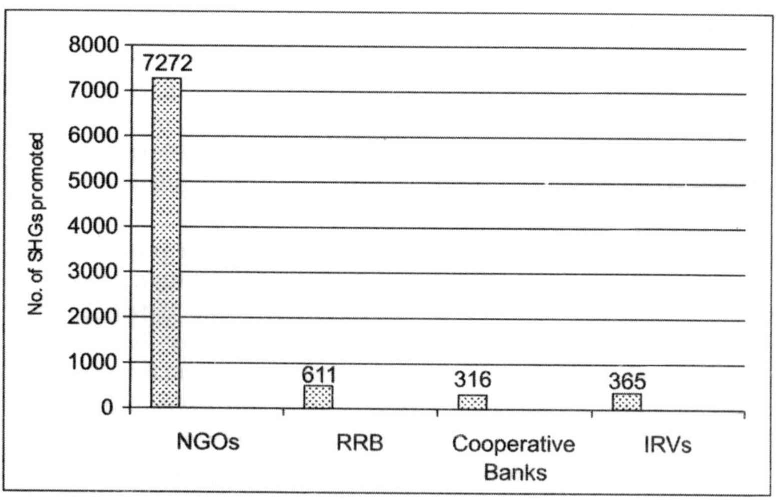

Figure 4.6

Number of SHGs Credit Linked

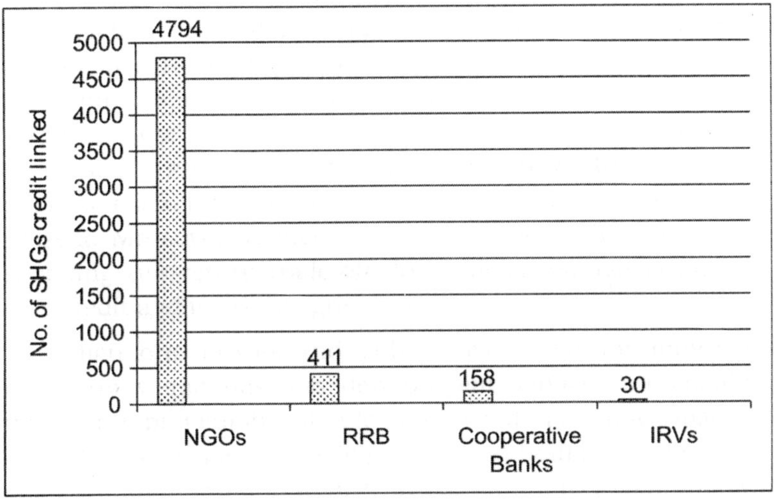

An analysis of support provided to SHPIs by NABARD indicates that the progress has not been encouraging in Rajasthan. Out of ₹ 4.21 crore sanctioned to SHPIs, only ₹ 1.05 crore has been released. Out of the target of 22,767 SHGs, only 8,564 (38%) groups were actually promoted and only 5,393 (24%) were credit linked.

Poor performance of credit linkage and group formation might be attributable to low financial support to SHPIs in absolute terms. Even though NABARD's objective was to supplement SHPIs finances through its financial support, it seems that SHPIs are promoting SHGs only from NABARD's financial support.

Figures indicate that only ₹ 4.21 crore was sanctioned to promote 22,767 SHGs in Rajasthan. This translates to ₹ 1,848 per group for promotion and credit linkage. This too was to be paid in 3–4 instalments to SHPIs. Actual cost of promotion of one SHG is estimated to be around ₹ 8,000 over a period of 3 years. Therefore, SHPIs found it difficult to remain financially sustainable and had to quit before completion of the projects.

Apart from NABARD, Small Industries Development Bank of India (SIDBI) has also been involved in promoting microfinance by lending to NGOs and MFIs to on-lend to microfinance clients.

Voluntary Organizations

In every district, there are about 5 to 10 voluntary organizations that are organizing SHGs either on their own or in collaboration with government. Most of the voluntary agencies have promoted 50 to 100 SHGs. However, there are a few agencies that have substantial number (300 to 1,800 SHGs) of groups. For example: PEDO in Dungarpur, Lupin Foundation in Bharatpur, PRADAN in Dausa, Dholpur, IBTADA in Alwar, ASSEFA in Baran and Banswara, URMUL in Bikaner, Sewa Mandir in Udaipur, Navyuvak Mandal and Bhoruka Charitable Trust in Churu, IIRD in Baran, Kumarappa Institute of Gram Swaraj (KIGS) in Tonk, CECOEDECON in Tonk, Jaipur and Baran, SRIJAN in Tonk and Bundi and a few others have large microfinance programmes.

Interestingly, not many NGOs can be found in districts like Nagaur, Karouli, Barmer, Pali, Jalaur, and Rajsamand, which have been found to fall lowest on SHG Saturation Index 2010. It is interesting to note that except for larger NGOs, other focus more on other social mobilization issues like health, education, advocacy, human rights, etc. Microfinance is typically not their core proposition. Therefore, expecting such smaller NGOs to create new products and to build a long-term vision for SHGs may not be appropriate.

SHG's Products and Services

The SHGs provides mainly two types of microfinance services, viz. Savings and Credit to their members. In few places, SHGs have also taken up micro-insurance services.

Savings

One of the objectives of the SHGs is to promote thrift/savings among members. SHG members save a specific amount every month (equal amount by each member) and the savings are either used as credit to members or are deposited in bank account (which ideally should be used for inter-loaning). A reserve is kept aside to meet emergency need of the members.

In Rajasthan, a trend is emerging, wherein members deposit voluntary savings in the groups, taking a lesson from self-help groups in South India. This trend should be promoted at larger scale since it provides an option to park surplus savings and not look for alternative saving mechanisms.

Average Saving Per Member Per Month

As per a study conducted by CmF in 2009–10, the normal monthly saving per person in SHG group has been found to vary from ₹ 20 to 100. About 60 per cent groups have been found to save up to ₹ 50 per person/month. Rest 40 per cent groups have been found to save ₹ 80–100 per month/per member. The average saving per member has been found to be ₹ 60 per month[115] which has increased from ₹ 35 per month in 2007. Data from DWCD[116] reveals that average monthly savings of SHG members per month as of March 2009 was ₹ 45 in plain region, ₹ 43 in desert region and ₹ 32 in tribal region.

Average Savings Per Group

In Rajasthan, as per analysis of SHGs promoted by SSV (Sakh-Se-Vikas) partners, total savings (which includes savings in bank plus amount inter-loaned in the group) has been found to be varying from ₹ 1,174 to ₹ 2,500.[117]

The total savings reported in banks of 2,17,007 groups by March 2010 was ₹ 180.19 crore.[118] Assuming that 40 per cent of savings lay idle in bank account,[119] it can be estimated that cumulative saving of SHGs by March 2010 has been ₹ 450 crore. This translates to average saving per group of ₹ 20,751 or average saving per member of ₹ 1730.[120] This conforms to findings of SSV partners.

Comparison of Average Saving Per Group

As per March 2009 figures, the average saving of non-SGSY group in banks was ₹ 6,786 and average savings of SGSY group was ₹ 9,412. The average saving of SGSY group was 23 per cent more than the state average and 27 per cent more than non-SGSY groups. The average saving per SHG is ₹ 9,504 in PSB, ₹ 4,966 in RRB and ₹ 5,958 in cooperative bank.

Estimated Savings of SHGs in Rajasthan (2008–15)

Total savings (money lying in bank account plus that inter-loaned) has been estimated and projected below using some assumptions which are discussed in footnotes.

Table 4.7

Estimated Savings of SHGs in Rajasthan (2008–15)

Particulars	*2007–2008*	*2008–2009*	*2009–2010*	*2010–2011 (Proj.)*	*2011–2012 (Proj.)*	*2012–2013 (Proj.)*	*2013–2014 (Proj.)*	*2014–2015 (Proj.)*
No. of functional SHGs (CmF est.)	1.6	2.1	2.6	3.1	3.6	4.1	4.6	5.1
Assume: saving per member per month	35[121]	45[122]	60	70	80	90	100	110
Savings of SHGs during the year (₹ crore)				225[123]	312	415	531	662
Total savings of SHGs	102	307	450[124]	675	988	1,402	1,934	2,596

Milestone Setting for Banks in Rajasthan

Self-Help Group has to be primarily savings-led model. Therefore, more and more inter-loaning should be promoted among the groups and the practice of parking deposits in banks should be discouraged. However, current practice of banks to impound savings is found to be in direct conflict with long-term vision of savings-led model. Moreover, credit disbursed by banks, compared to saving accumulated by SHGs, is not in tune with expectations. Given this context, banks should aim at milestones discussed in Table 4.8 to promote financial inclusion in Rajasthan.

Table 4.8

Milestones for Banks (2008–15)

Milestones (All figures in ₹ crore)								
Particulars	*2007–2008*	*2008–2009*	*2009–2010*	*2010–2011*	*2011–2012*	*2012–2013*	*2013–2014*	*2014–2015*
Target% of savings lying idle in bank	51%	45%	40%	35%	30%	25%	20%	10%
Target Savings of SHGs with Banks	52.23	138.37	180.18	236.28	296.27	350.57	386.73	259.60
Total savings of SHGs	102.41	307.48	450.45	675	988	1,402	1,934	2,596
Credit to saving ratio	0.99	0.54	0.49	1	1	1	1	1
Credit disbursed by Banks during year	101.68	167.34	219.02	675	988	1,402	1,934	2,596
Credit outstanding to total saving ratio	2.44	1.13	1.11	3	3	3	3	3
Credit outstanding to SHGs by banks	250.04	347.99	501.3	2,025	2,963	4,207	5,801	7,788

As indicated in Table 4.8, firstly, banks should ideally try to reduce SHG savings lying idle in bank accounts so that it can be used for inter-loaning. This would result in more and more funds for inter-loaning and only a minor portion of total savings of SHGs in the bank account.

Secondly, banks should ideally try to improve the 'credit disbursed to total SHG saving' ratio as indicated above. This would happen if annual number of SHGs credit linked is increased substantially and the repeat linkage is encouraged.

Credit

SHGs use their savings to advance loan to group members. Though the amount (members' savings in SHG) is usually small and is not sufficient to meet the total credit need of all members, but the practice of using group savings for loans to members is extremely important and useful. It promotes mutual trust and a financial discipline among members. Considering the total credit outstanding as of March 2009 on one hand and total SHG bank savings as of March 2009 on other hand, it can be deduced that 40 per cent of the outstanding loan to SHGs actually came from their own deposits in banks.[125]

Purpose of Credit

The poor need credit for various purposes. Members of Self-Help Groups have two avenues of raising credit through group membership: inter-loaning and bank loan. An analysis of usage of credit is given in Table 4.9 below.

Table 4.9

Purpose of Credit

Purpose of Credit	*Percentage*
Domestic (comprises: household expenses, debt redemption and social expenses)	90
Illness	54
Agriculture	25
Income generating activities	24
Education	22

An analysis of data provided by DWCD Base Line Survey indicates that almost 90 per cent of SHG members availed credit for domestic purposes while 54 per cent of members availed credit for illness.

Interestingly, only 24 per cent had availed credit for income generation activities. This may be due to the practice that funds used in inter-loaning are lent at higher interest rates[126] than that loan of bank loan. Such practice of having different lending rates for different sources of finance is not appropriate and should be abandoned. Capital employed in an entity is pooled together and invested at same discount rate irrespective of the sources of finance. Similarly, in SHGs, irrespective of the sources of finance (read, inter-loaning and bank credit), lending rates should ideally be the same.

Further, an analysis of data provided by DWCD Base Line Survey indicates that 37 per cent of bank credit availed by SHG members is for income generating activities. This indicates that SHG members feel more comfortable with bank credit (as compared to inter-loaning) when availing loan for income generation activities.

Inter-loaning Among SHGs

In SHGs promoted by SSV partners, percentage of SHG savings inter-loaned within members has been found to be around 90 per cent.[127] This indicates that savings lying idle in bank is less than 10 per cent.

In SHGs promoted by DWCD which is leading SHPI in Rajasthan, percentage of savings lying idle in bank is 33 per cent[128] in 2009–10. By March 2009, as per analysis of Base Line Survey of DWCD, on an average, 73 per cent of groups had done inter-loaning.

However, internal studies by CmF, Jaipur indicate that well over 50 per cent of savings of SHGs, especially in case of credit linked SHGs is deposited in banks. Therefore, in this entire report, it has been conservatively assumed that fund lying idle in bank accounts is 40 per cent of total SHG savings.

Average Credit Per Member

Not many studies have been conducted that research the credit availing pattern among SHG members in the groups. Further, using macro-level data to compute the average credit per member may be misleading owing to the fact that in majority of cases, credit is not distributed among SHG members on need basis. An analysis of data provided by DWCD Base Line Survey indicates that majority of credit distributed among group members is in following two ways:

1. Distributing credit equally among all group members irrespective of their needs.
2. Distributing credit to only 1–2 persons in the group.

Such practices of distributing credit are unhealthy, since they do not promote group solidarity and peer pressure. Only when more than 60 per cent of group members avail credit, that peer pressure and group solidarity comes into play. As per analysis of DWCD data, only in very few cases credit has been distributed to 6–8 members (among total of 12 members).

Therefore, neither a credible study exists for such an analysis nor a credible approach exists for analysis of computing average credit per member.

SHG Federation in Rajasthan

Many Self-Help Groups in Rajasthan have come out of their first phase of formation. Now many SHPIs are in consolidation stage and are exploring the idea of promoting second and third tier structures (people's institutions, e.g. SHG clusters and SHG Federations) of SHGs to make their microfinance programmes self-sustaining.

In Rajasthan, the SHGs are grouped together in clusters to build social capital of women. Clusters are usually formed by clubbing 10–15 SHGs across 2–4 villages or a gram panchayat. Currently, geographic proximity of SHGs plays a key role in determining the membership of SHGs in such clusters. These clusters are generally unregistered and operate as a tier between the federation and SHGs.

About 10–20 such clusters aggregate to form Federations, functioning mostly at sub-block level. The Federations are mostly registered as societies, or trusts or companies (Sec-25 of Companies Act). There are also many un-registered federations in Rajasthan. Thus, a SHG Federation normally has 100–250 SHGs as its members comprising total of 1,500 to 4,000 women each.

In Rajasthan, SHG federations are, unfortunately, promoter centric and do not follow an area approach or need-based approach. In other words, SHPIs club together SHGs promoted by themselves to promote a federation structure. Interestingly, all SHG Federations in the state have been facilitated by voluntary organizations. Government departments like Department of Women and Child Development and Department of Rural Development (under SGSY) are yet to promote any SHG Federation.

However, there is a divided opinion (mainly among the promoters) on federations performing a financial intermediation role. Irrespective of the opinion, almost half of the SHG federations in Rajasthan are engaged in some form of financial intermediation role. Some of them term themselves as Community Based Microfinance Institutions (CBMFIs) and have been accessing bulk finances for on-lending. Some of the federations call themselves 'Mahila Banks' (women's banks). Federations have shown their willingness to develop performance standards, undertake self-rating and have also undergone quality assessment (rating) by a third party to access loans from financial institutions. Many federations have demonstrated both operational and financial self-sufficiency by covering their costs.

Number and Composition of SHG Federations in Rajasthan

There are about 312 SHG clusters and 42 SHG Federations in Rajasthan as of March 2010 (see Table 4.10).

Table 4.10

SHG Federations in Rajasthan as of March 2010

Clusters	312
Federations	42
No. of Promoters	24
Registered Secondary Federation	20
Under Trust Act	9
Under Cooperatives Act	7
Under Rajasthan Societies Act	3

Why SHG Federations?

Promotion of SHG federations has various motivations. The primary motivation is to strengthen the SHG movement. Federations, because of sheer volume of members, empowers poor to 'voice' their opinion and get things done, be it at government level or bank level.

The second motivation is from SHPI's perspective. SHGs clubbed together are easier to manage. As the number of SHGs increases, the promoter finds it increasingly difficult to monitor individual SHGs. However, clusters and federations present a platform to simplify monitoring of SHGs in a cost-effective manner.

The third motivation is to strengthen the poors' capability and empower them to an extent that they undertake business activity on their own. In other words, federations of SHGs undertake financial intermediation (bulk loan from Banks/NBFCs and on-lending to SHGs) by themselves without support of SHPIs, thereby releasing SHPIs resources, which can then focus on other key issues.

The fourth motivation is multiple utility of SHG federations. Apart from financial intermediation, SHG federations have also demonstrated significant progress in their engagements on other issues like education, health and sanitation, etc.

Benefits of SHG Federations

SHG federations serve a role of multi-utility vehicle for SHGs. Federations have been successful in supporting livelihoods of SHG members (by providing services like veterinary care, supply of agricultural inputs, cattle feed, etc.) and have been instrumental in improving bank linkage of SHGs. A major benefit of federations to SHGs and their members is the empowerment and the improved solidarity among SHG women. The SHG members, through federations, have got a 'voice' which help them to get heard in a bank, municipality office or any other government department. This has led to increased confidence among women that they too can make a difference in their society and their life.

Another benefit is lower cost of credit. Though the rate of interest in case of SHG federations is relatively higher by 2–4 per cent p.a., the SHG members save plenty of time and money which they would have otherwise spent in following up banks had they approached the banks alone. Through federation structure, SHGs have been able to access insurance services, which they might not have fetched otherwise.

Another key benefit of SHG federation, not stated above, is simplification of record keeping and generation of regular reports through management information system (MIS), which is not possible at SHG level.

Issues Faced by SHG Federations in Rajasthan[129]

SHG federations in Rajasthan are in the very early stage and promoting agencies are making efforts to develop them as 'vibrant people's organizations'. Considering the fact that most of the SHG members and their leaders are poor, illiterate and socially marginalized, it will take some time before these federations emerge as strong organizations.

Some of the issues/areas for action regarding SHG federations in Rajasthan are:

1. Lack of a clear perspective and clear vision about federations among SHG members.
2. Lack of capacity in federation leaders on organization development, planning, management, etc.
3. Lack of resources (financial support) in the early stages of federation when their revenues are also not streamlined.
4. Availability of qualified staff (at the salary that federations can afford), and lack of appropriate legal structure to operate.

SHG federations in Rajasthan are currently promoter-centric, heavily guided by the perspective and organizational culture of the promoting organization. Federations should be as per the members' needs and, therefore, preferably location-centric or community-centric. The experiences tell that a federation does not become self-sustaining until it comprises 3,000 women (about 150–200 SHGs) and the area of operation is limited to 15 km radius.

Cost Benefit Analysis of SHG Federations

Cost of promoting and nurturing a SHG over a period of about 5 years is over ₹ 10 lakh.[130] This capital cannot be borne by SHG federation during formation stage. However, once the operation starts, SHG federations have been found to be running at operational self-sufficiency of about 76–113 per cent.[131] Taking into account the intangible benefits of federation to members, the benefits of federations are higher than its costs. A quantitative cost benefit analysis of SHG federations is not feasible owing to the fact that

1. it is difficult to attribute benefits occurring to one specific entity (SHG or SHG federation or even SHPI);
2. benefits involve lot of intangible benefits like women empowerment, enhancement of solidarity among women,

common 'voice', etc. which cannot be quantified but are key benefits of SHG federations.

Even then, if one were to estimate only incremental 'tangible' benefits attributable to SHG federations, one may conclude that benefits are higher than the costs.[132]

Revenue source of SHG Federations includes membership fees from members and interest income from on-lending. For example, in case of Saheli Samiti, Dausa and Savera Mahila Manch, Alwar, revenue sources are given in tables 4.11 and 4.12.

Table 4.11

Operating Income Sources of SHG Federations

Operating Income Sources	*% of Earnings*	
	Savera Mahila Manch, Alwar	*Saheli Samiti, Dausa*
Interest and fee income from loans	36.13%	0%
Income from other finance-related services	50.29%	95.09%
Miscellaneous income	13.5%	4.91%

Expenditure of SHG federations includes personnel expenses and administrative expenses. For example, in case of Saheli Samiti, Dausa and Savera Mahila Manch, Alwar, expenditure items were as follows:

Table 4.12

Operation Expenditure Sources of SHG Federations

Operating Expenditure Sources	*% of Earnings*	
	Savera Mahila Manch, Alwar	*Saheli Samiti, Dausa*
Personnel Expenses	78.47%	54.82%
Administrative Expenses	21.31%	45.18%
Other Operational Expenses	0.23%	0%

Loan Defaults by SHGs

In Rajasthan, repayment rate in case of SHGs has been understood to be higher than 95 per cent. Repayment rate is important because future bank linkage depends heavily on repayment rate of SHGs. Recent studies especially NABARD publication has informed that loan defaults are an emerging concern. However, no analysis has been conducted so far that goes deeper into the issue of SHG NPAs and SHG overdues. CmF recently concluded a study on SHG loan defaults to assess and analyse the status and reasons of the NPA and overdues of bank loans by SHGs in Rajasthan

Reasons for SHG Loan Defaults

The study reveals that NPA and overdue is a serious challenge to SHG bank linkage, which is a major propellant for growth of SHGs. The study highlights the following as the main characteristics of default SHG groups in Rajasthan.

First, the default groups have, in general, received inadequate attention to the processes of forging cooperative interaction among the members. Any social group evolves through phases of coming together, learning to work together, developing norms of engagement and finally being able to work together in an interdependent and flexible manner. Most of the groups in the study have not gone through such an evolutionary process. A brief summary of the major manifestations of lack of focus:

Aspects	*Observation*	*Remarks*
Process of group formation	Promoted to fulfil targets (esp. of govt. promoted SHGs) not only of numbers, but also of subsidy distribution; led to faulty selection of members (convenient members, relatives)	For BPL groups, target is chased by DRDA by putting pressure on banks to distribute loans
Development of group dynamics and evolution of group processes	Follows from above; reflected in irregular meetings/improper minuting of meetings; passivity of members; disproportionate accrual of benefits to only a few; gradual reduction in attendance in meetings	44 per cent of the groups show a decline over the years in the ratio of number of actual meetings to expected meetings

Cont'd...

Cont'd...

Leadership development	Permanent leaders, often the ones with power and resources; lack of knowledge on the part of the members about the rules and structure of leadership	Only 3 per cent of the groups surveyed ever changed their leaders

Second, the study found that there is widespread negligence among the default groups with respect to maintaining even the critical financial records regularly. This had led to misappropriation of benefits of the scheme by the leaders, who often are the only literate members. Only 10 per cent SHGs have all the required records regularly updated. One-fifth of the groups could not present their minutes books/attendance registers and, of those who could, 70 per cent have not updated them. Similarly, though 65 per cent of all groups surveyed could present their loan and savings ledgers, two-thirds of them have not updated the entries.

Third, there is a general lack of understanding of the strengths of SHGs and the ways of working with banks. Saving and inter-loaning are considered as two crucial functions of SHGs and as very critical to generating and consolidating cooperative group behaviour. However, only half of the SHGs reported any such lending using group fund and 9 per cent of these SHGs did not report any saving members. Lack of basic knowledge about banking and lack of financial literacy are the other two striking features of the defaulted SHGs.

Continuous drought situation, low levels of economic activity and poor income are found as the major triggering factors that accelerated the process of group degeneration and eventual default. About a fifth of the groups cited poor economic status of members as the major reason for defaulting repayment. Paradoxically, in one of the districts, many BPL groups ended up having multiple bank loans as they were reportedly pressurized to purchase animals as part of SGSY scheme. Most of these groups, obviously, ended as defaulters.

The poor households are not educated as to how to make the best use of subsidy. Many of the government promoted groups are formed by using the carrot of subsidy interpreted as 'free money' – to attract women to join groups. Groups have not been educated as to how subsidy reduces the cost of credit. This has led to negative promotion of subsidy support, which, in effect, has prevented the poorer households from taking advantage of schemes like SGSY.

Bank Linkage of SHGs in Rajasthan

Banks play a pivotal role in delivery of microfinance services to the poor through Self-Help Group Bank Linkage Programme. SHGs avail credit from banks apart from using own funds for consumption and livelihood promotion activities. We now look at banking infrastructure in Rajasthan, its growth trends and developments in SHG bank linkage programme and how it may affect the future of SHG movement in India. The discussion also covers the impounding of savings by banks, which is affecting the progress of SHG bank linkage today.

Banking Infrastructure

The state has a bank network of 4,655 branches comprising of commercial banks (3,042), regional rural banks or RRBs (1,052) and cooperative banks (561) as of March 2010. There are 43 commercial banks, six RRBs and 29 district cooperative banks in the state (Table 4.13).

The number of bank branches in the state has shown a steady increase over the years. It can be seen from Table 4.13 above that the bank branches have shown an increase in numbers over 2007, 2008 and 2009. The rural branches have increased by 1.9 per cent, semi-urban by 8.14 per cent and urban branches by 9.07 per cent over the last 1 year.

The population per branch in Rajasthan is 15,292 which have decreased gradually over the years (Table 4.14 and Figure 4.7).

Table 4.13

Number of Bank Branches in Rajasthan

Bank Name	*Branches (March 2007)*	*Branch (March 2008)*	*Branches (March 2009)*				*Branches (March 2010)*			
			Rural	*SU*	*Urban*	*Total*	*Rural*	*SU*	*Urban*	*Total*
Commercial Banks	2,508	2,668	995	786	1,080	2,861	1,014	850	1,178	3,042
RRBs	1,015	1,022	810	181	49	1,040	814	187	51	1,052
Cooperative Banks	534	549	189	286	83	558	189	287	85	561
Total	4,057	4,239	1,994	1,253	1,212	4,459	2,017	1,327	1,314	4,655

Table 4.14

Population Per Bank Branch in Rajasthan

Year	*March 2007*	*March 2008*	*March 2009*	*March 2010*
Population per branch	16,245	15,952	15,559	15,292

Figure 4.7

Population Per Bank Branch in Rajasthan

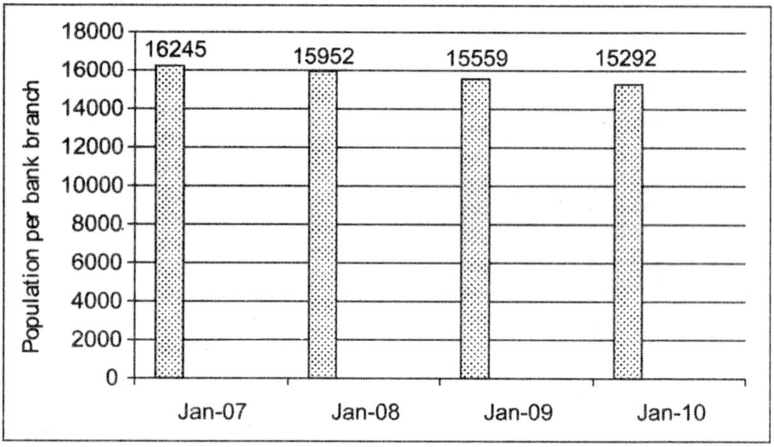

It is interesting to note that growth of branches in rural areas has not been commensurate with the population growth. This may be an indicator that branches of banks in rural areas are not as profitable as those in urban/semi-urban areas. Moreover, an analysis of growth of human resource in banks indicates that personnel are more inclined towards working in urban/semi-urban areas rather than in rural areas. This has resulted in very low bank personnel to branch ratio in rural areas. Therefore, low growth of bank branches in rural areas and further, lower number of personnel in rural branches has resulted in poor service for rural clients. This is validated by feedback received from members of SHG groups.

The total bank deposit in Rajasthan was ₹ 1,17,375 crore (SLBC, March 2009–10) registering a growth of 19.25 per cent over last year. The bank credit was ₹ 1,01,817 crore (SLBC, March 2009–10) registering a growth of 25.24 per cent over last year.

Population in District Per Bank Branch in Rajasthan

An analysis of population per district per bank branch in Rajasthan indicates that districts which are under-banked are the very districts that fall low on SHG 'Saturation Index'. This shows that SHG movement and bank presence in a district has high positive correlation.

In Rajasthan, Nagaur, Dholpur, Dausa, Karouli, Barmer and Jalaur are under-banked. These are also the districts where SHG movement has been found to be weak as per SHG 'Saturation Index'.

Moreover, Jhalawar, Dungarpur, Bhilwara, Bundi and Chittorgarh have strong bank presence. These are also the districts where SHG movement has been found to be strong as per SHG 'Saturation Index'.

Priority Sector Lending in Rajasthan

Analysis of priority sector advances indicates that though there is net increase in credit outflow to total priority sector, there is constant decrease in percentage of priority sector advances to total advances. Similar trends also reflect in advances to agriculture, i.e. though there is net increase in credit outflow except in 2009, there is constant decrease in percentage of agriculture advances to total advances.

In year 2009, total agriculture credit decreased by about ₹ 500 crore in Rajasthan. This is the year when loan waiver scheme was implemented for encouraging fresh loans to small and marginal farmers. The share of agriculture credit from banks has decreased from 34.56 per cent in 2007 to 27.4 per cent in 2010 (Table 4.15).

Table 4.15

Priority Sector Advances in Rajasthan

Parameters	*March 2007*	*March 2008*	*March 2009*	*March 2010*
Total Priority sector advances	34,388	40,854	43,033	49,493
% age of PS advances to Total Advances	56.65%	56.57%	52.93%	48.61%
Total Agriculture Advances	20,977	24,659	24,155	27,899
% age of Agriculture advances to Total advances	34.56%	34.15%	29.71%	27.40%
Total advances to weaker sections	5,981	7,666	10,300	1,3197

SHG Bank Credit Linkage

Analysis from SGSY and non-SGSY perspective – based on credit disbursed during the year.

There is substantial difference between figures reported by SLBC and NABARD. For example, if data from SLBC is trusted, then SHGs under SGSY have received a credit of ₹ 86.40 crore in 2008–09. However, as per data published by NABARD, SHGs under SGSY have received a credit of ₹ 44.59 crore in 2008–09. It is somewhat difficult to choose between the two sources of information. However, we decided to use NABARD data because it has been published.

In 2008 and 2009, the percentage of SHGs which have got credit linked has come down.

In Rajasthan, even though SGSY groups comprised only 8–16 per cent of total groups, the credit disbursed to them was 20–27 per cent. This is reversal of trend at national level. At all-India level, SGSY groups comprise around 25 per cent of total groups while the credit disbursed to them is only around 15 per cent. It indicates that the focus in Rajasthan is mainly on SGSY groups.

Table 4.16

Bank Typewise Credit Linkage
(number of SHG loans disbursed)

Year	*Commercial Banks*		*Regional Rural Banks*		*Cooperative Banks*	
	No. of SHG Loans	*Growth w.r.t. 2005–06*	*No. of SHG Loans*	*Growth w.r.t. 2005–06*	*No. of SHG Loans*	*Growth w.r.t. 2007–08*
2005–06	19,184		12,637		NA	
2006–07	18,445	–3.8%	13,923	+10%	NA	
2007–08	14,823	–22.73%	10,533	–24%	11,864	
2008–09	9,729	–49.28%	7,949	–25%	10,639	–10%

Source: Agenda notes of meetings of SLBC, Rajasthan

Commercial Banks and Regional Rural Banks

Overall the commercial banks' annual SHG-Bank linkage has fallen drastically as of March 2009. There are only four commercial banks that link more than 1,000 SHGs annually and they are SBBJ, Bank of Baroda, PNB, and SBI. Another two banks (OBC and CBI) have linked 576 and 543 SHGs during 08–09. Rest all banks have insignificant SHG-Bank linkage, i.e. less than 500 SHGs. All six regional rural banks have SHG linkage, however, the number of SHGs annually getting linked with RRBs are also showing a downward trend.

Cooperative Banks

As of March 2010, there are 29 District Cooperative Banks in Rajasthan covering all 33 districts. There are 5,259 primary agriculture societies – PACS (popularly called Gram Sahakari Seva Samities or GSS) in the state and there are 404 branches of cooperative banks across the state. Credit disbursed to SHGs during the year has decreased over last year, which is in conjunction with declining trend in number of SHG loans during the year.

Cross-sectional Analysis as of March 2009 – Comparison Among Banks

During 2008–09, Cooperative Banks surpassed commercial banks in terms of number of SHG loans, though in terms of amount of loan to SHGs, the commercial banks still have the lead.

Performance of Rajasthan Relative to that of Rest of India

Analysis indicates that performance is mixed (Table 4.17).

A study of NABARD annual report for 2007–08 and 2008–09 indicates that percentage share of Rajasthan in India has increased on parameters like:

1. Savings of SHGs with banks (which is not desirable and thus, a negative trend);
2. Bank loans disbursed to SHGs during the year (positive trend);
3. Bank loans outstanding against SHGs (positive trend).

Table 4.17

Percentage Share of Rajasthan Over All-India Figures

	2007–08			*2008–09*		
	Rajasthan	*All India*	*% Share of Rajasthan*	*Rajasthan*	*All-India*	*% Share of Rajasthan*
Savings of SHG with banks (₹ lakh)	5,223	3,78,589	1.38%	13,837	5,54,562	2.50%
Bank loans disbursed to SHGs during the year (₹ lakh)	10,168	8,84,926	1.15%	16,734	12,25,351	1.37%
Bank loans outstanding against SHGs (₹ lakh)	25,004	16,99,991	1.47%	36,655	22,67,984	1.62%

Average Credit Per SHG Disbursed During the Year 2008–09

Analysis indicates that average for Rajasthan is 35 per cent less than all-India average.

Average Credit Disbursed Per SHG[133]

Average credit disbursed in PSB is ₹ 80,252, in RRBs is ₹ 44,240 and in Cooperative Bank is ₹ 45,559. Average credit is ₹ 56,368 which is 35 per cent less than national average.

Saving Bank Accounts of SHGs in Rajasthan[134]

The number of SHGs having bank accounts in Rajasthan has increased from 22,742 in March 2003 to 2,17,007 by 31 March 2010.[135]

In Rajasthan, by March 2009, total 1,92,479 SHGs had their accounts in various banks. It included SHGs formed under SGSY (29,495 SHG, 15%) as well as non-SGSY SHGs (1,62,984 SHGs, 85%). Total saving of all these SHGs deposited in Banks was ₹ 13,837.49 lakh with average of ₹ 7,189 per SHG. However, it may be noted here that the savings of SHGs are supposed to be used as loan to members by the group.

Number of SHGs with savings bank account is 1,92,479 out of which 84,767 (45.6%) are in public sector scheduled commercial bank (PSB), 1,898 (1%) are in private schedules commercial bank, 59,625 (31%) are in RRBs and 46,189 (22.4%) are in cooperative banks (Table 4.18 and Figure 4.8).

Table 4.18

Number of SHGs Having S/B Accounts and Amount of Savings in Banks

Banks	*No. of SHGs Having S/B Accounts*	*Amount of Savings in Banks (₹ Lakh)*
Scheduled Commercial Banks	86,665	8,124.01
Regional Rural Banks	59,625	2,961.50
Cooperative Banks	46,159	2,751.98
Total	1,92,479	13,837.49

Figure 4.8

SHGs Having S/B Accounts and Amount of Saving in Banks

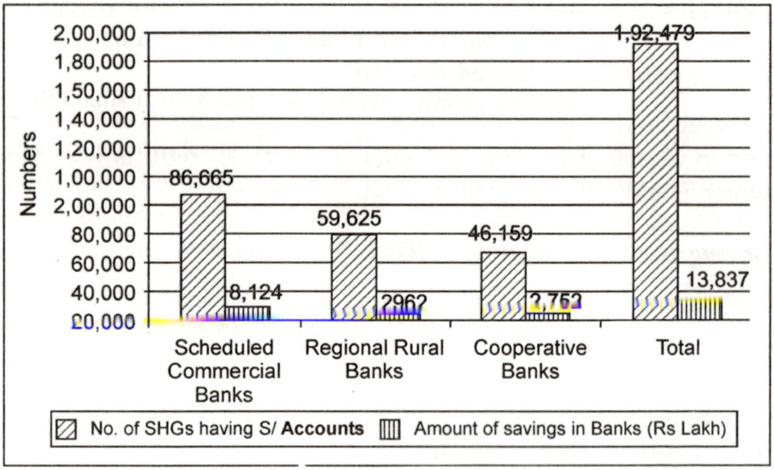

Amount of SHG Savings in Banks

Commercial banks are leading in having SHG saving with 59 per cent share, followed by RRBs with 21 per cent share and cooperative banks with 20 per cent.

Leading Banks in Rajasthan in SHG Bank Linkage

In terms of PSB, SBBJ serves highest number of SHGs, i.e. 29,850 (35% of total SHGs in public sector scheduled commercial bank) followed by PNB with 15,910 and BoB with 14,220. In terms of RRBs, Baroda Rajasthan Gramin Bank (BRGB) leading the way with 19,960 SHGs (43% of total SHGs in RRBs) followed by Rajasthan Garmin Bank with 11,764 SHG and MGB Grameen Bank with 10,554 SHGs.

Issues in SHG Bank Linkage Programme

Impounding of Savings by Banks

Many SHGs and SHG promoting organizations have raised the issue of 'impounding of savings of SHGs by banks' while providing them the credit. Impounding is disadvantageous to the SHGs as they pay higher interest rates even when their own savings are lying idle in banks. Besides the basic idea of meeting the credit needs of members from their savings get defeated if the savings are held by banks.

Main observations of the study conducted by Centre for Microfinance, Jaipur

The bankwise data gives clear indication that impounding of SHG savings is a practice across banks. In all the banks the savings of credit linked SHGs in banks were found to be more than that of non-credit linked SHGs.

- More than 80 per cent of the total savings of the SHGs especially in the case of credit linked SHGs is deposited in the banks.
- The average savings of SHGs in banks is ₹ 7,890 as of March 2009. Further, it is ₹ 3,714 for those which are not credit linked while ₹ 10,779 for those which are credit linked. It shows that SHGs who are taking credit from banks also deposit higher amounts in the bank. This indicates the impounding of SHG savings by Banks.

Though the credit linked SHGs are 59 per cent, their share of total SHG deposits in the bank is 80 per cent. It clearly illustrates that SHGs which are credit linked have to deposit more savings with banks.

The prime purpose of Self-Help Group movement is to use the savings in groups to advance loans to members (because these members do not have access to banks for credit and have to take loans from moneylenders on highly exploitative terms). But over a period of time, both SHG promoters and banks have kept this basic principle aside, and now SHGs are encouraged by promoters (and compelled by banks) to keep their savings with banks. In Rajasthan, ₹ 138 crore of SHG savings was sitting with banks by end of March 2009. This amount is almost 40 per cent of total savings by SHGs. Actually, this amount should have been rotating as loan to members.

It would be unfair to blame only banks for keeping the SHG savings with them, though branch managers of banks make all efforts to impound the SHG savings while giving loan to SHGs. But largely it is SHG promoters who do not educate SHGs and do not make necessary efforts of using the savings of members for advancing loan to them. It is very hard to justify when SHG members keep their saving in saving account (earning 3% per annum) and same members continue borrowing from banks at 12 per cent and moneylenders at 36 per cent per annum. With this calculation in 2008–09, SHGs as a sector, earned an interest of about ₹ 4.8 crore on their savings of 138 crore in banks and paid ₹ 15.2 crore to banks as interest on the same amount, thus making a net loss of ₹ 10.4 crore. This raises a question for both SHG promoters and banks on the purpose of SHG movement.

The situation is getting worse every year because as on March 2010 the SHG savings in banks were reported at ₹ 180.18 crore while the credit to all SHGs (including SGSY) was reported at ₹ 219 crore.

Further analysis of bank's data reveals that, in Rajasthan, the average credit outstanding is 2.64 times of total savings in banks. Comparing this figure with average credit to margin money ratio of 56 times[136] reveals that banks impound savings in case of SHGs.

Table 4.19

Credit Outstanding vs Savings Ratio for SHGs as of March 2009: Commercial Banks

Bank	*Total Savings*	*Total Outstanding*	*Credit: Saving Ratio for SHGs*
BoB	3,636.9	3,221.04	0.88
SBI	376.61	5,234.22	13.89
SBBJ	484.61	4,565.66	9.42
PNB	675.34	2,344.77	3.47
DENA	1,364.68	3,159	2.31
UCO	977.82	302.42	0.31
Total	13,837.49	36,654.6	2.65

Table 4.19 indicates that SBBJ and SBI are not impounding savings and are giving higher priority to SHG lending. On other hand, Bank of Baroda and UCO Bank fall way below the standards. These banks are impounding SHG savings.

RRBs too seem to be impounding savings. Jaipur Thar Gramin Bank has credit to saving ratio of 1.4 which means that only ₹ 1.5 of credit is given to SHGs for every ₹ 1 of saving of SHG in bank. This indicates that Jaipur Thar Gramin Bank is running almost risk free as it keeps 67 per cent of collateral for each loan disbursed to SHGs (Table 4.20).

Table 4.20

Credit Outstanding vs *Savings Ratio for SHGs as of March 2009: Regional Rural Bank*

Bank	*Total Savings*	*Total Outstanding*	*Credit : Saving Ratio for SHGs*
Baroda Rajasthan Gramin Bank	779.69	2,715.41	3.5
Hadoti KGB	173.19	569.86	3.3
Jaipur Thar Gramin Bank	638.29	884.26	1.4
Mewar Aanchalik GB	197.68	472	2.4
MGB Grameen Bank	713.09	1,505.14	2.1
Rajasthan Gramin Bank	459.56	1,566.34	3.4
Total	2,961.5	7,713.01	2.6

Cooperative Banks

The outstanding amount of cooperative bank is 2.96 times the saving amount.

The overall analysis clearly reflects that all three agencies, i.e. PSB, RRBs and cooperative are having similar ratio of outstanding in respect to savings (except SBI and SBBJ). Cooperative banks as a group fare a little better. Furthermore, the savings of SHGs are also lying in large chunks with PSB. First-hand conclusion is that many banks are more interested in savings mobilization from SHGs rather than giving credit. On the other hand, performance of SBI and SBBJ can be an example for the microfinance sector as they maintain appreciable outstanding ratio of 13.89 and 9.42 times respectively.

Banks should instruct their branch managers that they should not keep the savings of the SHGs seeking credit from banks. Banks must encourage withdrawal of savings by SHGs and its use as inter-loan among members.

Lack of Awareness among Banks' Staff

In linkage-banking programme, often the SHGs find it difficult/time consuming (necessitating repeated visits to the bank branch) for opening account/getting credit linked. Continuous efforts are needed to build awareness/knowledge of rural branch staff (who is frequently changed and new staff takes over) about the linkage banking programme and the simplified/user friendly procedures needed for their account opening/credit linkage, etc. The banks also need to bring about necessary changes in the working of their rural branches to accommodate this development. With introduction of business correspondent model by RBI, the experience of SHGs is expected to improve over time.

Inadequate Monitoring

At present, progress is monitored more on 'number of groups' linked. While it is important to track the number of groups linked, the 'number of repeat loans' and 'size of loans' should also be important indicators of monitoring.

Focus on Achieving Targets

State government has been focusing on achieving 'number of SHG' target only, rather than achieving 'real objectives of SHG bank linkage programme'. The focus should be towards achieving 'quality' rather than 'quantity'.

Lack of SHG Database in Rajasthan for Planning and Monitoring

A database of SHGs does not exist in the State. Figures from various government departments, NGOs, SLBC and NABARD are sometimes conflicting and sometimes fail to give any direction. A reliable, credible database of SHGs at state level will help in policy making and development of credible schemes.

Notes

1. 'Microfinance and NGOs', article available through Kumarappa Institute of Gram Swaraj.
2. 'The Role of Central Banks in Microfinance in Asia and the Pacific: Overview – ADB.org'. *Asian Development Bank: Fighting Poverty in Asia and the Pacific – ADB.org*. Web, 17 June 2010. <http://www.adb.org/Documents/Books/Central_Banks_Microfinance/Overview/chap_02.pdf>.
3. Ledgerwood, Joanna, *Microfinance Handbook: An Institutional and Financial Perspective, Sustainable Banking with the Poor,* accessed online at http://books.google.co.in
4. Ibid.
5. Ibid.
6. Ibid.
7. Ibid.
8. Ibid.
9. Ibid.
10. Ibid.
11. Ibid.
12. Ibid.
13. Ibid.
14. Ibid.
15. Ibid.
16. Ibid.
17. Ibid.
18. Ibid.
19. Ibid.
20. Ibid.

21. Ibid.
22. Ibid.
23. Ibid.
24. Ibid.
25. Ibid.
26. Ibid.
27. 'Microfinance and NGOs', op. cit.
28. Ibid.
29. Thakur, Sarojini Ganju and Tiwari, Anand Mohan, 'Whether SHG-based micro-credit programmes can remove poverty? A case study of SHG-based programmes in Patan District of Gujarat', article available through Kumarappa Institute of Gram Swaraj.
30. Ibid.
31. Ibid.
32. NABARD, 'Status of Microfinance in India 2007–2008' Publication available through Kumarappa Institute of Gram Swaraj.
33. Reddy, C.S. and Manak, Sandeep, 'Self-Help Groups: A Keystone of Microfinance in India, Women empowerment and social security', article available through Kumarappa Institute of Gram Swaraj.
34. Ibid.
35. Ibid.
36. Srinivasan, N. 'Microfinance India, State of the Sector Report 2008'.
37. Ibid.
38. Reddy, C.S. and Manak, Sandeep, op. cit.
39. Ibid.
40. Ibid.
41. Ibid.
42. Ibid.
43. Ibid.
44. Ibid.
45. Ibid.
46. Ibid.
47. Ibid.
48. Ibid.
49. Ibid.

50. Ibid.
51. Ledgerwood, Joanna, op. cit.
52. Ibid.
53. Ibid.
54. Ibid.
55. Ibid.
56. Ibid.
57. Ibid.
58. Ibid.
59. SHGs outstanding credit as of March 2009 was ₹ 347.9936 crore while credit disbursed during last year was ₹ 219.02 crore. Assuming that in conservative scenario, only 30 per cent of credit disbursed to SHGs was repaid in last year, then the total credit outstanding to SHGs till March 2010 would be ₹ 501.3 crore. Comparing this with conservative estimates of outstanding credit of MFIs as ₹ 527 crore one can conclude that MFI credit has surpassed SHG Credit outstanding.
60. Primary Survey conducted by CmF, Jaipur.
61. For example, gross remuneration paid to managing director of SKS for year ended March 2009 was ₹ 3.28 crore and that to CEO of SKS for year ended March 2010 was ₹ 2.45 crore. In comparison, gross remuneration paid to managing director of India's second largest private bank ICICI for year 2009–2010 was ₹ 1.62 crore. In another example, the managerial remuneration of the managing director of Share Microfin Ltd was around ₹ 2.29 crore. In 2008–09 it shot up to ₹ 8.08 crore, by far not only the highest remuneration in the microfinance sector, but way above the remuneration obtained by the CEO of the largest private sector bank ICICI Bank as discussed above. The remuneration paid to the managing director was around 7 per cent of the total personnel cost of SML in 2007–08 and shot up to 15 per cent of the personnel cost of the company in 2008–09.
62. 'Microfinance Gateway. What Is Microfinance?' Web, 20 June 2010. <http://www.microfinancegateway.com/section/faq>.
63. Ledgerwood, Joanna, op. cit.
64. 'Microfinance Gateway. What Is Microfinance?' op. cit.
65. Ledgerwood, Joanna, op. cit.

66. 'Microfinance – 10 Lessons from the International Experience.' *India Microfinance Business News*. Web, 20 June 2010. <http://indiamicro finance.com/microfinance–10-lessons-from-the-international-experience.html>.
67. Ibid.
68. Ibid.
69. Ledgerwood, Joanna, op. cit.
70. Ibid.
71. Ibid.
72. Ibid.
73. 'Microfinance – 10 Lessons from the International Experience.' op. cit.
74. Vandenburg, Paul, 'Poverty Reduction through Small Enterprises, Emerging consensus, unresolved issues and ILO activities', article available through Kumarappa Institute of Gram Swaraj.
75. Ibid.
76. 'Microfinance Gateway. What Is Microfinance?' op. cit.
77. 'Types of Risks Faced by Microfinance Institutions – Part 1.' *India Microfinance Business News*. Web. 30 June 2010. <http://indiamicr ofinance.com/types-risks-faced-microfinance-institutions.html>.
78. Ibid.
79. Ibid.
80. Ibid.
81. Ibid.
82. Ibid.
83. NABARD, 'Report of the Committee on Financial Inclusion, Chapter 11 Micro-insurance'. Web, 30 June 2010. <http://www.nabard.org/report_comfinancial.asp>.
84. Ibid.
85. Ibid.
86. Ibid.
87. Ibid.
88. Ibid.
89. Ibid.
90. Ibid.
91. Ibid.
92. Ibid.

93. Ibid.
94. Ibid.
95. Ibid.
96. Ibid.
97. Vandenburg, Paul, op. cit.
98. Thakur, Sarojini Ganju and Tiwari, Anand Mohan, op. cit.
99. Ibid.
100. Ibid.
101. DWCD 2009–10.
102. Three voluntary agencies Lupin, BCT and URMUL have formed SHGs under ICDS programme.
103. Under SGSY, total SHGs reported are 2,09,412 but it was found that many of SHGs are actually not formed but reported. Therefore, all SHGs having passed grade 1, and SHGs formed but yet to be graded (about 20% of graded SHGs) are reported here. On enquiry, it was told that 75 per cent of the groups are formed by NGOs and 25 per cent by others.
104. NABARD had reported 7,897 SHGs formed by NGOs from their support till 2007, additional 3,172 SHGs were formed later.
105. DPIP project evaluation. Anecdotal reports claim that only about 30 per cent CIGs formed under DPIP are functioning.
106. Internal Research of CmF.
107. Cooperative Department has reported 44,047 SHGs formed but it appears that all those SHGs who have accounts in cooperatives (irrespective of who has formed those SHGs) are reported by the department. So there is some double reporting here.
108. Others: Watershed Development (9,400); Literacy Mission (12,977); RCDF (5,168); Forest (145).
109. Ledgerwood, Joanna, op. cit.
110. Assuming growth in rural population at 2.6 per cent p.a., rural population was 4.32 crore in 2001 in Rajasthan (Source: Population Census 2001). It is also assumed that average number of members per household, which was found as 5.6 in Population Census 2001, still holds good.
111. Study of SHGs in 7 districts of Rajasthan by CmF.
112. Number of BPL households in Rajasthan as of March 2010 is 21,19,352. Source: bpl2002.raj.nic.in

113. SGSY Progress Report 2007–10 Department of Rural Development GoR.
114. www.dpipraj.gov.in accessed on 18th August 2010.
115. Study of SHGs in 7 districts of Rajasthan by CmF.
116. The Baseline Survey of Women SHGs, DWCD.
117. Average saving per member in Ibtada is ₹ 2,131, in Pradan is ₹ 1,174, in Srijan is ₹ 1,870 and in PEDO is ₹ 2,500.
118. Page 34, 105 Meeting Agenda of SLBC, Rajasthan, 2010.
119. In SHGs promoted by DWCD which is leading SHPI in Rajasthan, percentage of savings lying idle is 33 per cent in 2009–10. However, internal studies by CmF Jaipur indicate that well over 50 per cent of savings of SHGs, especially in case of credit linked SHGs is deposited in banks. Therefore, conservatively, it has been assumed that fund lying idle in the bank accounts is 40 per cent of total SHG savings.
120. Assuming 12 members per SHG.
121. Rajasthan Microfinance Sector Report 2007.
122. DWCD Base line survey of women SHGS, March 2009.
123. Assuming 12 members per SHG with ₹ 60 average saving per month per member and 2.6 lakh SHGs.
124. CmF had projected total SHG savings of ₹ 384 crore in Rajasthan in Rajasthan Microfinance Report 2007. By March 2010 the total SHG savings is estimated to be ₹ 450 crore owing to increased average saving per member per month from ₹ 35 in 2007–08 to ₹ 60 by 2009–10.
125. Total credit outstanding by March 2009 = ₹ 347.9936 crore and total bank savings by March 2009 = ₹ 138.37 crore (*Source:* NABARD microfinance report, 2009).
126. Analysis of DWCD Base Line Survey indicates that in majority of cases, interest rate charged is 2 per cent p.m. on borrowing in case of inter-loaning funds. While interest rate charged is less than 1 per cent on borrowing in case of bank credit.
127. As per feedback from SSV partners, viz. PEDO, Pradan, Srijan, Ibtada, GDS, etc.
128. Data from DWCD for 2009–10.
129. Comments of SHG federation leaders at 'Future Search: Secondary Institutions in Community-based Microfinance' held on 20 August 2009 at Jaipur.

130. Internal Research, CmF Jaipur.
131. Even though the sample size is low, it can be assumed to represent whole set. SHG federation called Saheli Samiti, Dausa has been found to be running at operational self-sufficiency (OSS) level of 76 per cent and financial self-sufficiency of 76 per cent. Savera Mahila Manch has been found to be running at OSS level of 113 per cent and financial self-sufficiency of 75 per cent.
132. A back-of-the-envelope computation of incremental benefits attributable to SHG federations of Saheli Samiti, Dausa and Savera Mahila Manch indicate that present value of incremental benefits are way higher than total costs incurred at today's value, indicating positive net present value of investment in SHG federations.
133. Analysis of data in NABARD Microfinance 2008–09 Report.
134. Based on analysis of data in NABARD 2008–09 Report.
135. Page 34, 105 Meeting Agenda of SLBC, Rajasthan, 2010.
136. Typical margin on working capital loans or capital expenditure loans is 15 per cent–25 per cent in banks.

5

Women's Perspective on Microfinance

Field Survey, Analysis and Interpretation

There are various models of microfinance institutions, some of which have already been mentioned, such as the SHG model. The following section deals with the people's perspective on microfinance institutions which were involved in the research survey in Rajasthan, and the activities which they carry out. A brief introduction of Grameen Bank is given as they are the pioneers in microfinance.

Grameen Bank

Grameen Bank was first established in Bangladesh by Professor Muhammad Yunus, and is a model of microfinance which relies upon mutual trust, accountability, participation and creativity. Its mission is to target the poor, particularly women, and it views credit as a fundamental human right. Grameen Bank rejects the use of any collateral against its clients, and instead relies upon trust as opposed to legal contracts. Grameen provides loans for self-employment and income generating activity more so than for consumption. It was created in order to provide financial banking services to the poor who were rejected by conventional banks and considered 'not creditworthy'. The bank provides its services directly at the doorstep of its clients, following a philosophy that the poor should not have to travel to the bank, but that the bank should make itself accessible to the poor. Loans are given to groups of borrowers, thus relying upon a system of mutual peer pressure to ensure the reliability of the borrowers and the repayment of the loans. Loans are received on a continuous basis; as soon as one loan is repaid, a borrower can receive another, and the loans are repaid in weekly or bi-weekly instalments. Grameen, likewise, offers both obligatory and voluntary savings, services for its borrowers. Grameen aims to reach sustainability whilst at the same time maintaining the interest rate as close to the market interest rate as possible. Building social capital is likewise one of Grameen's priorities, and it does this through creating groups and centres, and developing leadership through holding annual elections for these.

Development Profile of the Selected Districts

Within the overall development scenario of the state of Rajasthan, the five districts chosen for the study represent different levels of development too. It must be noted that the state falls in the medium category in terms of Human Development Index (HDI) with 28 of its 32 districts having index values between 0.537 and 0.799.

In Rajasthan, *Tonk* ranks twenty-fourth in HDI being below the state average, and it has lower values than the state index for health, income, and education. *Jodhpur* gets closer to the HDI index average ranking 9th. Nevertheless, all indexes without exception are below the state indexes even if it ranks 19th in education, 8th in health, and 14th in income. *Udaipur* is not far from the trend of Tonk with an HDI index clearly below the state average, ranking 20th in HDI. However, it presents an interesting paradox with relatively high rank in education development but is among the lowest ranks in health and income. Amongst all the districts its position is 13th in education and in income, and 27th in health. *Jaipur* is the most developed district with the fourth highest HDI in the state out of 32; it ranks fourth in education, 10th in health and third in income. In addition *Alwar* shows average values in all indexes. Its HDI value is clearly over the state index and the values in education, health and income are widely situated in the average indexes (see Table 5.1).

Table 5.1

Human Development Indicators of Selected Districts

District	*Education Index*	*Health Index*	*Income Index*	*HDI*
Tonk	0.688	0.443	0.582	0.571
Jaipur	0.833	0.688	0.814	0.778
Alwar	0.747	0.776	0.710	0.744
Udaipur	0.761	0.413	0.611	0.595
Jodhpur	0.725	0.725	0.609	0.686
Rajasthan	0.755	0.735	0.640	0.710

Source: Human Development Report Rajasthan (an update – 2008), Directorate of Economics and Statistics, Yojana Bhawan, Jaipur.

The research survey included one cooperative society, one microfinance company supported by NGO and three NGOs who are involved in the formation of SHGs. All the five institutions are rural based and are working with rural women except HPPI who have some works in the small town of Thanagazi (Alwar). Therefore, we can say that we have studied three types of microfinance institutions namely cooperative, company and NGO based.

In the cooperative model the society is generating funds through recurring deposits from its members and then giving it as loans to its members.

In the company model, the MFI is taking big loans from formal institutions such as Rashtriya Mahila Kosh/NABARD/ Banks, etc. and then lending it to the small groups called Joint Liability Groups. A Joint Liability Group (JLG) is an informal group comprising preferably of 4 to 10 individuals coming together for the purposes of availing loan either singly or through the group mechanism against mutual guarantee. The JLG members would offer a joint undertaking to the MFI that enables them to avail loans. The JLG members are expected to engage in similar type of economic activities like crop production. The management of the JLG is to be kept simple with little or no financial administration within the group. JLGs can be formed primarily consisting of tenant farmers, small farmers cultivating land or members of SHGs without possessing proper title of their land.

- Members should be of similar socio-economic status and background carrying out farming activities and who agree to function as a joint liability group.
- The groups must be organized by the like-minded people and not imposed by the bank or others.
- The members should be residing in the same village/area and should know and trust each other well enough to take up joint liability for group/individual loans.

Size of the JLG

The group should be formed preferably with 4 to 10 members to enable the group members to offer mutual guarantee.

These groups do not do any savings but get loans from MFI based on joint liability of the group. The MFI worker takes weekly meeting of the JLG to take instalments and give new loans to the members. The mode of payment is weekly as against SHG which generally has monthly repayments or at the time of harvest.

The SHG model promoted by NGOs has already been discussed in detail previously.

Profile of Sample SHG and Members

In this chapter, we will discuss the profile of the SHGs and members mainly based on the information collected through the structured questionnaires. Wherever necessary, we will substantiate the quantitative information with insights drawn from FGDs and personal interviews.

Age of Groups

As shown in Table 5.2 and Figure 5.1, the average age of the groups in the overall sample is four years. This average can be rationally explained and it is very interesting. The SHGs are usually groups supported by NGOs whose projects last between 4 and 5 years. These projects who take one year to settle down and start being efficient in rural areas, are backing groups' creation and development. And the more the groups grow, the more their savings increase. However, once the NGOs move away after a certain period of time, we notice that the SHGs have trouble managing such big amounts of money. The members, therefore, choose to give out all the money, and then they disband. And thereafter, they restart again. And thus, we observe an average life cycle of about 4 to 5 years. In addition, another reason also explains the SHGs' short period of life, which is drought that takes place every 4 years. So it is also about giving money to face difficulties in case of hard drought. Among the districts, Alwar and Jodhpur reported a slightly younger sample with an average age of two years. The reason to it is that they are at the beginning of the so-called SHGs development cycle. In the case of Udaipur which reported relatively older groups with average age of almost nine years, it is explained by the fact that there is an NGO which established long-term projects and is still present. There is, therefore, a strong outside support that increases SHGs' lifespan in Udaipur.

> The key to ending extreme poverty is to enable the poorest of the poor to get their foot on the ladder of development. The ladder of development hovers overhead, and the poorest of the poor are stuck beneath it. They lack the minimum amount of capital necessary to get a foothold, and therefore need a boost up to the first rung.
>
> **Jeffrey D. Sachs** (American Economist and Director of the Earth Institute at Columbia University)

Table 5.2

Average Age of Sample Groups

(Figures in percentage)

Age of Group	*Tonk*	*Jaipur*	*Alwar*	*Udaipur*	*Jodhpur*	*Total*
< 1 year	0	0	0	0	0	0
1–2	12.5% (1)	40% (4)	90% (9)	18% (2)	70% (7)	47% (23)
2 < = 5	87.5% (7)	60% (6)	0	9% (1)	30% (3)	35% (17)
5 < = 8	0	0	10% (1)	18% (2)	0	6% (3)
8 < = 10	0	0	0	18% (2)	0	4% (2)
> 10	0	0	0	36% (4)	0	8% (4)
Average age (in years)	4.25	2.7	2	8.8	2	4

Figure 5.1

Average Age of Sample Groups

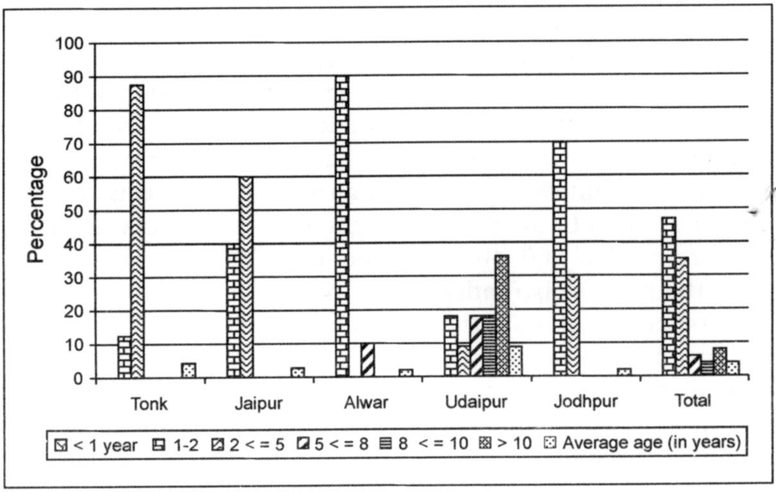

Size of SHGs

Coming to membership size of the SHGs in the sample, as reported in Table 5.3 the average size for the five districts put together is 12, though it ranges between 10 in Tonk and 15 in Udaipur.

Table 5.3

Average Membership of SHG

Districts	*Average Membership*
Tonk	10.7
Jaipur	11.5
Alwar	5.7 (JLG)
Udaipur	15.2
Jodhpur	11.1
All	12.12 (100)

Note: Average membership does not include Joint Liability Groups.

Social Category of Members

Based on information collected, social categories of members are shown in Table 5.4 and Figure 5.2. The interpretation of the coming results is mainly linked to geographical patterns. Indeed, Udaipur being the tribal belt of Rajasthan, we see that the sample SHG drawn from this area has 55 per cent members from tribal communities. Jaipur, Alwar and Jodhpur make up the most important part of the SHG members from other backward castes with respectively 60, 40, and 75 per cent. The analysis shows us that the results also reflect the social distribution between the different castes in Rajasthan. Tonk has a relatively larger share of SC members in the sample SHGs–50 per cent. It results from the overall sample a clear over-representation of OBC members, going past the 50 per cent. As for SC and ST members, they approximately share an equal part with respectively 19 and 17.5 per cent. Eventually, the representation of others category in the overall sample is only 12.5 per cent.

Table 5.4

Percentage Distribution of SHG Members by Social Category

(Figures in percentage)

District	*SC*	*ST*	*OBC*	*Others*	*Total*
Tonk	50% (10)	0	30% (6)	20% (4)	100% (20)
Jaipur	0	20% (4)	60% (12)	20% (4)	100% (20)
Alwar	30% (6)	10% (2)	40% (8)	20% (4)	100% (20)
Udaipur	0	55% (11)	40% (8)	5% (1)	100% (20)
Jodhpur	10% (2)	0	75% (17)	5% (1)	100% (20)
Overall	19% (18)	17.5% (17)	51% (49)	12.5% (12)	100%

Figure 5.2

Percentage Distribution of SHG Members by Social Category

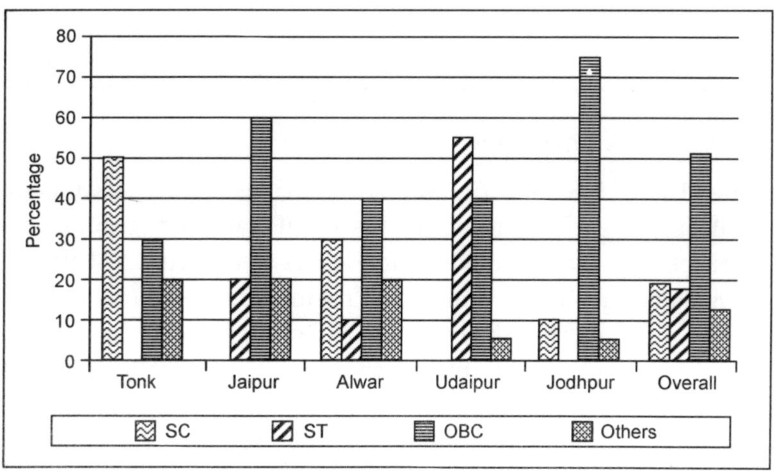

Distribution of SHG Members by Type of House

The Table 5.5 scrutinizes the type of houses which predominates in each district. Kaccha, literately translated would basically mean a house 'without concrete roof' whereas Pacca, on the contrary, would mean a house 'with concrete roof'. By and large, the general trend shows us that the Pacca house is more widespread throughout the different districts, with a result of 40 paccas out of 100. Tonk, Jaipur and Alwar present high results in this direction. However, Udaipur and Jodhpur set apart with more than half of any kind of living being 'Kaccha'. Eventually it is to notice that a relatively important part of SHG members have both a Kaccha and a Pacca. We can deduct that this distribution by type of house translates the slow economical development that is taking place in rural areas, with an evident increase of domestic facilities.

Table 5.5

Distribution of SHG Members by Type of House

	Tonk	*Jaipur*	*Alwar*	*Udaipur*	*Jodhpur*	*Overall*
Kaccha	6	1	7	11	10	35
Pacca	11	18	9	1	1	40
Both	3	1	4	8	9	25

Literacy and Education

The Table 5.6 and Figure 5.3 provides a fair idea about education level of total members of sampled groups. The members' literacy and education levels as depicted in Table 5.6 reveals about 46 per cent of the members questioned are illiterate, meaning that they cannot read or sign their name. This is a clear indication that unless there is significant handholding from the promoter agencies in writing the books of accounts, the groups themselves will not be totally able to independently manage their financial record keeping and also will not be able to know what is written in the record in most of the cases.

However, as we have an in-depth look, we observe that this trend is not truly homogenous. Indeed, whereas we have an illiterate rate average of about 46 per cent for all districts, Tonk and Jaipur clearly present figures below average, with 30 and 10 per cent respectively. This is a direct achievement of SHGs' work, whose members motivated new entrants to write or sign their name. It is also equally due to the coming of young persons, newly married, between 21 and 30 years old that came from developed areas. This affirmation comes to be confirmed as we look at Jaipur and Tonk's economical development. On the contrary, the incidence of illiteracy is particularly high in Alwar (70%), followed by Jodhpur (75%) and Udaipur (45%), where there are poorer areas.

> My vision for the future? Two things: to make credit a human right so that each individual human being will have the opportunity to take loans and implement his or her ideas so that self-exploration becomes possible. And second: that it will lead to a world where nobody has to suffer from poverty – a world completely free from poverty.
>
> **Muhammad Yunus**
>
> (Bangladeshi economist and founder of the Grameen Bank)

Figures in the bracket indicate the number of members whose literacy level was mapped which is 100 per cent of total membership in the sample groups.

Distribution of Main Source of Household Income

When it comes to members, labour, agriculture and MNREGA are the main sources of income with respectively 27.5, 27, and 18 per cents of the sample population (Table 5.7 and Figure 5.4). Interestingly, we notice that even though labour was the main source of almost every all household's income, agriculture would arrive in second position in every district, exception

Table 5.6

Distribution of SHG Members by Literacy and Education Level

(Figures in percentages)

Level	*Illiterate*	*Literate*	*5 Class*	*8 Class*	*9 Class*	*10 Class*	*12 Class*	*BA BEd*	*MA*	*MA BEd*	*BA*	*Total*
Tonk	10% (2)	55% (11)	5% (1)	10% (2)	0	0	5% (1)	5% (1)	0	5% (1)	5% (1)	100% (20)
Jaipur	30% (6)	30% (6)	10% (2)	10% (2)	5% (1)	5% (1)	0	0	10% (2)	0	0	100% (20)
Alwar	70% (14)	15% (3)	5% (1)	10% (2)	0	0	0	0	0	0	0	100% (20)
Udaipur	45% (9)	50% (10)	5% (1)	0	0	0	0	0	0	0	0	100% (20)
Jodhpur	75% (15)	10% (2)	10% (2)	5% (1)	0	0	0	0	0	0	0	100% (20)
Overall	46% (46)	32% (32)	7.5% (7)	7.5% (7)	1% (1)	1% (1)	1% (1)	1% (1)	2% (2)	1% (1)	1% (21)	100% (100)

Figure 5.3

Distribution of SHG Members by Literacy and Education Level

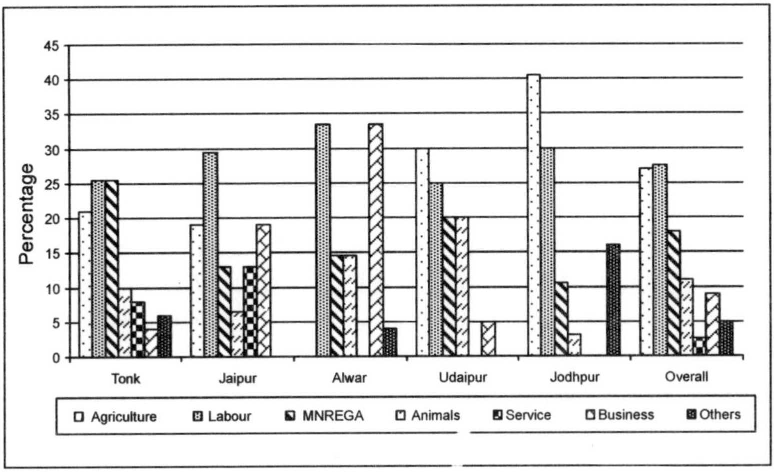

made of Tonk, where MNREGA plays an important part. The assessment remains equal, meaning that about 70 per cents of the population works in land-based activities. As for Alwar, business – 33.5 per cent – is as much important as labour as for the main source of income. Alwar is near to Delhi and enjoys the huge number of people migrating to the capital for their livelihood. Their main activity is therefore, business and labour. In addition, we observe that business also plays a relatively great part in the case of Jaipur, with the very same importance proportion of members having agriculture and business – 19 per cent, as their main source of household income. The proximity with state capital Jaipur also plays an important role. Animal husbandry and MNREGA work are reported by a relatively larger proportion of SHG members in Alwar and Udaipur. However, as we have an overall view, we clearly take in that the service sector does not represent a significant share in the different sources of income.

Table 5.7

Percentage Distribution of Main Source of Household Income of SHG Members

(Figures in percentage)

Source of Income	*Agri-culture*	*Labour*	*MNREGA*	*Animals*	*Service*	*Business*	*Others*	*Total*
Tonk	21% (11)	25.5% (13)	25.5% (13)	10% (5)	8% (4)	4% (2)	6% (3)	100% (51)
Jaipur	19% (6)	29.5% (9)	13% (4)	6.5% (2)	13% (4)	19% (6)	0	100% (31)
Alwar	0	33.5% (7)	14.5% (3)	14.5% (3)	0	33.5% (7)	4% (1)	100% (21)
Udaipur	30% (18)	25% (15)	20% (12)	20% (12)	0	5% (3)	0	100% (60)
Jodhpur	40.5% (11)	30% (8)	10.5% (3)	3% (1)	0	0	16% (4)	100% (27)
Overall	27% (46)	27.5% (52)	18% (35)	11% (23)	2.5% (8)	9% (18)	5% (8)	100% (190)

Source: Members' survey.

Note: Figures in brackets are the respective column total of households.

Figure 5.4

Percentage Distribution of Main Source of Household Income of SHG Members

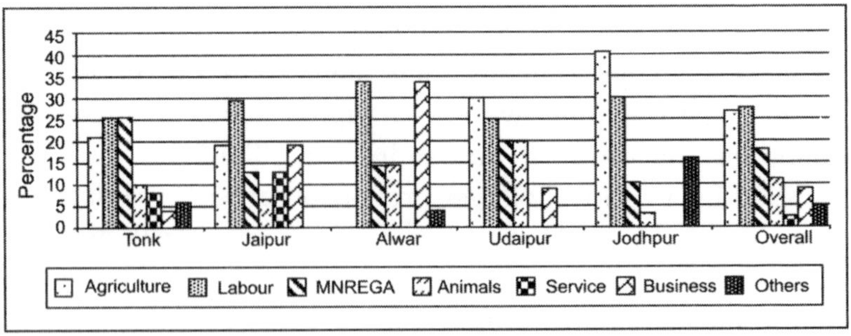

Economical Status: Land and Animal Husbandry (Table 5.8 and Figure 5.5)

As we look into economical status, it appears that lands and animal husbandry are the main indicators, attesting the situation in which SHG members live. The Table 5.8 can be divided in two. First as we take an interest to land, we discern that Tonk, Alwar, Udaipur and Jodhpur are holding almost 90 per cent of all land of sample members. However, major part of it is unirrigated, therefore non-farmable, and so useless in most of the cases. We can see that irrigated area is gradually declining except in Jaipur which is the exception to the rule, with about 70 per cent of its land irrigated. It is to highlight here the crucial importance of water and its access, in these very dry regions. This also shows the level of poverty existing in rural areas where SHGs members belong to poor section of the society. Second, as we analyse the second part of the table, we notice instantaneously the weight of

Table 5.8

Economical Status: Land and Animal Husbandry

(Figures in percentage)

Districts	*Lands (in bigha)*		*Animal Husbandry*					
	Irrigated	*Unirrigated*	*Cow*	*Buffaloes*	*Bull/ Ox*	*Camel*	*Goat/ sheep*	*Total*
Tonk	23.5% (27)	76.5% (88)	21,5% (6)	39% (11)	3.5% (1)	0	36% (10)	100% (28)
Jaipur	69% (84.5)	31% (37.5)	22% (4)	44% (8)	0	0	34% (6)	100% (18)
Alwar	0	100% (5)	14.5% (2)	57% (8)	0	0	28.5% (4)	100% (14)
Udaipur	40% (30)	60% (45)	22.5% (11)	26.5% (13)	22.5% (11)	0	28.5% (14)	100% (49)
Jodhpur	0	100% (970)	34.5% (9)	0	15.5% (4)	4% (1)	46% (12)	100% (26)
Overall	11% (141.5)	89% (1,145.5)	24% (32)	30% (40)	12% (16)	0.5% (1)	34% (46)	100% (135)

goat (34%) and buffaloes (30%) in animal husbandry. In Rajasthan, one of the richest states in India, the cows used to cover the milk production, but because of the market forces it has come to be covered by buffaloes. With the growth of Dairy, buffaloes were introduced to produce milk as they gave richer milk, with more fat content, and at a cheaper price. This tendency is common to each district except Jodhpur, which still presents a higher result for cows' husbandry. In addition, Udaipur has a relatively high share of bull/ox husbandry (22%) compared to the rest. As a general comment, we can say that people do not have many animals because of the unirrigated lands. Where there are rocky lands, we observe the development of others fields.

Figure 5.5

Economical Status: Land and Animal Husbandry

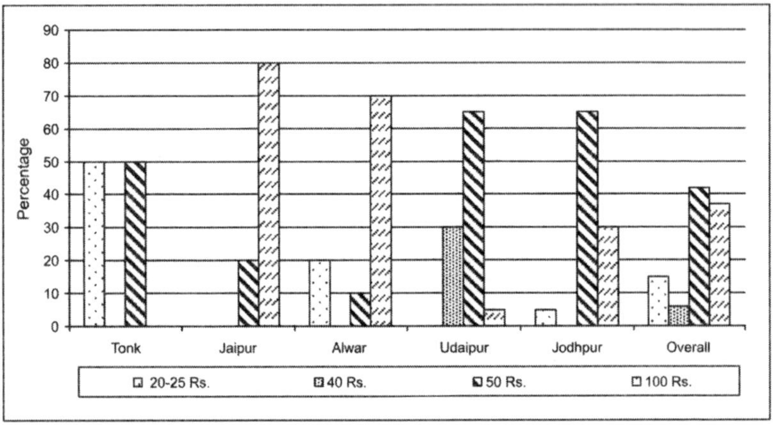

Monthly Savings by SHGs (Table 5.9 and Figure 5.6)

The overall dynamic clearly shows that ₹ 50 is the average amount saved each month, with 42 per cent. The result is simply a consequence of SHGs organization. SHGs start with ₹ 10 or 20 and once everything is settled down, they can increase the amount. In general terms it is about ₹ 10 per year, but it also depends on socio-economic condition of the members. Out of all savings realized by SHG in the different districts, we note that the saving average amount is of ₹ 50 in Tonk, Udaipur and Jodhpur with respectively 50, 65, 65 per cents. As for Jaipur and Alwar, the results are more important, with 80 for the first and 70 for the second. The overall view also shows that the smallest share in monthly savings (₹ 20–25) is not insignificant and represents 15 per cent of all savings. From this point of view, the share of ₹ 40 is almost non-existent. Now, if we look at the average in total savings, we can observe that Udaipur presents the highest number with 3,626. Tonk and Jodhpur show averaged figures around ₹ 1,500, which is gently below the overall average of around ₹ 2,000. This comes to confirm the economical differences existing between each district. Eventually, Jaipur is not far from Udaipur, getting close to the ₹ 3,000 mark with almost ₹ 2,800.

Table 5.9

Distribution of Monthly Savings by Districts

(Figures in percentage)

Monthly Savings (₹)	*20–25*	*40*	*50*	*100*	*Average Total Savings (in ₹)*
Tonk	50% (10)	0	50% (10)	0	1,324.5
Jaipur	0	0	20% (4)	80% (16)	2,772.5
Alwar	20% (4)	0	10% (2)	70% (14)	896.5
Udaipur	0	30% (6)	65% (13)	5% (1)	3,626
Jodhpur	5% (1)	0	65% (13)	30% (6)	1,454.5
Overall	15% (15)	6% (6)	42% (42)	37% (37)	2,014.8

In addition, as we relate the age of SHGs with their monthly savings, we see that the relation is direct. The older, the more the group saves bigger amounts of money. However, it is brought to notice that among others factors, the government's target SHG formation scheme led to lots of corruption and misappropriation of funds, which has, as a consequence, raised communities mistrust regarding SHG implementation in rural areas. Another point we noticed during the discussions with the villagers is that savings have been dramatically increasing for two years with the MNREGA (3rd highest source of income) programme initiated by the government.

Figure 5.6

Distribution of Monthly Savings by Districts

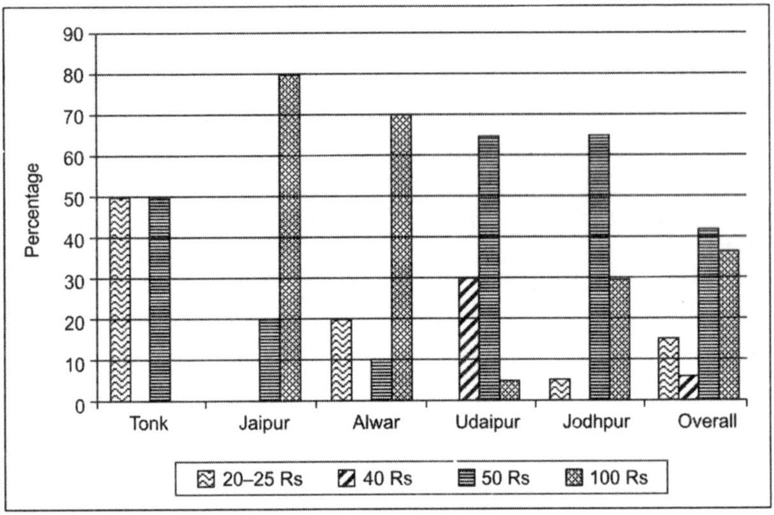

Loan Received from SHGs

The survey also revealed that 80 per cent of all the SHG members are taking loans, if we consider all districts. This clearly highlights the change induced by SHG groups' creation that availed extending the financial possibilities of SHG members. But it is not satisfying as the expectation is that all members should take SHGs loan. The reasons for this may be that firstly, the members do not need loans and secondly, maybe the loan is too small or finally maybe the groups do not have confidence in some members, being afraid that they will not repay the loan. As we look more in details of Table 5.10, we see that the overall tendency matches with the local results in each district, except in Tonk, where only half of the members got a loan from SHGs. It is also noticed that Udaipur SHG members all benefited from loans.

Table 5.10

Loan Received from SHGs

(Figures in percentage)

	Tonk	*Jaipur*	*Alwar*	*Udaipur*	*Jodhpur*	*Overall*
Yes	50% (10)	85% (17)	65% (13)	100% (20)	95% (19)	80% (79)
No	50% (10)	15% (3)	35% (7)	0	5% (1)	20% (21)

Purpose of Loan

The survey with SHG members revealed that out of the members who have availed loan, a high percentage used it for meeting animal husbandry expenses with an overall rate of 24.5 per cent, and 55.5 per cent in Alwar, 24 per cent in Udaipur, and 24.5 per cent in Jaipur. The second most important purpose of SHG loans is dedicated to domestic purposes, as it represents 21 per cent within all districts. In Tonk, it reaches 42 per cent, 28.5 per cent in Jaipur and about one-fourth of total loans in Udaipur. Loans taken are all emergency loans and short-term loans for which the members used to go to moneylenders or relatives earlier. The SHGs are now fulfilling this task by supporting members in urgent needs. Moreover, the loans are productive loans (animal husbandry, agriculture, etc.) and at the same time, vital as we see that loans for domestic and health purposes are rising. It is a major issue, as this investment is central for all the other purposes. Jodhpur stands aside of this trend with more than half the loans availed dedicated to agriculture (52.5%). In addition, it is pointed out that of the rest, health, marriage and paying instalment still have a relative importance in almost all districts. Indeed, Jaipur shows quite a relatively elevated rate in paying instalment (21%), related to the other purposes (Table 5.11 and Figure 5.7).

Table 5.11

Distribution of SHG Loans by Purpose

(Figures in percentage)

Purpose (informative amount in ₹)	*Tonk*	*Jaipur*	*Alwar*	*Udaipur*	*Jodhpur*	*Overall*
Domestic Purpose	42% (16)	28.5% (15)	0	22.5% (31)	7.5% (3)	21% (65)
Average Loan (₹)	1,875	3,253	0	4,002	6,333	3,092
Education	10.5% (4)	5.5% (3)	0	0	5% (2)	3% (9)
Average Loan (₹)	1,525	8,266	0	0	5,000	4,930
Health	18.5% (7)	11.5% (6)	0	12% (17)	7.5% (3)	10.5% (33)
Average Loan (₹)	1,871	6,075	0	5,594	5,666	3,841
Marriage	8% (3)	4% (2)	0	14.5% (20)	0	8% (25)
Average Loan (₹)	2,883	34,500	0	7,450	0	8,666
Agriculture	10.5% (4)	0	0	10% (13)	52.5% (19)	11.5% (36)
Average Loan (₹)	2,925	0	0	6,562	1,047	1,706
Animal Husbandry	2.5% (1)	24.5% (13)	55.5% (24)	24% (33)	15% (6)	24.5% (77)
Average Loan (₹)	1,000	9,026	14,166	6,862	6,333	7,477
To Pay Instalment	2.5% (1)	21% (11)	0	9% (13)	0	8% (25)
Average Loan (₹)	300	4,000	0	6,696	0	2,199

Source: SHG Member survey.

Note: Figures in bracket is informative amount in rupees.

Loans' Details Per District

As we can see from a general overview, the SHGs applying a 24 per cent interest rate share, to a lesser extent, a biggest part than those applying a 12 per cent interest rate. In rural areas it is

Figure 5.7

Distribution of SHG Loans by Purpose

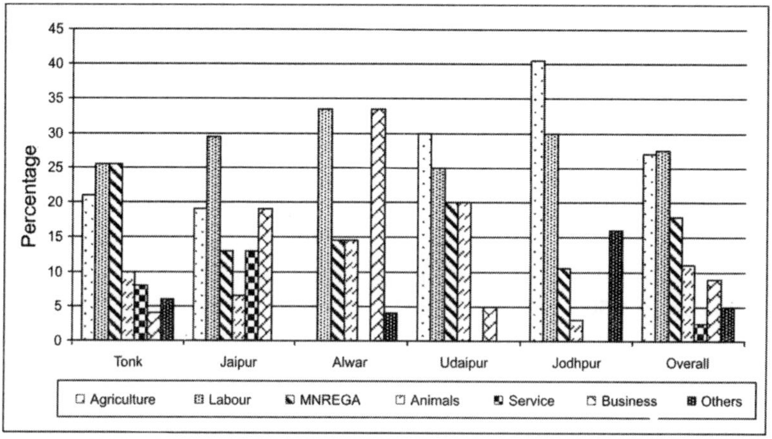

common that interest rates vary from 24 to 60 per cents. So we see that almost half of SHGs are charging interest rates below the market rate. That is a good sign, showing that SHGs are doing a good job and supporting development in rural areas. Tonk and Jaipur are among the majority, exclusively applying a 24 per cent interest rate, whereas Alwar and Jodhpur as a whole have rather a 12 per cent interest rate system. Udaipur has equal share of both interest rates. In addition, only Alwar district has largely implemented flat interest rates (90%). It is because the SHGs are working with a microfinance organization which supports them. It is a different logic from the one of NGOs, as they facilitate access to loans but they don't form SHGs. As for the others district, the loans were established with a reducing interest rate, bringing the overall average to 82 per cent for the reducing interest rate, and 18 per cent for the flat one. Eventually, only one SHG in Tonk is not applying penalty if there are any failings in repayment, taking distance with the others sample SHGs which wholly apply it. This is very positive as it demonstrates that financial discipline reached to be established (Table 5.12 and Figure 5.8).

Table 5.12

Loans' Details Per District

District	*SHG Applying a 24% Interest Rate*	*SHG Applying a 12% Interest Rate*	*SHG with Flat Interest Rate*	*SHG with Reducing Interest Rate*	*SHG Applying Penalty*
Tonk	100% (10)	0	0	100% (10)	10% (1)
Jaipur	100% (10)	0	0	100% (10)	100% (10)
Alwar	10% (1)	90% (9)	90% (9)	10% (1)	100% (10)
Udaipur	50% (5)	50% (5)	0	100% (10)	100% (10)
Jodhpur	10% (1)	90% (9)	0	100% (10)	100% (10)
Overall	54% (27)	46% (23)	18% (9)	82% (41)	82% (41)

Source: SHG Member Survey.

Figure 5.8

Loans' Details Per District

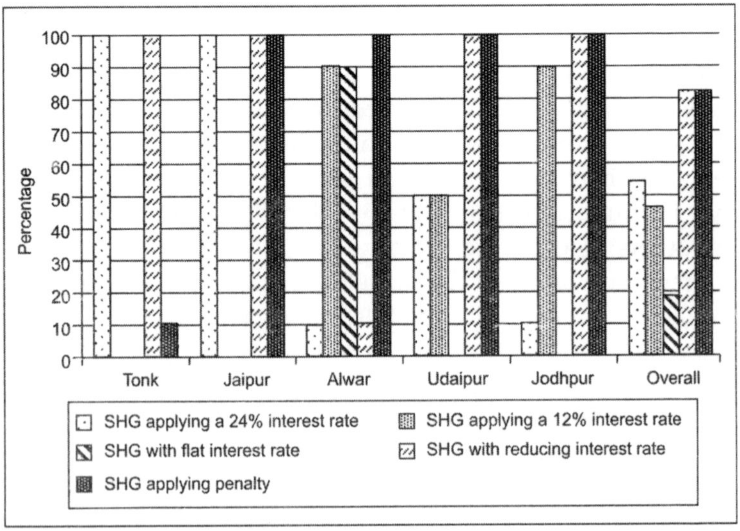

Problems in Loan Recovery

As we bend over the problems of loan recovery, the district of Tonk brings up the lack of money as the main obstacle to repay loans. However, this has to be nuanced as it means that they could not repay the whole loan on time, and would ask for a delay in the repayment, after which they were able to do so. As for Tonk, it is to highlight that it has 50 per cent of the problems in loan recovery due to the lack of money, or better said to late repayment. Moreover, we see that 37 per cent report that they did not have any problem in recovering loan. Indeed, the overall average percentage that attests of no problems in loan recovery is 42 per cent, which shows that SHGs providing loans at lower rates are doing a good job and supporting development in rural areas. As for family problems, these are inherent in daily life and, therefore, can happen to anyone. Eventually, as we look at the 'objectives unfulfilled' column, we can deduce that all people used the money for forecasted objectives and then they earn something out of it, proof of a high transparency. And they were able to fulfil them as the access to loan is facilitated through SHGs and as the corruption, which impeaches to reach the forecasted objectives, does not exist in SHGs operations (see Table 5.13 and Figure 5.9).

Table 5.13

Problems in Loan Recovery

(Figures in percentage)

District	*Family Problem*	*Lack of Money*	*Obj. Unfulfilled*	*No Problem*	*Total*
Tonk	12.5% (1)	50% (4)	0	37.5% (3)	100% (8)
Jaipur	38% (8)	19% (4)	0	43% (9)	100% (21)
Alwar	32% (9)	32% (9)	0	36% (10)	100% (28)
Udaipur	31% (9)	34.5% (10)	0	34.5% (10)	100% (29)
Jodhpur	0	0	0	100% (8)	100% (8)
Overall	29% (27)	29% (27)	0	42% (40)	100% (94)

Figure 5.9

Problems in Loan Recovery

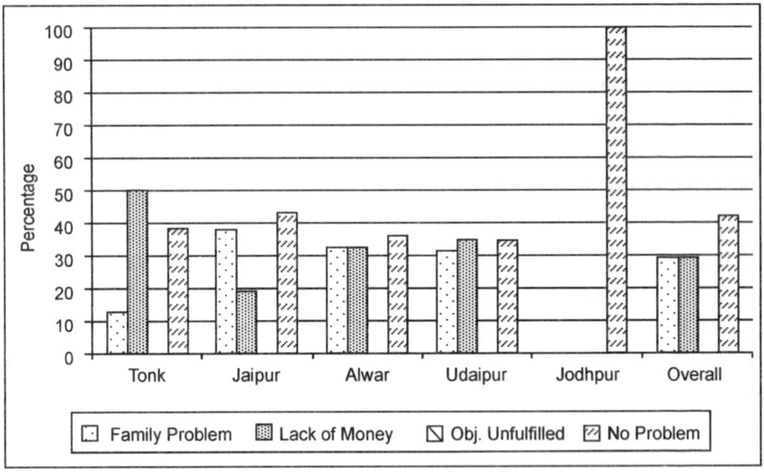

Loan Received from Banks and Distribution by Purpose

The propensity is much larger – 90 per cent – for those who did not get loan from banks in every district. It clearly shows the status of relationship that banks have with SHGs and NGOs. Only 10 SHGs were able to take loans from the banks, which did not show themselves as very cooperative and interested in working with SHGs. Udaipur presents the relatively most important part in receiving loans from banks with 60 per cent of the total amount (Table 5.14). As for the districts that have SHGs holding bank loans, we observe that they are essentially used in agriculture and animal husbandry. This is the direct consequence of the state scheme which obligates bank to give loan directed to land activities. Tonk has the largest share in agriculture with 50 per cent, whereas Udaipur had the loans received from banks more headed for animal husbandry – 80 per cent. By and large, we clearly notice that Bank loans are much less in number than those coming from SHGs. We comment regarding this table the measure the government had taken, which was to financially include all Indians by 2012, and we see that in our survey only 10 per cent had some relationship with the bank (see Table 5.15 and Figure 5.10).

As we establish relationships between all the data we collected through the survey, we see that low literacy level is visible also in bank accounts and loans received as well as in bank operation. About 80 per cent of the SHG members cannot read or write properly, thereby, they do not have any bank accounts and therefore, have not taken bank loans. Alwar shows again a different reading as women hardly go to the bank as the organization supporting them, works as a bank.

Table 5.14

Loan Received from Banks (Figure in Percentage)

District	*Tonk*	*Jaipur*	*Alwar*	*Udaipur*	*Jodhpur*	*Overall*
Yes	3	0	0	6	1	10
No	7	20	20	14	19	90

Shanti Devi lives in Barodiya village; Tehsil Niwai of Tonk district along with her two sons and daughters-in-law. The main occupation of Shanti Devi's family was agriculture, which was not sufficient to maintain the family and its ever-growing expenses. In these turbulent times, Shanti Devi saw a ray of hope in the form of an SHG which was being made at her village at that time. She attended one of the meetings and was inspired to save her hard earned money. Soon enough, she became the member of the Self-Help Group.

The other members were well aware of the financial crunch Shanti Devi was going through. They suggested that she should start selling the things which are required on a day-to-day basis. Soon Shanti Devi's savings multiplied. A loan was granted to her on behalf of the SHG to make a small shop in the premises of her own house. Nowadays her business is prospering and she has regained her respect in the neighbourhood.

Shanti Devi now leads a happy and contented life and ows all her happiness and success to the Self-Help Group.

Table 5.15

Distribution of Bank Loans by Purpose

(No. of persons)

Purpose	*Tonk*	*Jaipur*	*Alwar*	*Udaipur*	*Jodhpur*	*Overall*
Domestic Purpose	0	0	0	0	0	0
Education	0	0	0	0	0	0
Health	0	0	0	0	0	0
Marriage	0	0	0	0	0	0
Agriculture	50% (3)	0	0	50% (3)	0	100% (6)
Animal Husbandry	0	0	0	80% (3)	20% (1)	100% (4)
To pay Instalments	0	0	0	0	0	0
Business	0	0	0	0	0	0
Others	0	0	0	0	0	0
Total	30% (3)	0	0	60% (6)	10% (1)	10

Figure 5.10

Distribution of Bank Loans by Purpose

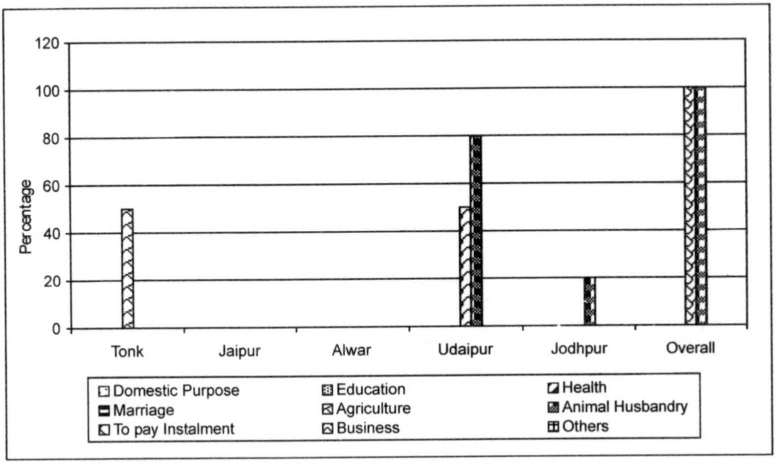

Problem in Opening Bank Account

If we look at the results of the study regarding the problems faced in opening Bank accounts, we note in the overall results that the 'no' answer is more. However, on a deeper analysis, we must take into account that this result does not reflect what the reality really is. Actually, it has to be clarified that many NGOs have supported the opening of bank accounts and therefore, facilitated in all the steps and procedure for the same. This fact has led to additional negative answers in Table 5.16. In practise this is not the case, as SHGs face many problems in opening bank accounts. The burden of SHGs is less, and since not many members of SHGs have ever opened individual bank accounts the group does not have much of experience. Tonk as well as Alwar are amongst those with a large number of answers being yes (18 out of 21).

Table 5.16

Problem in Opening Bank Accounts

	Tonk	*Jaipur*	*Alwar*	*Udaipur*	*Jodhpur*	*Overall*
Yes	8	0	10	2	1	21
No	1	10	0	8	9	28
No answer	1	0	0	0	0	1

Problems with Bank Operation

The survey with SHG members also revealed that out of the members, the majority consider 'paper work' as responsible for the problems with bank. This is confirmed when we see that it is the main attributed cause in Tonk (45%) and Jaipur (40%) (see Table 5.17 and Figure 5.11). As most of the members are illiterate, they find it hard to operate in the banks. However, it has been noticed that if there is regular training and support by the NGOs, many women are coming forward for doing bank operations. Another well-known problem is that bank managers are not fully aware, sensitive or trained in dealing with SHGs members, especially with illiterate and rural members. They mostly see dealing with SHGs as a waste of time and money. So in the case SHGs to succeed in opening a bank account, they are submitted to all kinds of procedures they are not accustomed to.

Similarly, we see that Jaipur on the other hand also shows the same percentage for the frequent visit being problematic with bank operations. Besides, Alwar and Udaipur also consider frequent visit as a problem with bank operations. Less cooperation between partners is also pointed out as it represents 34.5 per cent in Udaipur.

Table 5.17

Problems with Bank Operation

(Figures in percentage)

District	*Paper Work*	*Frequent Visit*	*Less Cooperation*	*Others*
Tonk	45% (13)	14% (4)	38% (11)	3% (1)
Jaipur	40% (2)	40% (2)	20% (1)	0
Alwar	36% (4)	64% (7)	0	0
Udaipur	31% (9)	34.5% (10)	34.5% (10)	0
Jodhpur	33.3% (1)	66.6% (2)	0	0
Overall	37.5% (29)	32.5% (25)	28.5% (22)	1.5% (1)

Figure 5.11

Problems with Bank Operation

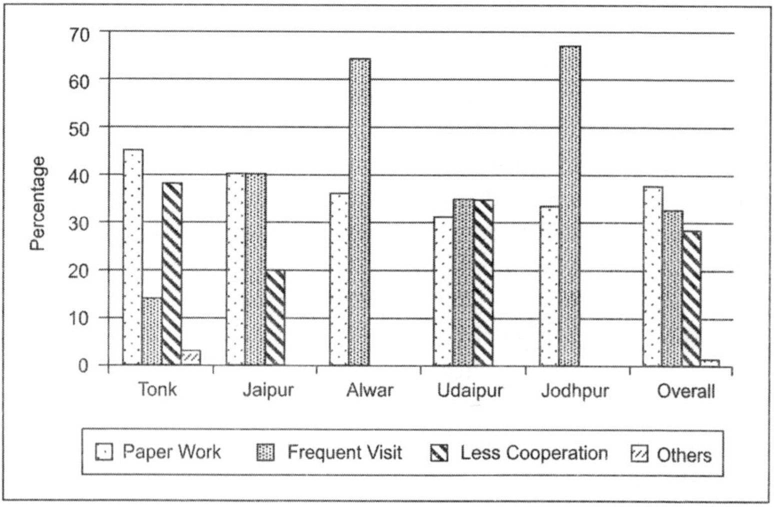

Distribution of Bank Operation

As we go deeper into the details of bank operation, we notice that there are more operations done 'occasionally' than regularly. Indeed, most of SHGs do not operate with banks regularly and only operate when they need money. Tonk, Jaipur and Udaipur fit into the tendency with respectively 80, 100, and 70 per cent of SHGs members having bank operations when needed. Generally bank operations are seen as a far too much complicated initiative. First, the banks usually are in towns, which implies villagers have to go there for any transaction, which is time consuming as well as expensive. Second, women cannot come alone and need to be accompanied, meaning that the male member will not be able to work on that day. And finally, it is also risky to bring money as it can be stolen. Therefore, the NGO's staff has to keep on supporting SHGs. We also observe that women manage to have a certain amount of money that does not need to be deposited in banks. As for Alwar, there is no bank operation as SHGs are working with organization specialized in giving money so that they do not have to deal with banks (see Table 5.18 and Figure 5.12).

Table 5.18

Distribution of Bank Operation

District	*When Needed*	*Monthly*
Tonk	80% (8)	20% (2)
Jaipur	100% (10)	0
Alwar	No Bank Operation	No Bank Operation
Udaipur	70% (7)	30% (3)
Jodhpur	0	100% (10)
Overall	62.5% (25)	37.5% (15)

Figure 5.12

Distribution of Bank Operation

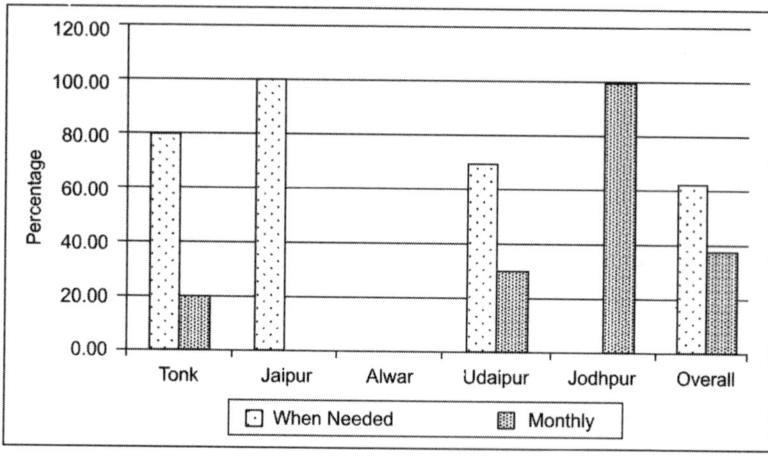

Why Join SHG

In a general way, savings is definitely the first priority with 65 per cent of opinions, after that it is the need of loan – 26 per cent, followed up with the community feeling – 6 per cent and the income generation – 3 per cent. More in precise terms, Tonk shows a high rate concerning savings – 90 per cent as well as Udaipur – 50 per cent. Alwar and Udaipur equilibrate it with 50 per cent in each district concerning the need of loan category. In Jodhpur, it is the income generation that has been chosen as the first priority of joining SHG, with 66 per cent. The basic purpose is to motivate people to save money for difficult times or for small expenses. It seems that the majority of members are convinced that saving is useful but do not appreciate the other functions of SHGs, such as the collective power, women empowerment, social capital, etc. This can be attributed to a lack of training or simply of understanding. It is also to point out the high dependency of SHGs with NGOs, which is mainly responsible for working more on one priority or another. Therefore, the priorities of the NGO become the priorities of the SHG (see Table 5.19 and Figure 5.13).

In addition, NGOs should work hard to inculcate these other feelings (income generation, community feelings, etc.) so that they become stronger. The SHGs members should understand that the support is not only in financial matters but also in social matters. The SHGs can be very strong entities.

Table 5.19

Why Join SHG

(No. persons)

District	*Savings as First Priority*	*In Need of Loan as First Priority*	*Income Generation as First Priority*	*Comm. Feeling as First Priority*
Tonk	90% (18)	0	0	10% (2)
Jaipur	30.5% (19)	4% (1)	0	0
Alwar	15% (3)	50% (10)	15% (2)	25% (5)
Udaipur	50% (10)	50% (10)	0	0
Jodhpur	22.5% (14)	15.5% (4)	66% (2)	0
Overall	65% (64)	26% (25)	3% (4)	6% (7)

Figure 5.13

Why Join SHG

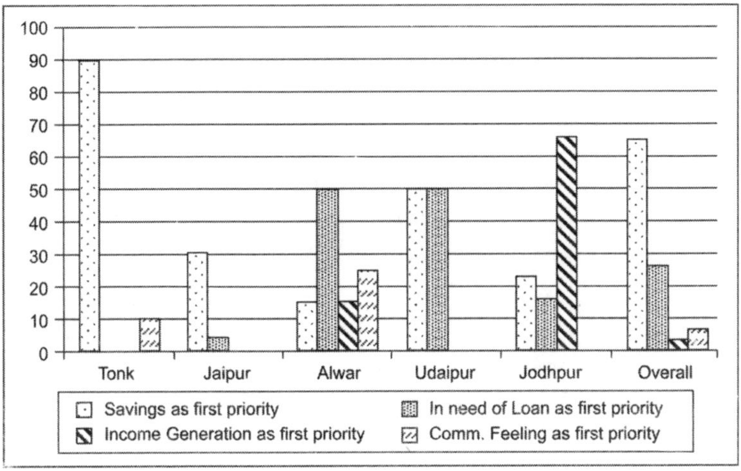

Works of SHG

During the case study, we asked the SHG members on the type of works they dedicated their time. First of all, it was clear that all SHGs are working according to their basic principles. In this sense, we can add that exploitation by money-lenders (the baniya) got reduced. If we consider the overall picture, the works economical development comes first with 17 per cent and then follows the association with bank and after that savings 15.5 per cent (see Table 5.20 and Figure 5.14). Now, if we look at each district we notice that SHGs from Tonk district work more at associating with banks, and Udaipur has SHGs involved in savings and in bank loans. Alwar goes well with the general tendency and has 60 per cent of its SHG members working for economical development. As for Jaipur and Jodhpur, they work equally in everything. As a general comment, we can say that basic purposes are being fulfilled and that the economical growth is a positive sign for the future of SHGs.

Table 5.20

Works of SHG

(Figures in percentage)

District	*Savings*	*In Need of Loan*	*Assos. with Bank*	*Bank Loan*	*Exploitation by Money-lender (baniya)*	*Eco. Dev.*	*Mutual Support*	*Other reasons*	*Total*
Tonk	20% (8)	12.5% (5)	25% (10)	0	12.5% (5)	12.5% (5)	17.5% (7)	0	100% (40)
Jaipur	14.5% (10)	14.5% (10)	14.5% (10)	14.5% (10)	14.5% (10)	14.5% (10)	14.5% (10)	0	100% (70)
Alwar	6.6% (1)	6.6% (1)	6.6% (1)	6.6% (1)	13.3% (2)	60% (9)	0	0	100% (15)
Udaipur	15% (10)	15% (10)	15% (10)	4% (3)	15% (10)	13.5% (9)	13.5% (9)	9% (6)	100% (67)
Jodhpur	16.6% (10)	16.6% (10)	16.6% (10)	0	16.6% (10)	16.6% (10)	16.6% (10)	0	100% (60)
Overall	15.5% (39)	14% (36)	16% (41)	5.5% (14)	14.5% (37)	17% (43)	14% (36)	2.5% (6)	100% (252)

Figure 5.14

Works of SHH

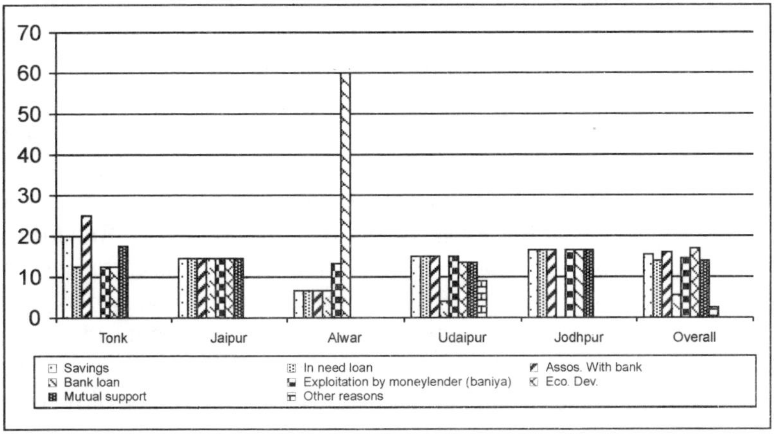

Dispute in SHG

Out of all the SHGs we are collaborating with, 70 per cent reported that they did not have any dispute within their group. Actually we can add that all members are satisfied with SHGs. The 30 per cent of 'yes' actually is a good sign, as it represents the discipline and the transparency that are being inculcated (Table 5.21). So we cannot consider that it is true dispute. Another reason is the fact that some members do not repay loan on time, leading to a pressure of the group, which is considered as a dispute, whereas it is in reality a need.

Table 5.21

Dispute in SHG

	Tonk	*Jaipur*	*Alwar*	*Udaipur*	*Jodhpur*	*Total*
YES	5	0	3	18	4	30
NO	15	20	17	2	16	70

Problems of SHG

As we look at the problems faced by SHG, illiteracy comes to be one of the major factors. Therefore, it is no accident that 'uneducated members' is reported to be the main cause of problems in SHG (see Table 5.22 and Figure 5.15). Indeed the overall figure is 44.5 per cent, far above the second main cause, which is the lack of responsibility – 21 per cent. Jaipur, Alwar, Udaipur and Jodhpur share the opinion and agree on the general trend, with respectively 57, 39.5, 50, and 44.5 per cent. NGOs' staff has to work hard in keeping of accounts to support SHGs. Regarding irregular meetings, the reason is that women are from rural background and, therefore, do not understand the very necessity of being regular in meeting with the other members of SHGs. Tonk is a good example, and it points out the irregular meetings as the main cause of problems in SHGs. As for the lack of responsibility they do not feel SHGs as very important. But actually, savings is just a means for all the rest (women empowerment, etc.). Bank problem for getting loan is also considered to be relatively important by Alwar – 28.5 per cent, and Jodhpur – 22 per cent. It is mainly due to a misconception of bank managers that they do not understand the impact of such groups. Eventually, irregular recovery has to be understood as late recovery, which is not a real problem.

The lack of responsibility as well as the factor 'uneducated members' can both be related to low literacy level. Indeed, members are not able to inculcate the feelings for SHG to its full extent. Thereby, their focus is mainly on financial matters. However, SHGs can also work for other added value activities, such as income generating activities, or social cohesion, etc.

> 'I have always said that micro-credits are of value because they give people a sense of their own worth. By working and producing they take their future into their own hands. Microfinancing has grown enormously in Latin America. Women are extremely important in this sector.'
>
> **Enrique Iglesias** (economist of Uruguayan-Spanish dual citizenship, once President of the Inter-American Development Bank)

Table 5.22

Problems of SHG

District	*Uneducated Members*	*Irregular Meetings*	*Lack of Responsi-bility*	*Bank Problem for Getting Loan*	*Irregular Recovery*	*Others*	*Total*
Tonk	30% (3)	40% (4)	10% (1)	10% (1)	10% (1)	0	100% (10)
Jaipur	57% (8)	0	28.5% (4)	0	14.5% (2)	0	100% (14)
Alwar	39.5% (11)	0	32% (9)	28.5% (8)	0	0	100% (28)
Udaipur	50% (10)	0	10% (2)	5% (1)	30% (6)	5% (1)	100% (20)
Jodhpur	44.5% (8)	5.5% (1)	16.5% (3)	22% (4)	0	11% (2)	100% (18)
Overall	44.5% (40)	5.5% (5)	21% (19)	15.5% (14)	10% (9)	3.5% (3)	100% (90)

Figure 5.15

Problems of SHG

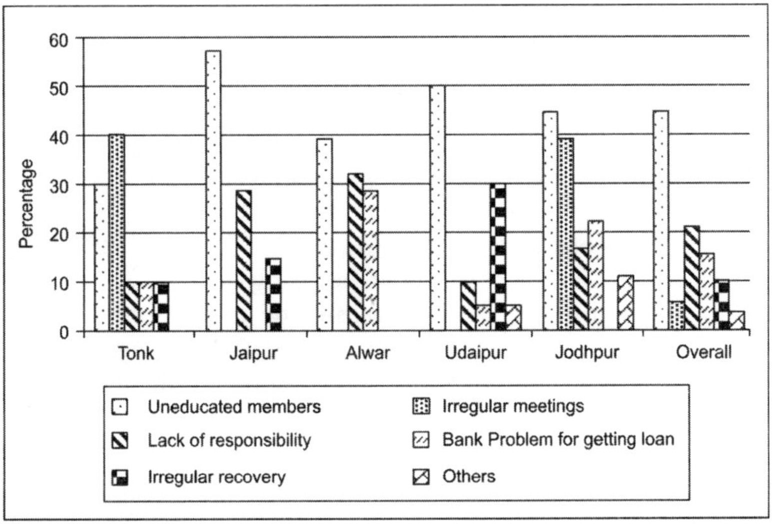

Training of Leaders and Members

As for the training of leaders and members, the study raised several questions that are enumerated below.

First of all, it appears important to put in perspective the magnitude of number of entrants which does not truly reflect reality, if we only restrict ourselves to percentage. Indeed, as this part of the survey offers a multiple choice answers, we have to decipher it as to obtain the most objective and realistic meaning possible. As we have a look at the different trainings that are proposed, we can initially observe that 'vocational training' is slightly a less unifier than other trainings which see high numbers of participants assisting. By and large, this training only represents 5 per cent of total participation to all trainings. This can be explained to a large extent by the fact that SHGs members do not see it as wonderfully useful. Indeed, vocational training always differs from the others as it proposes training in more or less direct link with the concrete job of SHGs. It can, for instance, be related to traditional craft activities. It would need to first establish training courses detailing all the steps as they are not directly related to farm activities, but also a sustainable financial support of the NGO, as the implementation of such an activity would mean funds to make it viable. We clearly understand that this cannot be financially sustainable. Therefore, the SHGs will not experience it as absolutely necessary and will neglect it in favour of other trainings considered as more interesting.

In addition, the other trainings are much more connected to SHGs work, to its structure and to its management. The SHGs' different steps of creation training, provides the basis instruction to create an SHG and see how it mainly works. As for the book-keeping training, it explains how to do one's accounts in the basic principles. Ultimately, the SHGs' management is meant to give a frame to SHGs' functioning and help institute rules within each group.

As we go through the analysis, let us take the training that apparently seems the most to attract people, the subject-formation training, which accounts for about 36 per cent of total entrants. This figure may appear high but it only represents 44 per cent throughout all the districts considered. This means that more than half the participants do not have access to it or are not interested, which is in both cases, a huge result (Table 5.23 and Figure 5.16).

Thus in Tonk, only 8 persons assisted the subject-formation training, that is less than half the total number of SHGs members. Alwar may give the impression that all SHGs members participated, at least, to one training if we look at the percentage (50% in each training). But actually, as explained previously, it is about a multiple choice questionnaire, so it may be the very same persons that assisted both trainings. The impact of the trainings on all members of SHGs is, as a result, significantly limited.

It is the same as for the impact of others trainings that must be put in perspective. Eventually, many general assessments can be drawn up. Firstly, these trainings directed to SHGs members, fail to elicit any response, as the gap between theory and reality is real. Moreover, the education level is a barrier to a large participation of SHGs members. Indeed, let us remember that about half of the members are illiterate and they cannot assist trainings that are using written material (book-keeping, etc.). In addition, another problem is the one of financing of the NGOs supporting these SHGs. A good many of them lack the resources to have all SHGs members participate, minimizing the impact of their own trainings.

We clearly see then, that the problem is twofold, and is situated as much on villagers' side who cannot assist in all these trainings (only 50%), as on NGOs' side, which are limited in their actions by the lack of resources.

> 'This is not charity. This is business: business with a social objective, which is to help people get out of poverty.'
>
> **Muhammad Yunus**
>
> (Bangladeshi economist and founder of the Grameen Bank)

Table 5.23

Training of Leaders and Members

(Figures in percentage)

District	*SHGs' Steps of Creation*	*Book-keeping*	*SHGs' Management*	*Vocational Training*
Tonk	40% (8)	40% (8)	35% (7)	0
Jaipur	30% (6)	5% (1)	30% (6)	20% (4)
Alwar	50% (10)	0	50% (10)	0
Udaipur	50% (10)	50% (10)	50% (10)	10% (2)
Jodhpur	50% (10)	50% (10)	50% (10)	0
Overall	36% (44)	24% (29)	35% (43)	5% (6)

Figure 5.16

Training of Leaders and Members

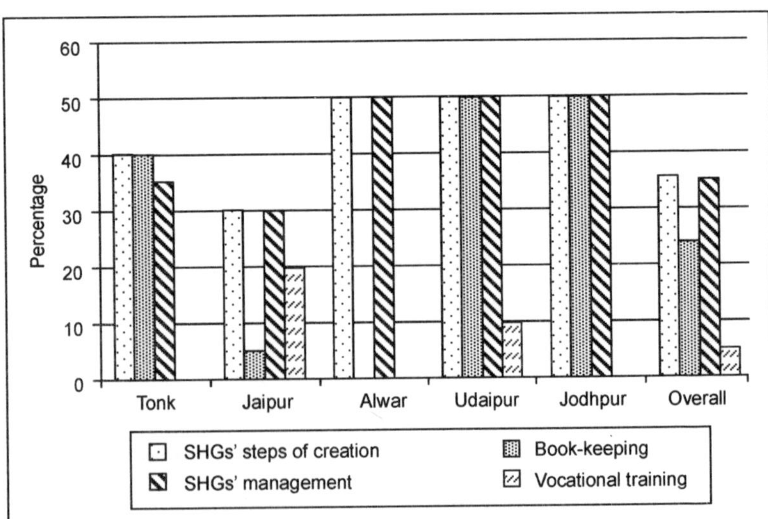

Efforts to Improve SHG

As for the efforts to be made expressed by SHGs sampled members, training arrives in first position with almost half of the answers. This means that SHG members are aware of the fact that one of the major problem is the lack of training, in order to make up for illiteracy, bank accountancy, etc. Tonk, Jaipur, and Udaipur are heading the trend with respectively 54, 57, and 46.5 per cent (see Table 5.24 and figure 5.17). Management is however also a great source of concern – 21.5 per cent. It is about all matters regarding the intern life of SHGs such as the meeting and book-keeping which should be concern of everyone. So it is positive to observe that this is seriously considered by SHGs members. Eventually, funds – 28 per cent corresponds to the restricted vision that SHGs' main function is to support financial matters. Again, as said before, SHGs must let members know about the great social impacts SHGs can have.

Table 5.24

Efforts to Improve SHG (Opinion by District)

(Figures in percentage)

District	*Training*	*Management*	*Funds*	*Others*	*Total*
Tonk	54% (14)	30% (8)	8% (2)	8% (2)	100% (26)
Jaipur	57% (19)	7% (2)	32.5% (11)	3.5% (1)	100% (33)
Alwar	32% (10)	26% (8)	42% (13)	0	100% (31)
Udaipur	46.5% (20)	32.5% (14)	16% (7)	5% (2)	100% (43)
Jodhpur	42% (13)	10% (3)	45% (14)	3% (1)	100% (31)
Overall	46% (76)	21.5% (36)	28% (47)	3.5% (6)	100% (165)

Figure 5.17

Efforts to Improve SHG (Opinion by District)

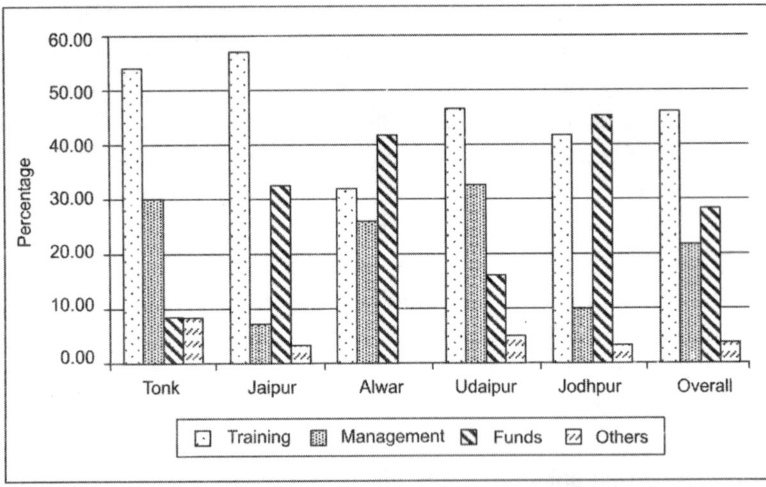

> 'Micro-credit and microfinance will however reach the maximum number of poor clients only when it is recognized as a national priority and integrated into the financial sector. Our goal is far beyond extending more credit to more poor people. Our goal is to figure out how to work together in partnership to build financial sectors that work for everyone and in particular for those that are trying desperately to climb the economic ladder to get out of poverty.'
>
> **H.E. Mr Dirk Jan Van Den Berg**
>
> (Permanent Representative, the Netherlands Mission to the United Nations)

Observations from Focused Group Discussions (FGDs)

Some of the crucial aspects of the study cannot be fully explained without taking qualitative features in consideration. In the present sections we have tried to address some of those crucial aspects of SHG functioning with equal emphasis on functionaries of Self-Help Group Promoting Institutions (SHPIs) and SHG members perspective. The following section summarizes the insights from these.

bank transactions, use of group fund, transactions in meetings, etc. In other words, leaders become owners of groups. The leadership, in almost all the cases, stayed with the same member since the formation of groups. The few cases of change in leadership were mainly due to death of a leader or change in his/her place of residence.

Record of Groups

Record maintenance in SHGs consists of two critical functions:

1. *Record writing* is generally done by facilitator of groups (staff of NGOs/Aanganwadi workers in case of ICDS). Rural women cannot do record writing due to high illiteracy levels;
2. *Record maintenance* which is done by office bearers/members of groups. Record maintenance implies safe keeping of records and ensuring that all transactions are recorded, etc.

In sample groups, both functions were found to be underperforming. Above sections indicated that record writing was poor while maintenance was worse. In more than 80 per cent of samples, records were found to be lying with facilitators. It will not be an exaggeration to mention here that facilitators seem to be owners of records, as it is up to them to write or not write the transactions while the elected SHG leaders and members have no idea of the actual transactions. Ignorance on the part of members can also be one of the reasons. Further, the records in many places have not been maintained once the worker stops showing interest. SHG members, interestingly, believe that it is better that facilitators take control as they are assured of getting a loan sanctioned. There is complete dependence on the facilitator which has very serious repercussion.

Process of Accessing Bank Loans

The process of accessing bank loan presents very interesting insights. It is needless to mention that loan amount is for members to fulfil their needs, both for consumption and production. Since the loan is for the use of members, the amount should ideally be in accordance with the need. But this is not the case especially in SGSY group, where large amount is involved.

In the case of SGSY loans, it was observed that loan amount is generally decided only after the bank manager informs that a specific loan amount can be applied for. After this, the group decides upon each member's share and just after disbursement, the loan is distributed. In many SHGs it has been noticed that the President and Secretary take the lion's share of the loan and distribute the rest among the members. In one case we found a president who is a member of 3 SHGs uses credit for further lending. It was also observed that in many cases of SGSY groups, loan was sanctioned without the actual need of the groups. This is primarily done to fulfil the target of SGSY which is being monitored at the district level in District Level Coordination Committee (DLCC). After the sanction, the group is being asked to complete the formalities.

Role of Grading

Grading is a process which measures credit worthiness of a group. There are parameters set by NABARD for general SHG bank linkages and by DRDA for SGSY groups. In case of non-BPL group, grading is done by branch manager/officer while in case of SGSY groups the process is executed by a committee comprising of branch manager, block development officer of the block in which SHGs falls and concerned SHPIs. The objective of the process is to measure the quality of group and accordingly recommend the loan amount. Ideally, this is a very suitable mechanism to measure the quality of groups and if this process is executed properly, there is high probability to filter out poor quality groups for which no loan should be sanctioned and hence default up to maximum extent can be avoided. Bank branch has a very critical role in this process.

Theoretically speaking, all sample groups have undergone the process of grading as shared by respective branch manager and concerned staff of SHPIs. But this all was on paper with no ground checking of groups, i.e. visits to see the actual functioning of groups on parameters prescribed. Most of branch managers said that branches have insufficient staff and hence to visit each SHG and see their function is not possible; so we asked the staff of SHPIs to come with all the records. Grading was done based on the records which needless to say, cannot give a true picture of SHGs. In other cases, even records were not verified and loan sanctioned to fulfil the target of SGSY groups; so say some branch managers.

Based on the interactions with branch managers, staff of SHPIs and discussion with SHG members, we may say that lack of grading is one of the most prominent factors which pave the ways to weak groups.

Repayment Schedule

As stated before, many members said that monthly repayment schedule was not convenient for them and they preferred to repay every 2–3 months. But it was customary that repayment will be monthly. In many cases we found that repayment do not match with cash flow of members' households. Further investigation revealed that the SHPIs have instructed them (SHG members) to repay monthly. In fact, improper repayment schedule is one reason for weak groups in many cases, but generally not properly recognized either by SHPIs or banks.

Impact of Microfinance in India on the Millennium Development Goals (MDGs)

Through a number of impact analyses it has been proved at all the levels that microfinance programme contribute with cross-cutting outcomes directly and in numerous ways to the achievement of the MDGs. This includes verifiable impacts on the economic situation mainly of poorer households and related effects on poverty reduction, education and health as well as the social status of women or the informal financial systems, etc.

Poverty Alleviation

One of the more high-profile approaches to poverty reduction is the provision of microfinance. Finance is often used by poor households to engage in micro-enterprise activities, especially in the informal economy. Microfinance is a useful way of channelling money to the poor and overcoming the obstacles they face in obtaining credit from formal financial institutions, such as banks. There is considerable anecdotal evidence that demonstrates the dramatic positive impact on the poor people.

The improved access to microfinance services results in income increases in SHG households which indirectly contributes to an improvement of living conditions, nutrition situation as well as to a reduction of poverty in the SHG households.

An increase in financial, productive and physical capital was also noticed. Indeed, a very high share of SHG members have changed their saving habits and substantially increased their saving rates to accumulate financial capital. The access to micro-credit enables many households to invest in productive assets to intensify and diversify their income generating activities. Increased savings and capital formation improve the self-financing capacities. They even out the household's cash flow and generally contribute to higher socio-economic risk absorption capacities and decreased vulnerability, especially of the poor people.

Decreased dependence on moneylenders was a central achievement. The access to financial services clearly leads to a reduced dependency on informal moneylenders. This has positive effects on the lowering of interest rates and thus the reduction of capital costs.

In addition, an increase of income and diversification of income sources has to be pointed out. Indeed, an increasing share of the beneficiaries diversifies their income sources, especially on the side of non-agricultural activities. The use of the microfinance services contributes substantially to an increase in income. Poor households may use their additional income to further intensify and diversify economic activities, for savings as also for increased expenditure on better nutrition, medical care, and access to schooling, housing and clothing.

Regarding the number of meals which directly gives an account of the poverty level, we see that there was a decline in the proportion of client households having one or two meals per day and a substantial increase in the proportion of client households having three meals a day, across all wealth ranks including the 'very poor' and 'poor'. Thus, microfinance contributed to an improvement in the pattern of food consumption of the client households.

As we look at the healthcare, overall, the proportion of client households having treatment at private hospitals increased sharply at the expense of other modes of treatment. This was also true in the case of 'very poor' and 'poor' households also. It is interesting seeing also that MFI clients showed preference for purchasing clothes 'at any time' rather than at festivals, across all the wealth ranks in end line.

Regarding school education, it is to be spotted that large proportion of client households moved from low-cost education to high-cost education, partly because of the graduation of children from primary to secondary and college education and also partly because of the keenness of the clients to send their children to better schools.

Education

Improved access to microfinance services and an increased income level enable poor SHG households to invest in education and thus in the future of their children. With the availability of increased financial resources people are obviously investing more in the education of their children as one of their priorities.

Women Empowerment

Through the participation in group activities, members also became more assertive in confronting problem situations and social evils. More sample SHG members expressed their desire to resist unpleasant problem situations such as verbal abuse, physical violence, negligence, psychological and emotional abuse. The study results show a positive tendency of SHG members to protest against social evils like drinking, gambling and wife beating by husbands. Gambling as well as drinking was reportedly protested by a much higher proportion of the members during the post-SHG situation compared to the pre-group situation.

Similarly, now many members protested to husband beating the wife against some of them doing so during the pre-SHG situation. Slightly more than one-third of survey respondents indicated that there was a decline in family violence.

Microfinance helped women in contributing to their household incomes by pursuing activities like tailoring, dairy, agriculture, small flour mill and small grocery shops either on their own or with the help of their spouses. Other effects are also observable through the following points.

Women enjoyed full liberty in savings with the group and savings in their name without any inhibition. They were able to influence their husbands to contribute to the savings. Many were happy to say that savings in their name gave some social status at home and in the community.

Regarding utilization of savings for purchase of assets or ornaments women had the power, but none of them (excepting single women households), wanted to take decision without consulting their husbands or other elder members in the house. However, many of them reported that they enjoyed freedom of spending the savings on purchase of clothes and other household goods.

Although increased self-confidence does not automatically lead to empowerment, it may contribute decisively to a woman's ability and willingness to challenge the social injustices and discriminatory systems that they face. This implies that as women become financially better-off their self-confidence and bargaining power within the household increases and this indirectly leads to their empowerment. Finally, given that empowerment is a process, the impact of the microfinance programme may take a long time before it is significantly reflected on the observable measures of women's empowerment.

Decisions regarding utilization of loan, whether for husband's business or new activity or repayment of loan, were taken jointly by husband and wife. Savings out of income from business were spent on education of children and purchase of assets. The decision to spend the savings was taken jointly.

> My name is Rajbala Devi w/o Late-Parbat Singh. I am residing in village Dosod; Tehsil Behror of Alwar District (Rajasthan). My husband died ten years ago due to appendicitis. For his treatment I had borrowed money from the moneylender on the highest interest rate. We are three members in my family, my two sons and myself. My sons are studying in 10th and 12th class.
>
> I do not have any source of income and I have no land. Often I used to go for labour work and earned on an average of ₹ 50 to 100 per day. But it was not sufficient for my daily domestic consumption, which made my family suffering from poverty at a higher level. I was also unable to send my children for study. I was in a deep trouble and was worried thinking about the future of children. I was hopeless and my future was in dark as I was struggling with poverty.
>
> One day I heard that someone from HPPI came in village to provide loan according to their conditions. I also heard from my neighbour that Humana Microfinance Project is going to conduct a meeting on JLG programme in my village to discuss livelihood issues and the mobilization of savings and the subsequent disbursal of credit. After discussing my needs I joined one of the JLG. I applied for a loan amount of ₹ 10,000 on the specified rule of loan cycle by Humana People to People India. I bought a buffalo and I started to get a little income by selling milk. I used some of the money for repayment of Humana People to People India and rest for my domestic consumption. Now I am very happy with my children and I am repaying the weekly instalment of Humana Microfinance easily. I would like to say thanks a lot to Humana People to People India who have provided me micro-credit loan to strengthen my economic condition and sustainable livelihood.

The women told that they earned prestige and importance in their homes and their family members also helped them in domestic work. Their spouses listened to them and consulted them in domestic decision-making. Women, however, commented that the burden of their domestic work had not been reduced; their earlier spare time was now utilized for business purpose.

Empowerment at the household level also covered women's ownership of assets within the household, their involvement in enterprise management, contribution to income and involvement in decision-making.

Also, with the support of microfinance, women are now contributing to the income of the family. Women have started taking decisions on children's education, improving the condition of housing and purchasing household assets.

Many MFI women clients were emboldened by their participation in group meetings, to participate in the Gram Panchayat meetings and in 'morchas' (public demonstrations) for social causes. Some had successfully contested in the local Panchayat elections. The backing of the MFI and the Group gave women courage and self-confidence to fight for the success in their activities and for their economic betterment. In difficult – sometimes hostile – social milieu, they tactfully manoeuvred their way and attained success.

Livelihood

Livelihoods, meaning a persons' economic activity, is an area that is vitally important to SHGs. The loans that SHG members receive are intended to improve their livelihoods so that they can receive greater and steadier cash flows. In rural areas, livelihoods range from agriculture farming, animal husbandry, dairy and various other goods and services activities. Experience has shown that SHGs have had improved livelihoods to the extent of providing the leveraging needed to start an enterprise. However, the interventions to introduce new livelihoods or refine existing ones that could yield better economic results were done by external agencies.

Informal Financial Sector

The high level of dependence of the informal sector on non-institutional sources continued despite a rapid growth of banking network in India in the last five decades, in particular through micro-credit. The rural financial system at present presents an impressively large network of more than 1,50,000 retail outlets.

Despite such phenomenal expansion of the outreach of the formal banking structure, the All India Debt and Investment Survey (GoI), 1981, gave indications that the share of non-institutional agencies (informal sector) in the outstanding cash dues of the rural households was quite high, at 38 per cent. It was also seen that households in the lower asset groups were more dependent on the non-institutional credit agencies.

The main difficulty faced by banks in financing the very poor seemed to be the comparatively high transaction cost in reaching out to a large number of people who required very small doses of credit at frequent intervals. The same held true of the costs involved in providing savings facilities to the small, scattered savers in the rural areas. Feelings were mutual among the very small savers and borrowers in the rural areas as well, as they tended to view banking as an institutional set-up for the elite.

Even if they tried to reach the bank branch, the long distances and loss of earnings on being away from work while visiting the bank branch were hurdles and they were never sure whether they would get any service or not if they did approach the branch. The levels of mutual inconvenience and discomfort made the poor look at banking as an almost inaccessible service, and the banks felt that banking with the very poor was not a 'bankable' proposition.

Social Security

Poverty and ill-health have a two-way relationship. Poverty leads to, and aggravates physical living conditions, poor sanitation, hygiene, and insufficient nutrition. As disease spreads, it leads to lower productivity, prevents people from working and drains their resources, thus driving them deeper into poverty.

Microfinance clients, especially those who also receive health education, are some of the most active and productive members of their communities. They recognize that health is one of their most important assets, and (as the title of one of the market research reports put it) that 'staying healthy means fighting poverty'. Many work hard to stay healthy and to protect the health of their families.

However, while most microfinance clients have regular sources of income from their micro-enterprises, healthcare expenses often impede their ability to consistently meet their families' needs for food and other necessities.

Despite the fact that between 20 per cent and 50 per cent of the family budgets are spent on health, people tend to be more and more focused on the potential for accidents or serious illness and the high costs associated with their treatment.

Microfinance clients resort to several means to pay for services, depending on available cash from earnings or savings, the stage of the illness, and the expected cost and length of treatment. During months when income exceeds expenses, costs for minor illnesses and medicines can be more easily paid, even though this can create hardship in future months, when reserves are needed.

However, poor microfinance clients often experience wide swings in income and expenses over the course of the year due to their dependence on agriculture, climates with extremes of drought and rain, school calendars, and various annual celebrations and festivals with long-established social requirements. Unfortunately, times of higher revenue for the family do not necessarily coincide with times of the highest incidence of illness and thus the need for healthcare.

Role of Banks to Support SHGs

The attempts made by Commercial Banks to help these women through self-help groups has opened doors for them but certainly has had a limited reach as these banks are not able to relate to the poor women from urban as well rural areas to the extent required. To maximize reach, it is essential for banks to understand the pulse and the psyche of these women to initiate them into banking habits, which they are unable to perform successfully. Poor, illiterate women find it useful to deal with a bank only if its services are tailored to suit their needs. Banking with the poor and the illiterate requires special procedures and mechanisms suited to their culture, their needs and their economy. This entails simple procedures, designing schemes that allow for small savings, training and assistance in understanding and dealing with banking procedures, door-to-door service, banking policies that adapt to their crisis situations and credit based on savings performance or loan repayment instead of collateral. It is also to be understood that access to financial services alone is not enough for the poor people to transform their economic activities into profitable economic enterprises. Access to markets, information, technical know-how and social support services is as important as money, if the poor are to share in economic growth. All these factors limit the role that Commercial banks can play in their socio-economic empowerment.

Difficulties, Need and Solutions for SHGs

It is to be noted that though the sustainability of SHGs to effect such change is directly linked to their financial sustainability, research has shown that SHGs financial management is generally average or weak. Thus, it is vitally important that both government and NGOs work to bear all the costs in mind of interventions to make them sustainable, otherwise the SHGs will be overburdened and destined to failure.

Government regulations could help manage this risk and increase the emphasis on sustainability of SHGs. There are key areas of SHG financial management that need to be improved upon, such as internal controls, accounting, management stewardship, organizational efficiency and others. If the government were to enact a policy that would regulate the quality of SHGs and tied this to their eligibility for SHG Bank Linkage, then this would help bring about a more measured and responsible growth to the movement.

Both for SHGs and SHG federations there is a need to aspire to attain standards following the best practices. As the SHG federations are emerging as community-owned microfinance institutions, there is a need for significant investment in providing institution building support. These SHG federations being bodies like corporations as they are registered under an appropriate legal form must comply with the prudential and legal norms. There is a need for a well developed third party rating system for SHG federations before they are linked with financial institutions to act as an intermediary, as they handle large volume of funds from the bank linkage and also undertake savings from their members.

We clearly see that there is a need for establishing a computerized MIS for SHGs and SHG federations to monitor their performance on a regular basis. SHG federations must be able to publish their annual reports and share those with all their members.

Governance of SHG federations is a major challenge. For the SHG members to manage their own institutions with professional staff and large volumes of transactions will be difficult.

SHPIs must provide the needed support for the SHG federations to develop into sustainable institutions of the poor. Considerable investments would be needed to facilitate and sustain SHG federations across the nation.

6

Major Findings

Microfinance is an essential tool for:

- Creating social capital and advancing human development
- Clearly supporting the poor, especially the women

However, it seems to present limits which have to be overcome.

Rajasthan is the less targeted state by MFIs but we can observe that there was nevertheless a rapid increase of microfinance in this state. This is partly due to the millennium development goals context, which saw governmental programmes flourishing within India that benefited the microfinance (MF) growth. A great example of these policy programmes was the MGNREGS project that was a scheme allowing many households to meet their priority expenses such as education, health, etc. A major objective of MGNREGS was to reach financial inclusion, as the payments under this scheme were routed through official institutions, which is a positive step forward. Many schemes were built up in order to tackle poverty and not only just BPL's categories, integrating them in official institutions processes such as banks, but also in skill development training cycles and especially off-farm trainings. All in all, these programmes established a favourable dynamics in order to reduce poverty and encouraged financial inclusion.

However, as seen in the survey, the reality is that hardly 10 per cent of SHG members are totally integrated to the financial institutional system.

Government policies, thus, tended to focus on creating institutions of the poor afterwards, as it was perceived as more sustainable and effective. For instance, NRLM scheme worked in that sense:

- Building credit linkages of the poor with banks
- Building institutions for the poor
- Providing seed capital
- Encouraging savings

However, and it is observable through the study, we have been assisting for the last few years to a rollback of private banks from MF. Indeed, these banks faced expansion issues in rural areas, and were not able to find solutions to the problems, resulting in a narrowing of financial provisions.

Furthermore, we know that savings and credits have been found to be the very two prime financial services that the poor needs. Nevertheless, with the shrinkage of private financial channels, many MF informal systems started to grow here and there, being sources of credit from friends and relatives, the most important part of it. Those informal systems prevalent in Rajasthan, are numerous and therefore making it more uncertain the conditions for obtaining credits.

However, informal sources are still very much present because:

- Easy access to credits
- Timely disbursement
- No formality
- Flexibility in repayment

As seen, these scattered informal systems and the lack of institutional informal credit providers, resulted in the implementation of several NGOs establishing microfinance projects across India, and in Rajasthan.

However, the increasing number of MFIs did not come along with an increase of resources from donors that started to shrink. Therefore, it is crucial to understand the necessity for MFIs to become self-sufficient and diversify their services without losing sight of the social functions MF has. This evolution of MFIs towards self-sufficiency must be supported by international NGOs, governments or donors providing technical assistance, funding, and training to the MFI itself. This partnership is central in strengthening local institutions and providing the best services.

We also have seen that in this context, the SHGs then have known a remarkable growth, from 'social mobilizations' to genuine organizational financial systems. These initiatives participate to the strategy for women empowerment and poverty alleviation. The efforts are meant at developing these groups as 'vibrant people's organizations'. However, most of the members are poor, illiterate and socially marginalized, and, therefore, it takes time to make these groups organized into strong entities.

Moreover, emerging problems regarding loans' defaults appeared in a context where, however, the repayment rate keeps on being high. But still, loan defaults are an emerging concern that has to be seriously considered. In the same way, the lack of awareness of the rural branch staff about the linkage banking programmes and the simplified procedures needed for their account opening and credit linkage is impeaching on SHGs' empowerment and positive impacts for them to spread.

Through the survey we handled in the different districts we noticed several points that need attention, in order to improve SHGs' efficiency:

- Average life cycles of about 4 to 5 years for SHGs are directly dependent not only on the NGO's projects, but also on the weather variations;
- The average size for the five districts put together is 12;
- The social category of the SHG members is drawn on geographical patterns but also reflects the social distribution between the different castes in Rajasthan;

- The distribution by type of house translates the slow economical development that is taking place in rural areas;
- SHGs members cannot independently manage their financial record-keeping because of high illiteracy incidence;
- But, major part of the land is unirrigated, therefore non-farmable, and therefore useless in most of the cases, except in Jaipur; it highlights the crucial importance of water and its access;
- People do not have many animals because of the unirrigated lands. Where there are rocky lands, we observe the development of others fields;
- As for the savings, the older the group the bigger the amount of money saved;
- SHG groups' creation extended the financial possibilities of SHG members even if all members do not benefit from it;
- Loans taken are emergency loans and short-term loans for which the members used to go to moneylenders or relatives before;
- The loans are productive loans (animal husbandry, agriculture, etc.) and vital loans (domestic and health purposes, etc.);
- Loans from the banks are few, which show very little cooperation and interest in working with SHGs;
- Savings is the very first priority in joining SHGs ;
- There is no appreciation of the other functions of SHGs such as the collective power, women empowerment, social capital, etc;
- Basic purposes are being fulfilled and economical growth is a positive sign for the future of SHGs;
- As for training, the problem is twofold, and is situated as much on the villagers' side who cannot assist in all these trainings, as on NGOs' side, which are limited in their actions by the lack of resources;
- SHG members are aware that one of the major problem is the lack of training, in order to make up for illiteracy, bank accountancy, etc;

- As mentioned before, SHGs must let members know about the great social impacts SHGs can have.

Several observations from FGDs also must be pointed out, as to show what is at stake:

- SHG is an effective institution for poverty reduction and women empowerment but it can be only effective when it is promoted with right approach and process;
- Various research studies have revealed that lack of proper training to SHGs is one of the most important reasons for poor quality of groups across the country;
- Further many groups lost their interest in inter-loaning as they feel that the interest on their savings is too low or completely absent in comparison to bank rate of interest;
- Grading is a process which measures credit worthiness of a group. The objective of this process is to measure the quality of the group and accordingly recommend loan amounts. Bank branch has a very critical role in this process;
- Many members said that monthly repayment schedule was not convenient for them, but in fact improper repayment schedule is one reason for weak groups.

It is also important to point out the problems faced by MFIs is not only having constant funds available, but also in the increasing resource costs, etc. The tendency to extract commercial returns and possible opaque pricing models is keeping away the poorer clients.

Therefore, to remain rooted on the objectives of serving the poor and vulnerable, MFIs need to:

- Revisit their original objectives; and
- Ensure mission fidelity.

Growth, profits and high corporate image gain considerable value when accompanied by mission achievement. Financial inclusion should involve both savings and credit products. Thereby, the provision of savings' products will enable MFIs to offer a more complete suite of products to low income groups.

Problems Faced by MFIs

The MFIs face problems, some common across the sector and some unique to a particular set of institutions depending upon the form, size and business model. The common problems range from availability of funds, increasing resource costs, higher risks, limitations on human resource (HR) availability and also a passive policy environment. The specific problems relate to low access to commercial funds for 'not-for-profits' and poor soft fund support to 'for-profits'. Federations seem to face problems in raising resources forcing them to become state-dependent, except in the case of mutually aided cooperatives.

Banks do not seem to have a continuing long-term interest in the microfinance institutions. The flow of funds is uncertain and could dry up any time, impairing the ability of MFIs to carry on their business. When credit availability to the client is disrupted, then the credibility of MFIs suffers in the field. In the not very distant past, a decision of one of the major banks to stop loans to MFIs on account of certain internal reasons had created a very difficult situation for the partner MFI in the field. While MFIs assume that their credit facilities with banks would continue to be enhanced year after year, the banks face difficulties in increasing the credit exposure beyond a point on account of risk management policies. With only book debts of MFIs available as collateral, banks were wary of expanding their loan exposure and the recent increase in risk weight on loans from 100 to 150 per cent to unrated institutions would make the banks even more cautious.

The recently introduced capital adequacy norm for the NBFC-MFIs has been discussed intensely in the sector. The 15 per cent capital adequacy stipulated is felt to be rather high by some practitioners, who are concerned at the increased cost of capital and the overall cost of funds that might result. However, there are others who feel that 15 per cent capital adequacy ratio (CAR) fairly reflects the level of risk that is inherent in the business and the need for a larger quantum of promoters' funds being brought into business. Larger MFIs such as SKS Microfinance, Spandana or Share Microfin do not see the additional equity as a major issue. But smaller entities without recourse to external equity will find this increased CAR to be a stumbling block to their growth aspirations.

Funds for Lending

The Indian MFIs are highly leveraged and in some cases, precariously. The debt to equity ratio for 83 MFIs taken for detailed analysis by Sa-Dhan in its Side by Side Report 2007 was 15. The high leverage enjoyed by MFIs becomes possible through borrowing from multiple banks; at times, not making full disclosure to the lenders. Available bank funds are typically short-term. The maximum period for which loans are available is for two years with rare exceptions. The lack of long-term resources for MFIs compels them to provide very short-term credit to their clients; which is not appropriate for undertaking investment in income generating assets. As these loans given by the banks and financial institutions have regular repayment obligations, the counter-party loans given to the clients typically carry weekly instalments. There is a tendency among some lending banks to sanction and disburse loans to MFIs around the end of the accounting year in pursuit of their targets. This leads MFIs to draw and deploy the funds suboptimally for a period, till they find better avenues for deployment in loans to the needy clients. In some exceptional cases, the loans taken from the banks were invested back with them in short-term deposits at much lower interest. The hidden cost adds to the already increasing cost of funds.

The hardening interest rates and the inflationary conditions have the potential of impacting the profits and balance sheets of MFIs. Rising fund costs and client expectations of declining interest rates from growing MFIs are the two extremities of the pricing continuum. When the high leverages are taken into account, it seems difficult for MFIs to continue to absorb the incremental costs of borrowing. The market should expect to see a resetting of MFI interest rates following the banks resetting their rates.

Risks and Challenges

The emergence of new MFIs and rapid scaling-up in several regions is a welcome development from many points of view. A matter of serious concern is the initial set of assumptions made at the time of designing the MFI and its business model. Quite a few of the new MFIs assume breakeven within a period of three years, with turnover targets running into a few billion rupees. This kind of very high growth is possible only when lending funds, skilled staff and sound internal systems are in place with potential to scale up along with increasing business. The returns to equity assumed are significantly high. Equity placement at a premium even before commencement of business is under negotiation in some cases. But for the fact that these institutions are designed as MFIs, these business projections would not be an issue for debate. But high profitability and high growth are based on the basic assumption of ability of MFIs to charge high interest rates. Such business models need careful appraisal by the investors and funders from systems and HR availability angles.

Key-man risk is the biggest single risk facing the larger MFIs. Most MFIs, especially the larger ones are driven by a committed individual or at best, a small group. If these persons, especially the promoters, exit from the institution; then, what would happen to the business and to its clients, is a question that needs to be answered satisfactorily. Eight large MFIs had more than half a million clients (two of these had more than 1 million clients and one has reached 2 million clients recently). Such large number of clients is entitled to warranties of continued quality of service from the MFIs, regardless of who the owners and funders are. The key-man has to ensure that there is a proper chain of command, and a good second and third-line of management, which is capable to run the business professionally. But the evidence of such second and third-lines of management within the institutions is hardly available. This is an area of concern not only in India, but all over Asia. The Banana Skins Survey[1] 2008 listed management quality, corporate governance and staffing as the key risks at ranks 2, 3 and 4 out of the top five risks that are facing the microfinance sector in Asia. Apart from recognizing the criticality of management and governance in MFIs, more needs to be done to ensure that institutions do not deny their past when there is a change in ownership.

Governance standards in the microfinance sector, especially in NBFCs (with some exceptions), have not received favourable comment. Mission drift, cousin boards, lack of transparency, failure to induct independent professionals on boards, weak audit systems, lack of independent review of audit outputs and lack of client protection/grievance redressal mechanisms are some of the concerns with regard to governance. There are some MFIs that have taken significant measures to improve governance and have provided good models for others to emulate. In the recent past, the larger MFIs have been making conscious efforts to improve different aspects of governance. The induction of private equity has made significant contributions to this change. But there is still, a long way to go.

Human resources are scarce in the sector and the Banana Skins Survey highlights this as a key risk. Sa-Dhan has estimated the HR requirements at 2,40,000 of which those at area manager levels was 6,500 over the next five years. The competencies at the base level are not extraordinary. The requirements relate to diligence, proper people-friendly attitude, and adherence to systems and procedures. But raw recruits need to be trained and schooled in the base-level skills of finance and microfinance. Industry-ready personnel who would hit the ground running are not available. A combination of theoretical training and a practical internship is a must to produce competent field staff. As for higher levels, it is difficult to get experienced people in large numbers. The MFIs with expansion plans should recruit persons with educational background and other industry experience in managing human resources and customer relationships. Indian Institute of Banking and Finance (IIBF)[2] and Sa-Dhan have partnered in a project to offer a certificate course and a diploma course in microfinance. IIBF also has partnered with Centre for Microfinance, Jaipur to offer a certificate course in microfinance. NABARD also offers financial assistance to those taking up a certificate examination in microfinance in the Yashwant Rao Chavan Open University. More such initiatives are needed to meet the large HR needs of the sector. The HR recruitment and training model of SKS microfinance provides some insights into the level of mobilization that MFIs have to undertake in their quest for fast growth.

Financing institutions and investors have highlighted that the poor quality of information that is available in the MFI sector renders their decision-making risky and conservative. Few MFIs have a core banking solution which produces the kind of information that is required on a variety of business and finance-related parameters. In many institutions, accounting and record-keeping is on manual systems; in cases where computers might be used, no standard software that takes care of accounting and information generation, is in place. Investments in technology are more seen as a function of availability of grants than a business requirement. In a fast-commercializing microfinance sector, investment in appropriate technological solutions to take care of accounting and management information system (MIS) requirements is a prerequisite. Availability of commercial funds (equity, venture capital funds and bulk loans) might become contingent on fulfilment of IT enablement of accounting and operational processes.

Alternatives to Loans

Over the last two years, institutions have been observed to be moving from soft funds to commercial funds; and in commercial funds, from loans to private equity. The depth in the market in terms of capacity to absorb equity is very shallow. While there is a clear need to diversify the sources of funds in this debt-dependent sector, it does not mean a move towards equity.

Securitization of portfolio, structured-debt instruments, portfolio buyouts and even bond issues are some of the liability products that are under development. Axis Bank, ICICI Bank and Development Cooperative Bank have already bought portfolios from MFIs. Stanchart has been working on structured debts and bond issues. But these resource-raising measures, by and large would be available only to large and mature MFIs.

One of the problems that have been agitating the sector is the uneven playing field between the MFIs and banks. A number of poverty alleviation programmes and other developmental schemes are implemented through the banking system. Routing of concessional credit and subsidy schemes of government through the banks places them in a better position to acquire more clients, and also reduce the credit risk that is inherent in lending to vulnerable sections of population. MFIs argue that they should also be made eligible to receive and distribute poverty alleviation schemes of the government.

Interest Pricing and Transparency

Interest rate and loan-pricing continue to dominate the discussion in microfinance and MFIs. Clients have no alternative, but to pay the rate of interest as fixed by the MFIs for want of alternative sources of finance. Some cases of high-interest pricing, taking advantage of almost monopolistic conditions and the desperation of borrowers have been witnessed. The pricing of the loan product differed from one MFI to the other, and the clients have great difficulty in knowing the real cost of credit.[3] The loan terms are complicated and opaque, with a result that the borrower is unable to make a comparison and take an informed judgement on the affordability of the loan. The borrowers, more often than not, are influenced to look at the affordability of the instalment of repayment rather than the interest cost of credit. There is a need for transparency in interest pricing. The difference between a flat rate charge and declining balance interest charge has to be explained in terms of financial cost of the borrowing.[4] Practices such as taking a security deposit, collecting an instalment of loan in advance, charging a variety of loan-processing and monitoring fees and so forth, have their own implication on the financial cost-of-credit to the borrower. These needs are to be factored in and analysed for giving greater information to the clients. In an attempt to bring greater transparency to interest-rate setting, formation of a new non-profit organization has been announced in the Micro Credit Summit Conference in July 2008. This platform named Microfinance Transparency (MFT) would place all interest rates of all MFIs on a standard format and make the results comparable as annual percentage rates paid on declining balance. The rationale for its formation as explained by MFT '... goal of MFT is to promote transparency on product pricing information; MFT also operates on the foundational principle of transparency. All operational rules, all calculations, all data sources are made public. MFT also operates on the principle of reporting objective facts. No judgments are to be made, no rating scores given, nor are profits of MFIs to be reported'.

The obligation of having to repay every week that too, on very small loan sizes which average around ₹ 5,000 does not serve the poor well in terms of poverty alleviation. Available loan size required to bring people above poverty line would be around ₹ 50,000, if we take into account a capital to output ratio of 4:1.[5] Inadequate loan size compels borrowers to find additional sources of funds, provides space for competitors to enter and encourages multiple borrowing. Multiple borrowing may not solve the problems of the client fully, but would certainly impair the asset quality of MFIs and alienate the client over time. Performance of a social mission and achieving profitability that would satisfy equity investors seem to be in conflict. In the words of one of the industry leaders 'microfinance without a development mission is a waste of time and resources'.

The Investment Climate

The total amount mobilized via equity sell-offs by Indian MFIs had increased 25-fold from 2006 to 2007 and looks set to increase even further in future. Even with all these developments, the Indian MFI equity scene is nowhere near to reaching its investment potential or fulfilling its burgeoning requirement for equity. With the overall sector growing at a scorching pace, MFIs would need to sell much more of their equity to investors, to maintain current low levels of capital adequacy.[6] Yet, recent regulatory changes in the sector imply that equity financing will not just keep pace with other forms of financing, but will increase and fill new gaps. The RBI has mandated that all non-deposit-taking NBFCs – the legal form of choice for most large MFIs – increase their capital adequacy ratios from10 to 15 per cent by April 2009. Even when equity is ready to flow, there are few institutions that have the necessary readiness to receive and absorb equity. The critical requirements for receiving and absorbing equity in MFI are: (1) information base and transparency, (2) governance standards, (3) investment readiness in the form of business strategy, (4) professional management, and (5) revenue models. There is a view that the investments made today in the sector are more experimental than calculated business decisions. The lack of a market-based exit route and also the difficulty of producing high returns render equity investments in most of institutions, risky. The political risk remains a key concern for many investors. All investors approached for comments, ranked political risk as one of their top concerns.

Other challenges to expanding equity investments arise from regulation. While MFIs in India are registered under a variety of legal forms, equity investments are effectively restricted to MFIs registered as NBFCs. Due to the minimum capital requirement of ₹ 20 million for registering a new NBFC, along with the other legal requirements, converting an MFI into an NBFC from another legal form remains a difficult task. In addition, while larger MFIs in other countries have recently come to depend on deposits as a source of funds, it looks increasingly unlikely, that the RBI or government will lift restrictions which effectively prevent MFIs from accepting deposits from clients.

The investors on their part have several objectives. Some have social objectives and target a low return in exchange for achievement of social objective. There are some that are entirely commercial and target high rates of return. The return expectation ranged from 5 to 30 per cent on the equity investment. The other material factor is the holding period for such equity investment. This varies from 3 to 7 years. In a growing market, which is building volumes and serving reportedly, the vulnerable sections of the poor; a three-year investment threshold and a 30 per cent return on equity appear unrealistic. In fact, it will be unachievable except through charging high rates of interest from the poor clients. Though double bottom lines are desired in an investor, the equity funders look to financial performance as a non-negotiable outcome. The equity funds have investors backing them and have to post decent returns to keep them interested. The risks in equity investments are higher than in loans as the equity generates a return only after all other claimants are paid, and any capital appreciation and exit possibility depends on good financial performance. For the other stakeholders, contractual payments do not depend on financial performance (except some types of staff incentives). Hence, equity investors feel that their return expectations should not be envied as there is a real risk of total investment failing to recover even the capital. But there are other views on equity investments targeting the mature MFIs. Vijay Mahajan[7] points out 'Globally 3 to 4 billion dollars has been spent to bring the field to where it has reached now. For extreme profit-seeking investors to now cherry pick that part of this field which gives a high return, without any care as to what it does to the poor, is not acceptable'.

The investors, especially the bulk funders from the banking sector are extremely wary of the reputation risk that might arise from inappropriate behaviour on the part of the MFIs. This leads them to take extra precautions in terms of specific areas of governance, financial management and in some cases even interest pricing. Some institutions insist that the borrowing MFIs should cap their rate of interest to clients. Some others seek a seat on the board of the MFIs, in which the investments are made or the loans are extended. Overall, the investment climate is adversely impacted in the short-term by the introduction of changes to capital adequacy norms that have mandated a risk weight of 150 per cent to bank loans extended to unrated institutions.[8] MFIs which are not rated would become unattractive, as clients to the lending bank. As this pushes up the level of capital required carrying such exposure on their balance sheet, the banks would tend to increase the interest rate of such loans and also reduce the quantum thereof. This would adversely affect the growth plans of many of the existing MFIs.

This brings us to a discussion on the practice of rating of MFIs. As far as the Central Bank is concerned, banks can, in case of MFIs where the exposure is more than ₹ 50 million, accept ratings carried out by those agencies that are approved by RBI. Presently, CRISIL, CARE, ICRA and Fitch are the rating agencies whose ratings are recognized by Reserve Bank, and the financing banks can make use of the same for their risk assessment of larger borrowers and lower the risk weightage on loans.[9] M-CRIL has been present in the industry for a long time and has considerable experience of intense involvement in rating of the MFI sector. Yet, its ratings have not been recognized for this purpose (in the case of loans of ₹ 50 million and more) by the Central Bank. The ongoing discussion between M-CRIL and the RBI[10] should produce positive results bringing much-needed relief, both to MFIs and the lending banks. But the point is that the MFIs should commission ratings every year in their own interest so that they are in a position to access bank funds and raise comfort levels of investors and clients. The present trend of MFIs making the rating exercise an optional extra that is contingent on availability of donor funds must cease. The MFIs should get themselves rated in their own interest and should know from an independent source, the health of their organization. There are signs that MFIs are more ready to get ratings done on their own. Sanjay Sinha estimates that in 2008, about 50

MFIs would pay for their rating when compared to 20, which paid in 2007. The pressure from financing banks for rating reports (prodded by the credit risk assessment requirement under Basel II norms) is a factor in this move towards getting external ratings done.

Some of the banks have gone ahead with a deeper examination of the risk involved through portfolio study and systems audit, looking to the risks faced by the sector. ABN-AMRO has taken up the conduct of portfolio audit jointly with a couple of other banks. Such studies apart from providing information to lenders could provide valuable feedback to the MFIs.

Information Asymmetry

One of the problems facing the lender is the lack of full information about the borrowing institutions. Many MFIs have multiple borrowing relationships with multiple lenders. The terms at which these loan contracts are concluded differ from bank to bank. But information relating to the underlying quality of asset as also the operational aspects is not uniformly known to all the lending institutions. While each institution seems to have a part of the information, a totality of what the borrowing institution is about, is rarely available. Ratings referring to the position at a point of time can be too dated in a fast-developing microfinance sector. There have been attempts in the recent past to pool the information through an informal forum of lenders. The informal forum exchanges information about the MFIs, quality of asset, business models as also the processes that are adopted. Instances of deviant behaviour on the part of MFIs are beginning to be shared across like-minded lenders. The lenders increasingly feel the necessity for a more formal arrangement under which, sensitive information could be pooled and shared to make appropriate decisions. Further, more lenders together could jointly carry out portfolio audit; systems audit, and also place a common representative on the board of the MFIs to protect their interest. This, according to banks, is an acute necessity on account of the high leverages and high-debt dependence of MFIs on the banking system. There are suggestions for introduction of common reporting formats on which MFIs could provide periodic, operational and financial information to all the lenders. Any special requirements of individual banks could be separately met, as such requests are likely to be rare. This would save time on the part of the MFIs and the banks. Similarly, there is a move for a set of common minimum standards in financial and operational disciplines that would be insisted upon by all lenders so that the scope for MFIs arbitraging on these conditions between different lenders is avoided.

The private sector banks and the foreign banks are quite active in financing the MFIs rather than the SHGs. These banks have their own system of appraisal and audit as also dedicated personnel for management of microfinance portfolio. The feeling of these banks is that the sector is suffering from shortage of qualified professionals, weak information systems, weak accounting standards, multiple lending to same borrower by different MFIs, absence of credit information bureaus, relatively loose regulation, and unrealistic targeting by MFIs that are yet to mature.

Investment in Indian microfinance has increased dramatically, over the past year and a half. Despite this dramatic rise, investment will need to increase even faster if it is able to plug the gaps in financing, which have resulted from recent regulatory moves by the RBI and the overall growth of the sector. Intellecap has projected that the Indian MFIs would cumulatively require funds of the order of ₹ 243 billion, of which equity capital would be ₹ 21.6 billion and ₹ 223 billion would be the loans.[11] This level is about 5.5 times of the volumes expected to have been reached in 2008. Significant obstacles to the scaling-up of investment in Indian microfinance remain; yet, the strong growth in the supply of microfinance investment funds is an encouraging sign that market participants are up to the challenge. Clients would be better served through improved governance, efficiency and access to large source of funds. But the tendency to extract commercial returns and possible opaque pricing models would keep away the poorer clients. To remain rooted to the objective of serving the poor and vulnerable, MFIs need to revisit their original objectives and ensure mission fidelity. Growth, profits and high corporate image gain considerable value when accompanied by mission achievement.

Notes

1. This survey was carried out by Centre for Study of Financial Innovations, supported by Citibank and CGAP.
2. Indian Institute of Banking and Finance is an industry-level body that caters to the capacity building needs of bank staff and certification of their competencies. It offers diploma and certificate courses as well.
3. S. Mullainathan and Minakshi in a study on behalf of CmF, IFMR, found that among a sample of 200 microfinance borrowers, 58 per cent did not know of the interest payable as per the loan contract; 34 per cent about the correct instalment amount and 86 per cent about the total interest on the loan amount.
4. Excerpts from a note on interest pricing and implications of flat rate and annual percentage rate by Chuck Waterfield.
5. The draft guidelines proposed by the Ministry of Rural Development (under discussion, yet to be operationalized) for revamping the poverty alleviation programme, SGSY sets a minimum outlay of ₹ 1,00,000 to bring families above the poverty line.
6. As there is no law or regulation in India requiring organizations, which provide micro-credit to formally register or provide basic statistics on outreach, accurately assessing the growth of the overall sector is a difficult task. As a crude proxy, we may use the growth in the total number of clients for all MFIs reporting to the MIX market. According to this measure, the Indian microfinance sector as a whole, grew at a compound annual growth rate of over 100 per cent between the years of 2001 and 2006.
7. Vijay Mahajan, founder and MD of Basix, in an interview carried in Microfinance Insights, June 2007.

8. Excerpts from the RBI notification on the revised risk capital requirements.
9. The Central Bank has specified that 'while applying risk weights to exposure/limits of ₹ 5 crore and above, if such exposure is rated by any of the recognized credit rating agencies, the risk weights varies with the rating of the exposure. A better rated exposure attracts a better risk weight'. Master circular on Capital Adequacy issued to banks by Reserve Bank of India, DBOD.No.BP.BC.11/21.06.001/2008–09, dated 1 July 2008.
10. Sanjay Sinha, M-CRIL, explained 'The RBI has said that they would like to see default data in relation to the rating grades awarded by us and they will then consider adding our name to the list. We are in the process of collecting the necessary data from the leading lenders to MFIs'.
11. Inverting the Pyramid – The Changing Face of Indian Microfinance, Intellecap.

7

Conclusion, Suggestions and Recommendations

It is undeniable that microfinance has enormous potential to promote economic and social development among both the rural and urban poor, proof of which lies in the countless success stories of microfinance in India and in the developing and developed countries alike. It is true that microfinance may not target the poorest of the poor, yet it has done wonders for those who are economically active and who have the potential to prosper through self-employment. Not only does microfinance provide financial stability to those who are in dire need of it, it also promotes the idea of credit as being a fundamental human right, something which all people, regardless of their socio-economic status, should be entitled to. It champions social development by empowering women and promoting gender equality, as well as developing leadership and social capital within communities. However, it is important that institutions wishing to engage themselves in microfinance, conduct adequate research beforehand, concerning the local environment in which they wish to operate, the profiles of the potential borrowers and the risk associated with providing microfinancial services. Today, the goal of all microfinance institutions should be to achieve financial sustainability, whilst remaining socially relevant and productive. MFIs should strive to provide savings services to their clients, and to use savings mobilization as a means of self-funding their micro-credit operations. MFIs should seek mutually beneficial partnerships with international organizations or local NGOs, to increase the scope of knowledge and expertise in all areas. Finally, MFIs must ensure that they fully educate their borrowers about the concept of microfinance and the importance of repaying the loans and putting the money towards productive means, before the process of loan disbursement commences.

With all of these considerations in mind, institutions which undertake microfinance initiatives have many chances of success. In India, one goal of the microfinance sector must be to expand its operations uniformly throughout the country, providing all states with equal access to microfinancial services. Although there is still great room for expansion and growth within the microfinance sector in India, it has already proven a powerful tool in eradicating poverty. In the words of Muhammad Yunus, pioneer of microfinance:

> If you go out into the real world, you cannot miss seeing that the poor are poor not because they are untrained or illiterate but because they cannot retain the returns of their labour. They have no control over capital, and it is the ability to control capital that gives people the power to rise out of poverty.[1]

And so today, microfinance in India and beyond has the capacity to achieve exactly this, to raise millions of people out of poverty, and to provide them with a second chance that was never considered worthy for them before.

In conclusion, this chapter outlines the major opportunities and issues that need to be addressed for scaling up the microfinance sector in Rajasthan. The research confirms the potential of microfinance to organize two-thirds of rural households that are otherwise difficult to reach. According to the estimates there is a vast market for micro-savings, micro-credit, micro-insurance, and remittance services for the poor in Rajasthan. Achieving this will require concerted action from all stakeholders on various issues, some of which are listed below.

Greater Coverage of Poor Under Microfinance

Reach out to 'all poor families' and 'not restrict to only BPL'

Rajasthan has a peculiar economic status, where the average landholding is comparatively high (3.7 hectare in Rajasthan, 1.5 hectare in India) and the density of population is comparatively low. There are large numbers of families which are not in BPL list but are only marginally better off than BPL. A single year of drought is enough to pull them below BPL families' status.[2]

More importantly, the whole approach of SHG is based on affinity among members and on condition that members of a group have mutual trust and can use peer pressure on each other to ensure repayments, etc. Experiences all over, tell that exclusive BPL groups do not function well.

Therefore, focusing only on BPL families, while forming SHGs (as done under SGSY, DPIP and MPOWER projects), may not address the poverty alleviation or women empowerment significantly, as large number of families will be left out. The SHG movement in Rajasthan should reach out to all poor (about 60–70% households in rural areas) including BPL, small and marginal farmers, etc.

Strengthening SHG Movement in Weaker Areas

As discussed earlier, SHG movement has been found to be weak in districts like Nagaur, Dholpur, Dausa, Karouli, Barmer, Jodhpur, Pali, Jalaur, Alwar and Rajsamand. Also under-banked index of districts in Rajasthan, Nagaur, Dholpur, Dausa, Karauli, Barmer and Jalore have been found to be under-banked too.

The reasons for disparity of SHG movement among the states can be traced to opportunities in local economy, density of population, presence of NGOs and government support, etc. It has been observed that backward and disadvantaged districts have less number of SHGs.

This disparity can be tackled with two-prolonged strategies: First, to create a cadre of human resource including Community Resource Persons (leaders of SHG groups) in stronger districts in phases and train them to promote Self-Help Groups in weaker districts. Community Resource Persons (CRPs) are better placed in creating solidarity among group members and can pace up the movement in weaker districts; Second, to put special focus on weaker areas by allocating special funds for implementation of community based microfinance and livelihoods projects by collaborating with NABARD, Banks and Voluntary Organizations.

Adopting Common Approach

Currently, in Rajasthan, Self-Help Groups are promoted by many Government and Non-Government agencies with different objectives like women empowerment, poverty alleviation, delivery of credit, etc. The promoting agencies, even if they work in the same village, have different vision and expectations from SHGs. This creates operational problems and confusion at the community level. By becoming member of a particular group, a woman may get good amount of subsidy, which she may not get if she were a member of another group. This often leads to multiple memberships in SHGs and breaking up of some groups.

To tackle this issue, SHG movement in Rajasthan needs a common approach. Government and banks should look at all SHGs, irrespective of their pedigree, through a single lens. Discussed below are few strategies to use a common approach for all SHGs, irrespective of their originator, SHPI or the scheme they fall under.

Standardized Systems and Processes for all SHGs in the State

All SHGs, irrespective of their pedigree, should have uniform systems, processes, operations, bookkeeping, record-keeping, grading, auditing and quality standards. Such a standardized approach to all SHGs would lead to drawing of everyone's attention and focus on SHG movement rather than a select set of SHGs falling under a certain scheme.

Common Perspective

Savings First, Credit Later

The SHG movement started with 'thrift' as its core value and banks came in later with credit, primarily to augment SHGs' corpus. Objective was to meet credit need of SHG members to a larger extent. But now, primarily under government programmes, the SHGs are being formed to meet the targets and to avail bank credit only.

If such a trend continues, the sector and its core value of 'Self-help' will not grow. If the core value of 'Self-help' does not grow, then solidarity among groups will not be strengthened, which in turn will lead to breaking up of groups. Self-Help Group Bank Linkage Programme cannot afford such a trend and therefore, the groups must focus on savings by members first, so that they do not become dependent on bank credit for small needs. Bank credit is only meant to supplement the group savings. SHGs have to provide appropriate savings products to mobilize disposable cash surpluses of members and create a reserve for future.

Focus on Women Empowerment

The relevance and impact of Self-Help Groups on women empowerment and on livelihood strengthening has been proven all over country (Rajasthan as well). Good quality Self-Help Groups create mutual trust and a sense of solidarity among members. This raises their confidence to deal with socio-economic problems of their family and their village, all by themselves. Women empowerment can further be boosted by promoting the following four ideologies, which can be taken as indicators of success:

1. Zero tolerance of domestic violence in families of all SHG members in Rajasthan;
2. 100 per cent girl child enrolment in educational institutions in families of all SHG members;
3. 100 per cent institutional infant delivery;
4. 50 per cent participation of women SHG members at village development committees.

Milestones should be set for every year in order to achieve the stated objectives while progress should be tracked by measuring the indicators.

Promoting 'Area Centric' Federations of SHGs

Self-Help Groups on their own are tiny institutions (10–20 marginalized women from very poor families). They can best be effective to provide small social capital, small savings and small credit to members. They alone and individually are not in a position to bring larger change and impact on lives of the poor women unless they federate into next tier institutions and aggregate their demands and surpluses to market, to take benefit of 'economics of scale'. In Rajasthan there are about 42 federations of SHGs and the vibrancy of SHGs through the federations is commendable. In southern states like AP, Tamil Nadu, Karnataka, etc. there are thousands of federations of SHGs.

In Rajasthan, so far only NGOs have promoted SHG federations and the objective and perspective of different NGOs has been different. The quality and system of SHGs have been heavily influenced by the promoting institutions. It has been observed that SHGs promoted by a particular promoter federate leave aside SHGs promoted by other promoter within the same village. If this trend continues, it may lead to more than two SHG federations working in the same village. Therefore, efforts need to be made to promote area-centric federations rather than 'SHPI centric' or 'target-centric' federations.

In next 3–5 years, efforts should be made to federate the SHGs into village, cluster and block level federations. This task is very crucial and would require clear perspective, skills, patience and investments required for 'institution building'. There is good experience available on federating SHGs in the state and outside, which should be used in forming new SHG federations.

Rajasthan Microfinance Mission

State Government may consider setting up a body for SHGs in Rajasthan with equitable mix of government functionaries, SHPIs and SHG community leaders in form of 'Rajasthan Microfinance Mission or Rajasthan SHG mission'. The body would prepare a vision and a 5-year action plan to upscale the SHG movement in the state. All SHGs, irrespective of their pedigree, may fall under the purview of this body. Under this body, a cadre of quality auditors can be developed (at district level) which will help communities and bankers with an independent assessment. This cadre may be given the task of regular grading of the SHGs and providing necessary inputs to SHGs on a regular basis.

Deepening Financial Services and Financial Inclusion

Increasing Bank Credit through Self-Help Groups

Compared to the vast demand and potential of micro-credit, annual credit through SHGs from banks in Rajasthan (about ₹ 200 crore) is very low. The number of SHGs credit linked every year is also about 10 per cent. The repayment of SHGs to banks is more than 95 per cent on time. It is also observed that the SHG members start losing interest in group meetings, etc. if timely credit does not come to groups from banks.

SHGs have the potential and capacities to bridge the gap between banks and the poor. Therefore, banks should increase their credit through SHGs. This can be done by orientation and sensitization of branch staff, simplifying the procedure of opening bank accounts and credit sanction to SHGs, not impounding of SHG savings (while giving them loan), timely processing of loan application of SHGs, encouraging repeat credit linkages, adopting a common system of grading, appreciation of the quality of SHGs by providing credit to good groups on priority, etc.

In the recent past, there have been some positive experiences in the form of special emphasis by banks on rural credit and SHG bank linkage programme. In Dungarpur district, Bank of Baroda collaborated with local NGO and Centre for Microfinance (CmF) and adopted a focused approach for livelihood strengthening of SHG members through timely and adequate credit. This approach can work in other districts as well. Therefore, commercial banks should take up districts where they are the lead banks and adopt a focused approach where SHG promoting organizations ensure the quality of SHGs and the banks ensure timely and adequate credit.

Government has made micro-credit eligible under Priority Sector Lending of Banks. However, to give impetus to banks' engagement with SHG movement, government should allocate a certain percentage of priority sector lending target to SHG bank linkage. This target can be earmarked at 2 per cent of the total credit disbursement in a state of a particular bank. A committee along with SLBC may review the achievement of this target.

Credit Fund for SHGs

Annual credit from banks to SHGs in Rajasthan is stagnant in the range of ₹ 160–220 crore. Only about 60 per cent of SHGs have been able to take credit from banks in the last 10 years. Whereas the annual credit in states like Andhra Pradesh is to the tune of ₹ 5,000 crore.

Banks, State Government and leaders of SHG movement should explore possibility of setting up an 'exclusive SHG credit fund' and 'special purpose vehicle' (SPV) to deliver credit to SHGs in the state. Banks, State Government and SHGs can jointly float a company/fund to provide timely credit. Such a company may be professionally managed. SHG federations can effectively take up the role of 'financial intermediation', provided they are supported and strengthened. The SHG federations can facilitate the SHG bank linkage with credit rating services and ensure repayments. Proposed company can give bulk loan to SHG Federations which the federation can lend on to SHGs.

SHG-MFI Collaboration

MFIs currently operate in urban, semi-urban and with relatively economically better off people in rural areas. MFIs can target poorer segments by collaborating with SHGs. SHGs provide a ready platform for MFIs to scale up and impact weaker sections of poor. SHGs need more credit while MFIs look for disciplined clients with good credit record. MFIs can save on cost because SHGs are capable of taking care of back-end operations (e.g. collection, distribution, book-keeping, etc.) by themselves. However, for this to happen, MFIs may have to give a re-look at their cost structure and see where costs can be reduced so that the effective rate of interest to SHG members is below 20 per cent per annum on reducing balance basis.

Financial Inclusion through Information and Communication Technology (ICT)

Banking activities from origination and transaction to fulfilment and settlement can be completed using a mobile phone or smart cards. This is evident from success of FINO in India, M-Pesa model in Kenya, Tanzania and Afghanistan, where the poor are able to access formal financial services through branchless banking. Such a model for technology-based financial inclusion can also be implemented in India. The New Pension System offers a model of low-cost electronic accounts that banks can adopt – an agency could maintain accounts on a single electronic platform that different banks can access as per account holders' mandate, thereby lowering costs. These accounts could be tied to the unique identity numbers being generated under UID project. Access to these accounts could be through mobile phones held by airtime sellers, retail outlets, business facilitators, business correspondents, SHGs, post offices, etc. The accounts could also be used for payment of MGNREGS, pension and other government schemes to intended beneficiaries.

Building Dedicated Support Structure for SHG Movement

District Level SHG Resource Centres

There is a need for concerted efforts on promotion of new groups, quality improvement of existing groups, as well as the need for setting up systems to ensure that new groups are made keeping quality and quality standards in focus. This requires not only investments on the groups' trainings and exposures but also require a fleet of trained trainers and dedicated institutions working as resource centres preferably at each district level. These centres will act as technical support centres and a knowledge hub offering quality training programmes for those engaged in the sector, extend handholding support to promoters as well as community institutions; undertake studies on relevant issues and disseminate best practices. Some of the voluntary agencies having vast experience and human resource can take up the role of district/regional resource agencies.

Comprehensive Database of SHGs and SHG Federations

At present there is no authentic database available at the state level. The data provided by SLBC varies a great deal from the data provided by SHPIs and NABARD. A good number of SHGs get defunct which does not get recorded because there is no monitoring or tracking mechanism. The number of reported SHGs seems to be inflated by 50–60 per cent. There is urgent need for a comprehensive database of SHGs in Rajasthan. SHPI-wise or scheme-wise database may be of little use. What is needed is a comprehensive database of all SHGs, irrespective of their pedigree. Such a database platform can be interactive and process-oriented to ensure regular updating, rather than a stand-alone system for data compilation, e.g. all SHGs registered on the platform, only may be eligible for credit linkage. Grading certificate of SHGs can be generated online based on transactions.

Developing Human Resource

Most organizations practising microfinance have constantly been in need of trained staff. There is also a need for capacity building of existing human resource. For meeting this scale of requirement, new institutional innovations have to be attempted, which may include courses and training programmes for capacity building on microfinance and livelihoods. Various management and training institutes in the state need to collaborate with SHPIs and federations to take up training and educational programmes in the state.

Need for Investment in this Sector

Investment by Government and Banks

Considering the good impact that SHGs are having on households, both in terms of women empowerment and economic development, there is need to make necessary investments for institutional building. Currently most of the SHGs are formed by state government employees, where targets are given to them. The due process of SHG formation is not followed. It has been seen that a good quality SHG needs about three years handholding support and a capital expenditure of ₹ 8,000. Further, quality improvement of existing SHGs will require ₹ 5,000 per SHG. This translates to a total investment of ₹ 250 crore to improve the quality of existing SHGs and create good quality SHGs.[3] This investment may be viewed as a part of developing financial infrastructure. Government and banks should come forward and invest in building potential base of its future clients.

Livelihood Enhancement of the Poor

Over the last one decade, farmers in Rajasthan have been migrating to wage labour, effectively pushing agriculture and allied activities to second and third priority. This is attributable to slow growth in agriculture in Rajasthan. Slow growth in agriculture can be traced retrospectively to low level of private investment in agriculture and livestock, leading to low credit offtake in agriculture. Even though SHG members use small credit for procuring seeds, fodder and for buying animals, large credit or large investment is usually not done unless business development services (e.g. technical services, health services for animals, marketing services to sell their produce and so on) are present. Moreover, rainfed agriculture in Rajasthan and corresponding risk-return trade-off does not encourage farmers to take credit and invest in agriculture.

Therefore, private and public investment for improving productivity and business development services for enabling micro-entrepreneurship should be targeted in a phased manner. All stakeholders have a role to play. Banks should develop collaborations with people's institutions and technical service providers. SHPIs should encourage innovations to boost farm productivity.

Proposed Structure for Microfinance in Rajasthan

After taking into consideration the uniqueness of the state of Rajasthan and its problems in microfinance sector, the following structure for microfinance is proposed:

Step 1 Setting up of a separate statuary body like IRDA, TRAI for SHGs in Rajasthan with equitable mix of government functionaries, SHPIs and SHG community leaders in the form of 'Rajasthan Microfinance Mission' or 'Rajasthan SHG Mission'.

Step 2 *Building dedicated support structure for SHG movement:* District level SHG Resource Centres should be established. There is a need for concerted efforts on promotion of new groups, quality improvement of existing groups as well as the need for setting up systems to ensure that new groups are made, keeping quality and quality standards in focus.

Proposed Structure for Microfinance in Rajasthan

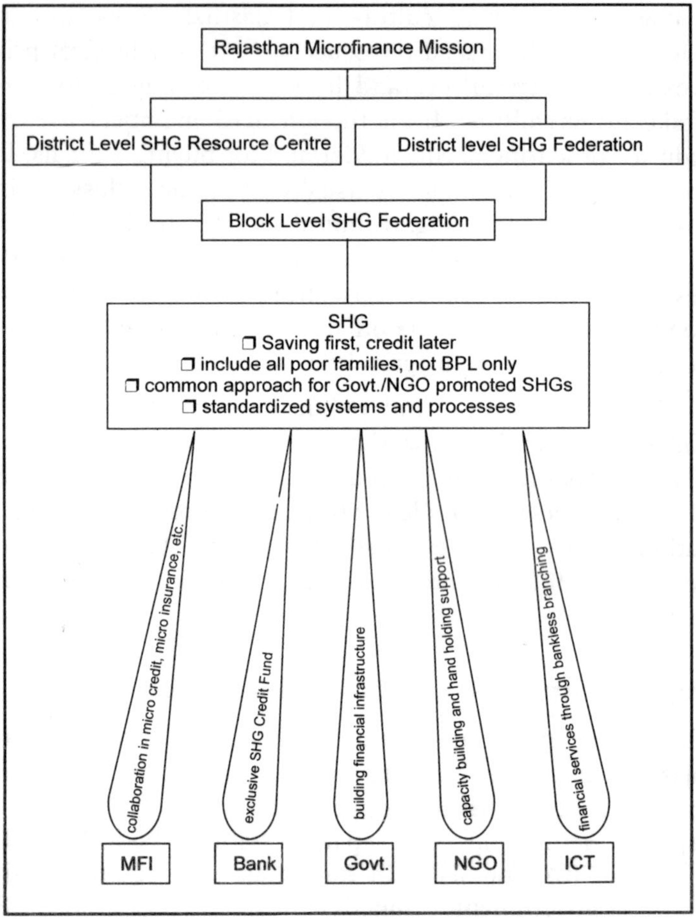

Step 3 *Strengthening SHG movement in weaker areas:* SHG movement has been found to be weak in districts like Nagaur, Dholpur, Dausa, Karouli, Barmer, Jodhpur, Pali, Jalaur, Alwar and Rajsamand. Also under-banked index of districts in Rajasthan, Nagaur, Dholpur, Dausa, Karauli, Barmer and Jalore have been found to be under-banked too. This has to be seriously addressed.

Step 4 *Developing and nurturing new and existing human resource* on microfinance and livelihoods through continuous courses and training programmes for capacity building.

Step 5 *Investment by government and banks:* This investment may be viewed as a part of developing financial infrastructure. Government and banks should come forward and invest in building potential base of its future clients.

Step 6 *Adopting common approach:* Currently, in Rajasthan, Self-Help Groups are promoted by many Government and Non-Government agencies with different objectives. To tackle this issue, SHG movement in Rajasthan needs a common approach. Government and banks should look at all SHGs, irrespective of their pedigree, through a single lens.

Step 7 *Standardized systems and processes for all SHGs in the state*: All SHGs, irrespective of their pedigree, should have uniform systems, processes, operations, bookkeeping, record-keeping, grading, auditing and quality standards.

Step 8 *Common Perspective: Savings first, credit later* – Primarily under government programmes, the SHGs are being formed to meet the targets and to avail bank credit only. If such a trend continues, the sector and its core value of 'Self-help' will not grow. If the core value of 'Self-help' does not grow, then solidarity among groups will not be strengthened, which in turn will lead to breaking up of groups.

Step 9 *Greater coverage of the poor under microfinance*: Reach out to 'all poor families' and 'not restrict to BPL only'.

Step 10 *Promoting 'area centric' federations of SHGs:* Self-Help Groups on their own are tiny institutions (10–20 marginalized women from very poor families). They alone and individually are not in a position to bring larger change and impact on lives of poor women unless they federate into next tier institutions and aggregate their demands and surpluses to the market, to take benefit of 'economics of scale'.

Step 11 *Deepening financial services and financial inclusion:* Increasing bank credit through Self-Help Groups – Compared to the vast demand and potential of micro-credit, annual credit through SHGs from banks in Rajasthan (about ₹ 200 crore) is very low. SHGs have the potential and capacities to bridge the gap between banks and the poor. Therefore, banks should increase their credit through SHGs.

Step 12 Banks, State Government and leaders of SHG movement should explore possibility of setting up an 'exclusive SHG credit fund' and 'special purpose vehicle' (SPV) to deliver credit to SHGs in the state.

Step 13 *SHG-MFI collaboration*: MFIs currently operate in urban, semi-urban and with relatively economically better off people in rural areas. MFIs can target poorer segments by collaborating with SHGs.

Step 14 *Financial inclusion through ICT:* Banking activities from origination and transaction to fulfilment and settlement can be completed using a mobile phone or smart cards, where poor are able to access formal financial services through branchless banking.

Step 15 *Livelihood enhancement of the poor:* Private and public investment for improving productivity and business development services for enabling micro-entrepreneurship should be targeted in a phased manner.

Notes

1. Yunus, Muhammad, *Banker to the Poor: Micro-lending and the Battle against World Poverty.* New York: Public Affairs, 1999. Print.
2. 114 NSSO survey 59th round.
3. Quality improvement of existing SHGs (about 1 lakh SHGs are lacking quality) needs an investment of ₹ 50 crore (₹ 5,000 per SHG). In terms of increasing outreach by about 50,000 new SHGs per year for the next 5 years, an investment of ₹ 8,000 per SHG is required which aggregates to a total of ₹ 200 crore. This translates to total investment of ₹ 250 crore.

Index